Cosmic Healing II

Taoist Cosmology and Universal Healing Connections

Mantak Chia
and *Dirk Oellibrandt*

Edited by
Colin Campbell

Copy Editor: Colin Campbell

Final Editor: Matt Gluck

Editorial Assistance: Sarina Stone

Design and Production: Saniem Chaisarn

Illustrations: Udon Jandee

Project Manager: W.U. Wei

© *North Star Trust*

First published in 2001 by:

Universal Tao Publications
274/1 Moo 7, Luang Nua,
Doi Saket, Chiang Mai, 50220 Thailand
Tel (66) (53) 865-034 & 495-596
Email: universaltao@universal-tao.com

ISBN: 974-87672-6-4
Library of Congress Catalog Number:

Manufactured in Thailand
First Printing, 2001

Table of Contents

Chapter IX

Chapter X

Chapter XI

Chapter XII

About the Author

Mantak Chia

Master Mantak Chia

Master Mantak Chia is the creator of the Universal Tao System and is the director of the Universal Tao Center and Tao Garden Health Resort and Training Center in the beautiful northern countryside of Thailand. Since childhood he has been studying the Taoist approach to life. His mastery of this ancient knowledge, enhanced by his study of other disciplines, has resulted in the development of the Universal Tao System which is now being taught throughout the world.

Mantak Chia was born in Thailand to Chinese parents in 1944. When he was six years old, Buddhist monks taught him how to sit and "still the mind." While still a grammar school student, he learned traditional Thai boxing. He was then taught Tai Chi Chuan by Master Lu, who soon introduced him to Aikido, Yoga and broader levels of Tai Chi.

Years later, when he was a student in Hong Kong excelling in track and field events, a senior classmate named Cheng Sue-Sue introduced him to his first esoteric teacher and Taoist Master, Master Yi Eng (I Yun). At this point, Master Chia began his studies of the Taoist way of life in earnest. He learned how to circulate energy through the Microcosmic Orbit and, through the practice of Fusion of the Five Elements, how to open the other Six Special Channels. As he studied Inner Alchemy further, he learned the Enlightenment of the Kan and Li, Sealing of the Five Senses, Congress of Heaven and Earth and Reunion of Heaven and Man. It was Master Yi Eng who authorized Master Chia to teach and heal.

When Mantak Chia was in his early twenties he studied with Master Meugi in Singapore, who taught him Kundalini, Taoist Yoga and the Buddha Palm. He was soon able to clear blockages to the flow of energy within his own body. He learned to pass the life force energy through his hands also, so that he could heal Master Meugi's patients. He then learned Chi Nei Tsang from Dr. Mui Yimwattana in Thailand.

A while later, he studied with Master Cheng Yao-Lun who taught him the Shao-Lin Method of Internal Power. He learned the closely guarded secret of the organs, glands and bone marrow exercise known as Bone Marrow Nei Kung and the exercise known as Strengthening and Renewal of the Tendons. Master Cheng Yao-Lun's system combined Thai boxing and Kung Fu. Master Chia also studied at this time with Master Pan Yu, whose system combined Taoist, Buddhist and Zen teachings. Master Pan Yu also taught him about the exchange of Yin and Yang power between men and women and how to develop the Steel Body.

To understand the mechanisms behind healing energy better, Master Chia studied Western anatomy and medical science for two years. While pursuing his studies, he managed the Gestetner Company, a manufacturer of office equipment and became well acquainted with the technology of offset printing and copying machines.

Using his knowledge of Taoism, combined with the other disciplines, Master Chia began teaching the Universal Tao System. He eventually trained other Instructors to communicate this knowledge and he established the Natural Healing Center in Thailand. Five years later, he decided to move to New York, where in 1979, he opened the Universal Tao Center. During his years in America, Master Chia continued his studies in the Wu system of Tai Chi with Edward Yee in New York.

Since then, Master Chia has taught tens of thousands of students throughout the world. He has trained and certified over 1,200 instructors and practitioners from all over the world. Universal Tao Centers and Chi Nei Tsang Institutes have opened in many locations in North America, Europe, Asia and Australia.

In 1994, Master Chia moved back to Thailand, where he had begun construction of Tao Garden, the Universal Tao Training Center in Chiang Mai.

Master Chia is a warm, friendly and helpful man who views himself primarily as a teacher. He presents the Universal Tao System in a straightforward and practical manner, while always expanding his knowledge and approach to teaching. He uses a word processor for writing and is totally at ease with the latest computer technology.

Master Chia estimates that it will take thirty five books to convey the full Universal Tao System. In June 1990, at a dinner in San Francisco, Master Chia was honored by the International Congress of Chinese Medicine and Qi Gong (Chi Kung), who named him the Qi Gong Master of the Year. He is the first recipient of this annual award.

He has previously written and published these Universal Tao books:

Awaken Healing Energy of the Tao - 1983
Taoist Secrets of Love: Cultivating Male Sexual Energy
co-authored with Michael Winn - 1984.
Taoist Ways to Transform Stress into Vitality -1985
Chi Self-Massage: the Tao of Rejuvenation - 1986
Iron Shirt Chi Kung I - 1986
Healing Love Through the Tao: Cultivating Female Sexual Energy - 1986
Bone Marrow Nei Kung - 1989
Fusion of the Five Elements I - 1990
Chi Nei Tsang: Internal Organ Chi Massage - 1990
Awaken Healing Light of the Tao - 1993
The Inner Structure of Tai Chi co-authored with Juan Li - 1996
Multi-Orgasmic Man co-authored with Douglas Abrams 1996 - published by Harper/Collins
Tao Yin - 1999
Chi Nei Tsang II - 2000
Multi-Orgasmic Couple co-authored with Douglas Abrams 2000 - published by Harper/Collins
Cosmic Healing I - 2001

Also many of the books above are available in the following foreign languages:
Bulgarian, Czech, Danish, Dutch, English, French, German, Greek, Hebrew, Hungarian, Indonesian, Italian, Japanese, Korean, Lithuanian, Malaysian, Polish, Portuguese, Russian, Serbo-Croatian, Slovenian, Spanish and Turkish. There is a Foreign Publishers listed in the Universal Tao Center Overview in the back of this book.

Acknowledgements

The Universal Tao Publications staff involved in the preparation, research and production of *Cosmic Healing II:Taoist Cosmology & Universal Healing Connections* extend our gratitude to the many generations of Taoist masters who have passed on their special lineage as an unbroken oral transmission over thousands of years. We particularly thank Taoist Master I Yun (Yi Eng) for his openness in transmitting the formulas of Taoist Inner Alchemy.

A special thanks to Joost Kuytenbrower and Inge Maasen for helping to structure this book and for sharing their writing skills with us.

We offer our eternal gratitude to our parents and teachers for their many gifts to us. Remembering them brings joy and satisfaction to our continued efforts in presenting the Universal Tao System. For their gifts, we offer our eternal gratitude and love. As always, their contribution has been crucial in presenting the concepts and techniques of the Universal Tao.

We wish to thank the thousands of unknown men and women of the Chinese healing arts who developed many of the methods and ideas presented in this book. We offer our graditute to Master Lao Kang Wen for sharing his healing techniques.

We wish to thank Colin Campbell for his editorial work and writing contributions on the first printing of this book, as well as his ideas for the cover. We appreciate his research and great labor. We wish to thank Matt Gluck for his editorial contributions on the revised edition of this book, as well as thanking our instructors, Dennis Huntington and Annette Derksen, for their insightful contributions to the revised version. We thank Dirk Gerd Al for his technical editing and clear writing throughout the book.

A special thanks goes to our ***Thai Production Team*** for their cover illustration and book design and layout: Raruen Keawapadung, Computer Graphics; Saysunee Yongyod, Photographer; Udon Jandee, Illustrator; and Saniem Chaisam, Production Designer.

Thanks to the testing institutes: Gerhard Eggelsberger, Institute for Applied Biocybernetics Feedback Research, Vienna, Austria and Dr. Ronda Jessum, Biocybernetics Institute, San Diego, California.

We also wish to express thanks to Cosmic Healing Certification Retreat Organizers around the world who have worked with us for many years and helped us prepare this manuscript throughout the Retreats: Beate Nimsky, Vienna, Austria; Serguei Orechkine, Moscow, Russia; Christopher Larthe, London, England; Masahiro Ouchi, Rye, New York; Dr. Angela C. Shen, San Francisco, California; Dirk Oellibrandt, Hamme, Belgium; Brita Dahlerg, Frankfurt, Germany and Lizbeth Cavegn, Zurich, Switzerland.

We wish to further express our gratitude to all the instructors and students who have offered their time and advice to enhance this system, especially Felix Senn, Barry Spendlove, Chong Mi Mueller, Clemens Kasa, Andrew Jan, Marga Vianu, Harald Roeder, Salvador March, Dr. Hans Leonhardy, Peter Kontaxakis, Thomas Hicklin, Gianni Dell'Orto, Walter and Jutta Kellenberger.

Words of Caution

The practices described in this book have been used successfully for thousands of years by Taoists trained by personal instruction. Readers should not undertake the practice without receiving personal transmission and training from a certified instructor of the Universal Tao, since certain of these practices, if done improperly, may cause injury or result in health problems. This book is intended to supplement individual training by the Universal Tao and to serve as a reference guide for these practices. Anyone who undertakes these practices on the basis of this book alone, does so entirely at his or her own risk.

The meditations, practices and techniques described herein are **not** intended to be used as an alternative or substitute for professional medical treatment and care. If any readers are suffering from illnesses based on mental or emotional disorders, an appropriate professional health care practitioner or therapist should be consulted. Such problems should be corrected before you start training.

Neither the Universal Tao nor its staff and instructors can be responsible for the consequences of any practice or misuse of the information contained in this book. If the reader undertakes any exercise without strictly following the instructions, notes and warnings, the responsibility must lie solely with the reader.

This book does not attempt to give any medical diagnosis, treatment, prescription, or remedial recommendation in relation to any human disease, ailment, suffering or physical condition whatsoever.

Chinese medicine emphasizes balancing and strengthening the body so that it can heal itself. The meditations, internal exercises and martial arts of the Universal Tao are basic approaches to this end. Follow the instructions for each exercise carefully and do not neglect the foundations, i.e, the Microcosmic Orbit and any other supplemental exercises. Also pay special attention to the warnings and suggestions in each chapter. People who have high blood pressure, heart disease or a generally weak condition should proceed cautiously, having prior consent from a qualified medical practitioner. Pregnant women should not practice Cosmic Healing. People with venereal disease should not attempt any practices involving sexual energy until they are free of the condition.

The Universal Tao is not and cannot be responsible for the consequences of any practice or misuse of the information in this book. If the reader undertakes any exercise without strictly following the instructions, notes and warnings, the responsibility must lie solely with the reader.

The correct way to work with Cosmic Healing II is to read and practice the techniques in Cosmic Healing I by Mantak Chia, to fully obtain the benefits of this new work.

Preface
Taoist Cosmology
Stellar and Planetary Connections

Dirk Oellibrandt

We are moving towards unprecedented changes, at the turn of the millenium. The accelerating speed of global change shows us that society is moving towards a climax of tension and contraction, the center of the evolutionary spiral where things are turning towards their opposites. The ability to adapt to this breathtaking process is essential to survive. These changes are not always caused by natural disasters or climatic alterations, but by the effect of centuries of the human drive for power, temporarily forming an unstable social atmosphere on the planet. This tension field is magnified by universal astrological conditions.

In the modern world, many people have barely enough energy to follow the speed and direction of these changes much less have enough creative energy remaining to consider and set down their true tasks. A major part of the world population spends too much of its precious energy trying to survive. Some do this by imitating and using political and social structures that are controlled by the commerical industrial groups. In this way they are destroying the roots of their own culture. Natural rhythms are changed by obsessive striving for material goods. Superficial pleasure takes over, disconnecting people from their spiritual roots and a natural way of life.

A new orientation in life and guidance by leaders who understand the order of the universe and can see truth in the midst of the realm of phenomenon and events, is one of the most urgent needs we all experience today.

This book does not pretend to and does not claim to solve these needs for you. We do, however, trust that these practices can help you to reconnect with who you really are and that it may help you in finding the way back to your origin. Once we reconnect to this source of intelligence, everything around us acquires a new and a deeper meaning.

This book offers parts of the Taoist cosmology about the planetary and stellar world, some personal insights and an introduction into Taoist planetary and stellar practice. Once you have integrated these into your life, they will help you to cultivate inner light and clarity.

We hope this book will inspire you and help you, so that you will feel more liberated and at peace with yourself. May it enhance your sense of 'coming home' as well. Although most information comes out of the ancient oriental tradition, we want to point out that the true information source is the *Tao* itself, the essential you ,including all countries, traditions, races and so much more.

Fu Hsi - Creator of the I Ching   (Drawing by Juan Li)

About the Authors

Dirk Oellibrandt

Dirk has been practicing the principles of oriental martial arts since the age of 13. His training combined with a great passion for nature helped him to develop a solid base with a high sensitivity for energies. In his evolution as a martial artist he became fluent with the Taoist specialties and Shiatsu. At 25 he began with drawing from the external martial arts and studied different forms of Chi Kung, Aikido, Tai Chi and Pakua. He also learned to apply his energy in the form of healings; he studied different shiatsu systems, oriental medicine, and osteopathic techniques. His most important sources of inspiration are Master Mantak Chia, Saul Goodman and Michio Kushi.

His gathered knowledge and experience from his studies, treatments and teachings combined with his inherent sense of the universal laws helped him to give life to a new approach to the field of bodywork and healing. He named it "4 DIMENSIONAL BODYWORK".

Dirk and wife Katrien direct an international organisation centered in Belgium called "DU MAI" to further this work. The unique philosophy underlying the Du Mai program combined with Dirk's vigorous and awakening teaching and treatment style has been a source of support and inspiration for many. Together with a team of colleagues including teachers and therapists he is exploring the dynamics between the universal laws and the constant re-creation of our human body. This approach suggests exciting possibilities and higher dimensions in the art of healing and bodywork.

内經圖

INNER
ALCHEMY
OF THE
TAO

Chapter I
Taoist Cosmology and Universal Healing Connections

Introduction

Taoism is a practice of studying and living the laws of the universe. It has its roots in a body of knowledge that many masters have gathered over thousands of years. According to ancient Taoist records, this practice has been the fruit of deep meditative practice by highly advanced practitioners who lived an intimate relationship with the universe and nature, often in remote and isolated places.

A major role in the discovery of a practical way to work with the energy of the universe was played by Fu Hsi, who has been credited in Chinese history with the discovery of the pakua and who has been seen as the creator of the I Ching, the most ancient Taoist book of wisdom. There is agreement among historians of Chinese culture that it was the Yellow Emperor, who played a major role more than 5000 years ago, in synthesizing Taoist practices in the domains of health and healing as well as in the healing love practice. He integrated a wealth of insights and practices from a wide variety of Taoist masters. This process of synthesis and accumulation of theory and practice continued to grow in subsequent millennia, until today. It is still evolving.

Taoist practice as we understand it is not religious in conventional terms, nor is it based on a creed or on transcendental principles.

It is a practice of self-awareness and self-transformation through which we gradually become one with the cosmos. In this process we realize and actualize ourselves, as within the physical body the energy body grows (in Taoism known as the soul body) and within the latter the spirit body (the light, diamond or rainbow body - see illustration on page 12) evolves. It is in this process of subsequent energy transformations, that we return to our origins and realize our original intrinsic nature of which peace and freedom are the natural fruits.

There is a firm insistence in the Taoist wisdom tradition that any advance in energy transformation or what in western culture is called spiritual advancement, needs to be well rooted in the earth: thus the initiation into the higher practices bears fruit, in the Taoist view, only to the extent that the practitioner is rooted and grounded. Taoist practice may help a person to lead a fascinating life and at the same time grow spiritually by realizing one's natural potential.

Essential to spiritual growth is that the Taoist practitioner cultivates a sense of purity, joyfulness in life and a sense of wonder, thereby regaining and enhancing the openness and excitement of a small child. Not surprisingly the virgin child stands in the Taoist tradition for purity and immortality. In this way the practitioner develops one's own sense of inner truth as a reflection of one's innate spiritual origin.

In the chapter which follows, we offer an approach which integrates ancient Taoist insights with knowledge and information from several more recent sources, exposing a wide range of possibilities. We hope that the information offered in the following chapters may help the reader to enhance his or her awareness, health and quality of relationships and may also serve to raise thereby, the quality of society in general. Knowledge of this material can also be used in personal healing and by those who engage themselves to help others to heal themselves. Promising effective results of this approach in thousands of treatments have encouraged us to share this information. In the near future a book may appear which will be specifically focused on the therapeutic possibilities of this work.

Three Ways

We propose that the reason for the generally poor quality of our lives and that of society is due to the perception we have of who we are, where we originated and what we are doing here on earth. The quality of our life as we live it does not reflect our full potential. In what follows, we describe three different kinds of people, typical of the most common visions and life-styles. Also we will see how we as human beings gradually entered into a process of degeneration and how we lost our divine nature. Many centuries of conditioning by institutional religion as well as by modern science have lowered our energy frequencies and have locked up humankind into a horizontal, materialistic culture in which sensitivity to our true origin has become obscured and we live cut off from the energies of heaven.

Thus we have become trapped into a rational, materialistic way of life. At the same time, as a result of our repression and disconnection we tend to be lost in guilt, we project negative emotions on others and look for truth outside rather than within ourselves. This book is designed to help us to reactivate the deep memory of who we are beneath the crust and overgrowth of the various forms of domestication and slavery that we have been subject to in the history of our civilization.

Horizontal Axis Dominant - Disconnecting from Heaven and our Spiritual Source

Religions / Scientific Conditioning / Unconscious Denial of Spiritual Orgin

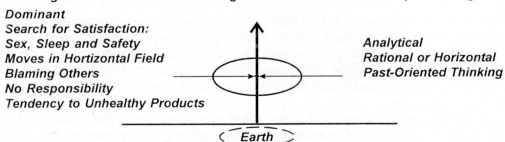

Materialistic Way of Life - Heaviness stuck on the Earth

Fig. 1.1 Horizontal Axis

This state of spiritual disconnection has been further aggravated by unnatural ways of living, moving and eating. Spiritual disconnection and materialist obsession are at the very core of modern society. Since we turned away from the higher intelligence of the universe, which is our only source of true knowing, we became like a space shuttle without external information, depending and hoping for good luck.

Thus most of us in the world of today live in an unawakened, half numb state, unconscious that we are caught in the past, afraid to look at ourselves and where we are here and now.

As this is the dominant state of social energy, it is not easy to avoid being trapped in it. Most people are resigned to this state and if you would ask them how they feel and how they are doing, they would tell you: "We are doing okay". Their lives basically revolve around eating, sleeping, mating, security and power. If they would look deeply inside and were honest to themselves, they would see that they are rather unhappy and feel empty inside. The deep fear of looking at this pain and emptiness prevent them noticing that they have gravely suppressed their godly nature.

As children of the universe we are not only created by the same intelligence and the same subtle substance, but if we allow it, we spontaneously will co-create its evolutionary process. We are not only children of the universe and its love which gave us life, we are also its fathers and mothers, whose love is co-responsible for the way it evolves. As an ancient expression says: "Embrace the universe as a mother embraces her firstborn child".

Once we truly take responsibility for ourselves, our health, our spiritual origin and our life task, we can start to wake up from this numb state. Then we become aware of the fear and mechanisms we have cultivated to prevent ourselves from getting in touch with our true selves. Only when we have the courage to look beneath the surface of our ordinary consciousness, will we be able to open up and walk the path to freedom and spiritual independence.

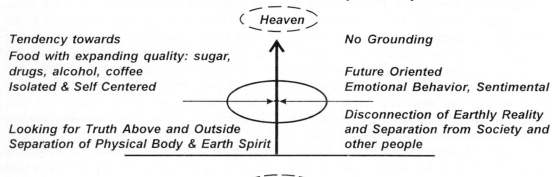

Vertical Axis Dominant - Connection to Heaven and Spiritual Reality
Disconnected from Earth and Physical Body

(Heaven)

Tendency towards
Food with expanding quality: sugar,
drugs, alcohol, coffee
Isolated & Self Centered

No Grounding

Future Oriented
Emotional Behavior, Sentimental

Looking for Truth Above and Outside
Separation of Physical Body & Earth Spirit

Disconnection of Earthly Reality
and Separation from Society and
other people

(Earth)

Physical Disconnection - Space Travelling

Fig. 1.2 Vertical Axis

The Flower Power period and the New Age movement may be seen as a reaction to the materialistic upsurge. However many followers of these movements, in their relative disdain of mundane and earthly material pursuits, have moved to the other extreme: a spiritualism without grounding 'roots' in the earth. Or they have the same fear pattern but now use a new emergency exit, which contains the same duality between heaven and earth and which has characterized most dominating religious and philosophical traditions.

People with poor groundings and a negative relationship with their body frequently face a host of problems in their daily lives regarding sex, money, health, self esteem and relationships. They often suffer from insecurity and have a weak relationship with the realities of life. They tend to seek ways to elude these realities, including their own physical existence, so that they experience a growing disconnection between body, mind and spirit. They do understand that they need to look for truth within themselves, as they carry the divine within. But they find this difficult because of the split which they have created within themselves between what is "above" and what is "below", between heaven and earth within themselves.

The pursuit in realizing freedom often causes such spiritual aspirants to imprison themselves in their search. As a result they are bound to end up as imbalanced as their materialist opposites. It is the deep pain they experience which pushes them to a spiritual path, free from all obstructions. Now the same ego is hidden behind a spiritual mask. When we turn our attention away from our body we cut the intelligence away from the 'matter'. In this way the body is ignorant, dependent and selfish. We dishonor the female nature, the holiest temple on earth. The higher frequencies are not balanced and integrated in the physical body, so the vital essence will gradually leave the body or will transform into high energy frequencies that can only be partly assimilated in the physical body. The balance of the energy will leave the body and find a new 'attraction'. Physically this person will start to weaken slowly and all kinds of symptoms will appear, ultimately leading to premature aging. Their heart-energy may be compared with to a flower which is not connected with the roots. Their spiritual condition is only momentary. They only live in the upper body, as they tend to ignore or are afraid of their sexuality; they lack a connection with the belly, their energy centre. As love and sex are not connected, their relationships tend to be emotionally unstable and superficial. Let us be true to ourselves; we were not given our bodies to deny them. We can all contribute to the quality of life on this planet by dissolving the denseness and separation in our mind and our social mentality. The problem is not only in the body, but also in the absence and denial of an understanding of the infinite and unfathomable true spirit and universal mind. Taoist masters realize that truth lies in a spiritual life which includes the physical body. By consciously fusing the spirit with the core of physical existence a new quality of life arises.

Taoist self-healing practices can significantly help such people: by teaching them how to get in touch with the spiritual nature of their body, to care for it and make it healthy and strong. This is essential for the growth of a healthy energy body.

The initial focus of Taoist practice is on creating a healthy and strong physical body, well rooted in the source of life, the energy of our 'mother' earth. At the same time Taoist practice acknowledges that the origin of our spirit is in heaven. Our soul has chosen to incarnate on earth and seeks opportunities to grow and evolve, by learning from the universe. Since everything finds its nature in Tao or the great spirit, the human body, soul and spirit can be seen as different densities of the same substance.

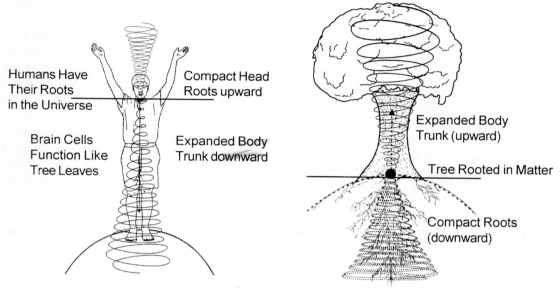

Fig. 1.3 Roots of Human and Tree

In view of our unawakened unconscious state, most of us tend to get trapped in one of the two poles: either by focusing on an earthly life at the expense of heaven or the other way around. This imbalanced polarity is well illustrated by the struggle between men and women.

Over the ages, Taoist masters have frequently obtained great insights in the art of cultivating their health and physical strength. Longevity was one of the fruits. In such a way they enjoyed much time and space to cultivate their spirit and to transform their physical and energy body into a light body. In the Taoist tradition this state of being has also been called "the crystal" or "the immortal body".

With the deepening of the grounding practice, the higher body can grow step by step and the emotions of daily life, with its ups and downs, gradually lose their uprooting effect. When one practices daily, a point may be reached where one feels the desire to withdraw from society, live away from the hustle and bustle of modern life, to facilitate a truly intimate relationship with the universe and nature for a certain period of time. This may speed up the transformation process, as has been demonstrated for centuries by monks of different spiritual traditions. Taoist masters have also advised their students to give up their withdrawn lives and return to "the world" to maintain their roots in the realities of daily life. This advice was given by a master, if he observed that his students needed to mature and that they needed to get a taste of social life and experience desire, so that they could compare these two 'directions' and appreciate the experience of true peace in their meditation practice.

Thus, before achieving a higher level of awareness and mastery over their energy, they were sent for a few years into a busy town to work as a dishwasher or do other menial jobs. If the student had reached the stage where he could maintain his inner peace, even under difficult circumstances, then he was seen as becoming a master himself.

For most people, withdrawal from society and from social relations and earthly life may only be advisable after having learned and integrated different stages and levels of energy transformation within society. If we withdraw from society without the necessary maturity and insight, the mind is often bound to remain restless, as it continues to look unceasingly for physical, emotional and mental satisfaction.

When a Taoist student has achieved a strong navel centre and enjoys a firm connection of heaven and earth within , then he can freely move "upward" and "downward" without getting lost. The relationship between heaven and earth may be represented by a vertical axis which goes up (heaven) and moves down (earth). Along this axis we can visualize the different centers and levels of energy and their transformations (body/soul/spirit). Because of the firm rooting, the Taoist way of energy transformation is a safe one. It has been tested for many centuries. The Universal Tao practice is actually a self-cultivation program we can make use of effectively and apply in our daily lives. The practices lead us step by step from an initial level to the highest or "immortality" practices. The Taoist way of life teaches you to reconnect and become aware of your true spiritual origin and bring this experience down into the lowest center of the physical body: the Lower Tan Tien. It brings spirit into matter or light on earth. After achieving this strong rooting process between heaven and earth (vertical axis), the practitioner can move freely into the materialistic world (horizontal axis) without losing his connection with the spiritual.

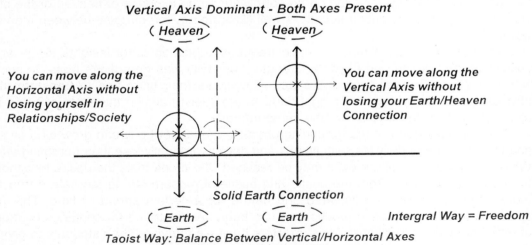

Vertical Axis Dominant - Both Axes Present

(*Heaven*) (*Heaven*)

You can move along the Horizontal Axis without losing yourself in Relationships/Society

You can move along the Vertical Axis without losing your Earth/Heaven Connection

Solid Earth Connection

(*Earth*) (*Earth*) *Intergral Way = Freedom*

Taoist Way: Balance Between Vertical/Horizontal Axes

Fig. 1.4 Both Axes

Three Sources of External Chi

According to the Taoist view, the energy of the universe is comprised of three different realms.

The subtle origin of the universe or the Tao is the source of all life, all beings, all things, all energy and their various manifestations.

In the Tai Chi (See fig. 1.5) the circle represents the oneness and the yin and yang energies represent the intrinsic polarity of all forms of energy. Yin and yang represent a unity of opposites, always balancing, completing, embracing and containing each other. The interaction between yin and yang created the Three Pure Ones or the three energy sources in the universe: the cosmic force, the universal force and the earth force. Knowing that these energies contain the pure light of the Tao, we recognize the Three Pure Ones in the Tai Chi Tsu. The circle represents the cosmic light energy while yang and yin represent the universal and the earth energy.

Oneness Unity   **Yin/Yang Polarity**   **Triple Unity - Universal**
                                                                      - Cosmic ⎱ **Chi**
                                                                      - Earth

Fig. 1.5 Tao of Triple Unity

Cosmic Chi is born out of the original Chi of the Tao and literally carries the intelligence and essence of life. Guided by this intelligence it spreads out into the universe and manifests in different densities and forms defined by the cosmic laws. This is how stars, planets, human cells, subatomic particles and all other forms of life take form and are nourished.

In particular, cosmic energy descends and materializes into the human baby, as it is attracted into the world by the magnetic field between the earth and the moon. Since most people have lost the ability to consciously and directly absorb the cosmic light, we can only do this in a materialized form: either by eating living substances that have absorbed cosmic light (plants) or by eating living creatures that have eaten the plants (animals). This means that we only consume light in the more or less materialized form: cosmic dust, which in turn becomes plants and animals. Evolution is leading us to return to consume from the source: cosmic light. In this way yin and yang have become one another, as the circle leads us back into light.

Taoist practice focuses on restoring this direct connection with the cosmic source (light particles) so that we regain the ability to directly live from light energy. In this way we become less and less dependent on eating animals and plants. There is abundant evidence that throughout the ages many Taoist masters have been able to live for months or even years without taking any food and without losing weight, while maintaining and even enhancing their vitality. Today, more and more people in different places all over the world and with different backgrounds are living only on water, tea and fruit juice. This practice is possible because such advanced practitioners tap into the original source of human life and all other forms of being: cosmic light.

.Both universal and earth energy have their genesis in the original energy of the Tao. The universal force of heavenly Chi is the radiating force of all galaxies, stars and planets of the whole universe. It is this all pervasive force which nourishes the cosmic force in nature and all life forms. The earth force is the third force of nature which includes all the energies of mother earth.

.This force is activated by the electromagnetic field originating in the rotation of the earth. It is also integrated into all aspects of nature on our planet.

.The earth energy is accessed through the soles of the feet, the perineum and the sexual organs. Earth energy nourishes the physical body. It supplies our daily life force and is one of the principal forces used to heal ourselves.

Human Energy in the Universe

In early times Taoist masters had an understanding of what a human being 'is', an understanding which is quite different from some present day theories. Human energy was understood to be the highest manifestation of the cosmic light. The primary responsibility of humankind as the highest manifestation of cosmic light, was seen as keeping the balance between heaven and earth.

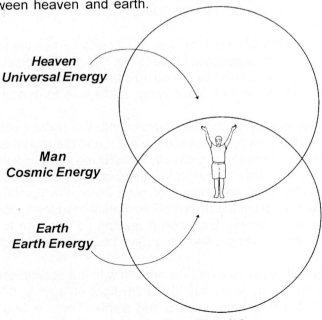

Heaven
Universal Energy

Man
Cosmic Energy

Earth
Earth Energy

Fig. 1.6

Today, responsibility is frequently experienced as a burden and not as an opportunity to grow. Supernatural powers of the 'Immortals' are not really extraordinary, as they are inherent to our natural position in the universe.

Each of us holds the memory of the true potential of life and of human responsibility.

Three Levels of Existence

The threefold nature of the universe manifests itself in many different ways. In the Taoist vision, everything we see and experience around us has gone through three different realms or spheres of existence.

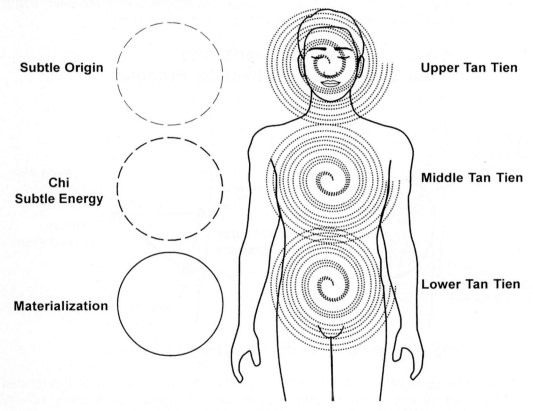

Subtle Origin

**Chi
Subtle Energy**

Materialization

Upper Tan Tien

Middle Tan Tien

Lower Tan Tien

Fig. 1.7 Three Tan Tiens in the Human Body

The subtle origin is the source of everything: heaven and earth. It contains the realm of Chi and all phenomena.
1. The subtle origin or pure law of existence (Tao).
2. Chi, the subtle energy.
3. All phenomena, interactions, transformations of Chi.

The three realms are inseparable. Once we understand this threefold nature and ex-perience its manifestation in our bodies, we have made a major step on our spiritual journey.

We have pointed to the necessity to open up the vertical axis and establish a deep rooting in both heaven and earth. The three principal energy centers in our body on this axis are called Tan Tiens. They are in reality the containers of the physical, soul and spirit energy. The way we become human is through a process of materialization (the body is the material densification of energy) in which the subtle energy of the Tao, connected to your spirit, has incarnated through your soul into your body. So heaven had descended into the earth and what is above and below have united.

The Tan Tiens (fig 1.7) each have specific energetic functions. The three main stages in Taoist spiritual cultivation are directly related to the Three Tan Tiens.

Three Tan Tiens and
the Three Step Cultivation Process

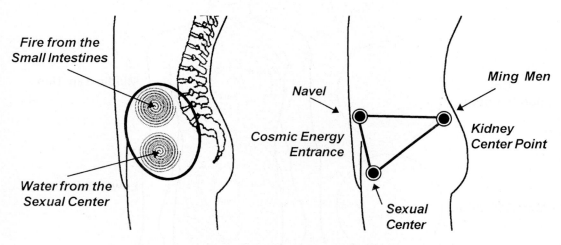

Fig. 1.8 The Lower Tan Tien is found within the triangle.

The lower energy center or Tan Tien is located behind and below the navel. It is located in the small intestine and is also called the lower fire. This center has a strong polarity because it governs the fire (small intestine) and the sexual water (kidneys) energy at the same time.

It is the center of the physical body and of physical strength. It contains a frequency of gross energy (compared to the two other two Tan Tiens). In the center point (see fig.1.8), the prenatal force is preserved by the power generated from the kidneys. When the lower Tan Tien is strong, digestion is easy, emotions and experiences are easily transformed and there is much sexual energy.

The center point contains the basic spark which was created when your father's sperm penetrated your mother's egg. If this spark continues to be active and strong, it provides life-force to the billions of cells throughout your body. The Lower Tan Tien is located in the triangle between the navel, the opposite point to the navel (in the spine between the second and third lumbar called the 'Gate of Life') and the sexual center. For men this is the prostrate gland and for women it lies in the top of the cervix between the ovaries.

Control of sexual energy and its transformation into life force is essential if we wish to raise our energy level in the lower Tan Tien. For men this implies that they need to preserve the life essence of the sperm during intercourse or masturbation. Through controlling ejaculation they can transform the essence of the sperm into Chi. For women it means that they learn to regulate and control menstruation, thereby transforming blood into Chi. For healers, it is very important to learn how to transform sexual energy into spiritual energy. Because this original balance between love and sex, or water and fire contains in itself the essence of healing and creation. Self-transformation is a condition for being able to help others on the path of transforming sexual energy into spiritual energy. Once the energy in the lower Tan Tien has become pure and strong, it will naturally ascend to the heart center and the middle Tan Tien.

When the lower Tan Tien transforms negative emotions, a purer higher frequency energy arises and radiates from the heart. The state of compassion and of love as a high energy state is the fruit of the virtues of all organs. This should not be mistaken for the dualistic sentimental love that all of us have experienced temporarily and taken for a peak love experience at some time in our life.

The true godly nature of our being and our love starts radiating through our higher self connection in and from our heart center. In this state there is an abundance of energy, as the heart center is directly nourished by the cosmic light. In this state a deep oneness with people around us can be experienced.

This higher energy and awareness level allows us to help others while not losing energy ourselves. This **light of compassion** which is born from universal love can be cultivated and will gradually attract more pure divine light and spiritual essence.

This spiritual essence is attracted by the crystals (the glands) in our head at the core of the nervous system. This compact, spiral-formed spiritual center is also called the upper Tan Tien.

In this process, the nature of our life changes and adopts a divine quality. The actions and directions you choose come from the laws of the universe and are no longer determined by animalistic behavior, emotional satisfaction or a drive for wealth and power.

The spiritual essence is gathered in the crystal body, a body that does not dissolve at the moment of death, a body that carries us to immortality.

The three step cultivation is a life long process of self cultivation that gradually takes us from the suffering of addiction and dependence, extreme emotions and ups and downs, into a life of freedom, spiritual independence and enlightenment.

The three step cultivation leads to:

☆ A healthy body and an abundance of life force.

☆ Control and balance on the emotional level and the growth of the **compassionate heart** center. This compassion is raised by cultivating virtues and by good deeds and is stored in the soul body.

☆ When the soul body matures, it acts as a baby sitter to help nurture the spirit body.

☆ Body, soul and spirit are united deep into the Tan Tien, enlightening the person.

☆ The ability to share this light and wisdom with everybody around them.

Since the soul carries the seed of the immortal or spirit body within, the development of the spirit body is the condition for breaking through the law and the wheel of incarnation. When the three bodies are established and spiritual energy is dictating the quality of life, the practitioner can transform energy from the physical into the soul body and from the soul into the spirit body.

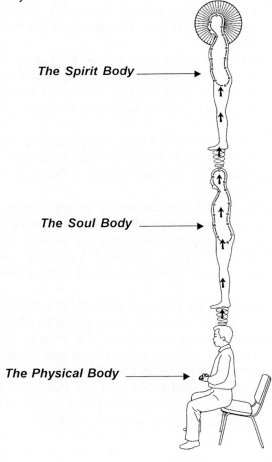

The Spirit Body

The Soul Body

The Physical Body

Fig. 1.9 Three Bodies

At the moment of death, the energy of the physical body will be partly or completely absorbed into the spirit body. This means that the physical body eventually dissolves. There are many records of Taoist masters who successfully dissolved their physical body rapidly, leaving only teeth, hair and nails.

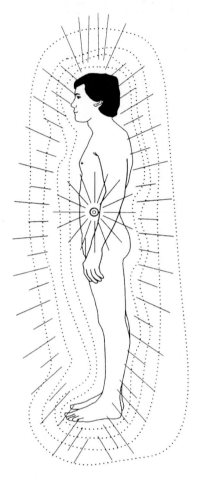

Fig. 1.10

In the condensed state the soul body is kept as a pearl of consciousness with the spiritual essence deep inside. This consciousness center creates a bright protective awareness field.

Chapter II
Universal Tao Basic Practices and Preparation Exercises

Introduction

In the Universal Tao, we teach Cosmic Healing within a system of exercise and meditation. As a part of this system, Cosmic Healing comprises the art of healing oneself and others and focuses on energy work for projecting Chi. One can easily learn the simple movements of Cosmic Healing without doing any other Universal Tao practices, but if one truly wishes to master the art of Cosmic Healing, it is important to have a firm foundation in the basic Universal Tao practices. Therefore in this chapter we will introduce you to the basic Universal Tao practices that are used in conjunction with Cosmic Chi Kung.

The preparatory practice consists of a few parts. Work through each part at your own pace and eventually join them together as a whole.

Always start with **warming the stove** at the abdomen and direct the fire down to the Sexual Center to transform the sexual energy. Next practice the Cosmic Inner Smile. The Cosmic Inner Smile is a powerful relaxation and self-healing technique that uses the energy of love, happiness, kindness and gentleness as a language to communicate with the internal organs of the body. Each organ is connected to a specific element and corresponds to a specific color, so that the kidneys are , for instance, connected to the water element and correspond to the blue color, whereas the heart is connected to fire and red, etc. This makes it very easy to guide the healing power into each organ by using the appropriate color. The practice also aids the transformation of negative emotions into positive energy. This transformation is a very powerful Chi Kung practice. A **genuine smile** transforms negative energy into loving energy that has the power to relax, balance and heal. By learning to smile inwardly to the organs and glands your whole body will feel loved and appreciated and enjoy more Chi. After the Inner Smile, practice Bone Breathing, Marrow Washing, Cosmic Healing and the Microcosmic Orbit.

Warm Up the Stove

1. Sit at the edge of a chair with your hands clasped together and your eyes closed.
2. Start with 'bellows breathing', moving your abdomen in and out quicly. Emphasize the exhalation by breathing out forcefully for 18 to 36 times. Rest, cover your navel and feel warm and nice.
3. Next do the "inner laughing" exercise, where you feel the abdomen vibrate inside you. Practice for a few minutes, allowing the movement of your inner laughter to grow

stronger. Then rest and use the mind and eye power to gather the Chi, now felt as a warm feeling behind the navel, into the Tan Tien. Picture a stove with fire burning behind your navel. Feel nice and warm.

Transform the Sexual Energy

Once you feel the Tan Tien warm enough, smile down and bring the warm Chi down to the sexual organs; women, down to the uterus; men, down to the testicles. It may feel like the sun shining on the water. The rays of the sun purify the water until it becomes steam and rises up high. Keep on smiling down to the sexual organs and feel the warm or fiery feeling from the navel area continue to flow down to the sexual organs, transforming the sexual energy into Chi. Raise the Chi up the spine into the brain; this will help activate the crown and mideyebrow.

Focus your awareness in the sacrum. At the very tip of the sacrum, the coccyx, there is a hole. Breathe into this hole until you feel some activity there. This may be felt as tingling, numbness or pulsing. If you can really activate this point it will have 'suction'. Be aware of the sacrum opening. Feel the hole in the tailbone (the sacral hiatus) having a suction-force; breathe into it until you feel it become activated. Once the sacrum is activated, you will very easily feel the suction and breathing in the cranium and mideyebrow also. Keep on gently smiling and softly breathing into the Tan Tien and feel the suction in the abdomen. Focus 95 % in the Tan Tien and 5 % in the sacrum, the crown and the mideyebrow. Be aware of the Tan Tien breathing and internally observe the pulsing and breathing in the sacrum, the mid-eyebrow and the crown. Do this 36 times.

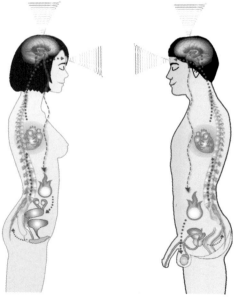

Fig. 2.1

Cosmic Inner Smile

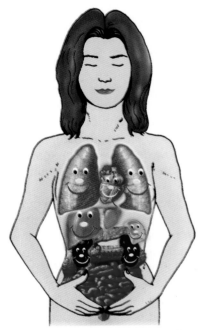

Fig. 2.2 Smile Down into the Organs

The Inner Smile begins at the eyes and the mid-eyebrow point and moves down to the heart. As you activate the heart, the loving energy will flow out and you will feel the energy of your Inner Smile flow down the entire length of your body like a waterfall. This is a very powerful and effective tool to counteract stress and tension.

1. Be aware of the **mid-eyebrow**, imagining that you are in one of your favorite places in the world, a place where you feel safe, relaxed and happy. Recall the sights you might have seen there, the sounds you might have heard, the scents, sensations and flavors that you associate with this place.
2. Imagine that one of your favorite people is standing in front of you, smiling to you with loving, happy, radiant shining eyes. **Smile** and slightly lift up the corners of your mouth.
3. Feel yourself responding to that special person's smile with a smile of your own. Feel your **eyes smiling** and relaxing.
4. Smile down to the thymus gland and picture a white flower blossoming. Gently inhale into the **thymus gland**, connecting your breath to the olfactory organ. Smell the good fragrance.
5. Aim your inner attention at your heart, picturing the image of the heart before your inner eye and smile to it. Smile until you feel the **heart smile** back to you. Picture your heart like a red tulip, gradually opening. This will activate the love and fire of compassion in the heart. Once you feel the red light and loving awareness it will activate the

cosmic **red healing light** or mist from above and around you.

6. Smile at the light or mist and very slowly, with a soft, long, deep breath draw the red mist, **love and compassion** into the mideyebrow, down through the mouth and throat, into the heart and gradually overflowing to the small intestine. Exhale, but retain the red light and the love and compassion in the heart and small intestine. At the same time exhale the cloudy, black or negative energy which holds hate, arrogance, heart-breaking traumas and irritation. Keep on doing this way of breathing for 18 to 36 times. Breathe until the heart becomes bright red before your inner vision and starts to radiate out to the tongue, mouth, nose, ears and eyes. Allow the red light to whirl around you and form a **red aura**. Feel your skin glowing with red energy.

7. Let the heart's loving energy radiate out to the lungs. Aim your attention at the lungs, picture the image of the lungs before your inner eye and smile to it. Smile until you feel the **lungs smile** back to you. Picture your lungs like a white flower, gradually opening and smell the good fragrance. This will activate the courage in the lungs. As soon as you invoke the white light and the courage into the lungs, you will also activate the cosmic **white healing light** or mist from above and around you.

8. Smile at the light or mist and very slowly, softly take a long deep breath and draw the white mist into the mideyebrow, the mouth and down to the lungs, gradually overflowing into the large intestine. Exhale but retain the white light and the feeling of courage in the lungs. At the same time exhale the cloudy, black or negative energy. Keep on doing this kind of breathing for 18 to 36 times. Until the lungs become bright white and start to radiate out to the nose, ears, eyes, tongue and mouth. Invite the white light to whirl around you and form a white aura covering your skin like autumn dew.

9. The **spleen**, pancreas and stomach correspond to the yellow color of the earth element. Connect to these organs and smile down into them from the mideyebrow. First connect to the heart, then attract the clear yellow light from above and around you. You might see the golden yellow aura of a wheat field ready for harvest. Expel feelings of worry; exhale the cloudy, sticky energy. Breathe in the golden yellow aura, filling your Spleen Center with **golden yellow light**. Repeat to complete 18 to 36 cycles, then allow the light to radiate out to your mouth, nose, ears, eyes and tongue. Wrap the **golden aura** around you, leaving a golden shine on your skin.

10. The **kidneys** and bladder correspond to the blue color of the water element. Gentleness is contained within the **blue healing light**. Inhale the blue aura into the kidneys. Expel feelings of fear or stress on breathing out. Allow your energy-field to expand, breathing in and out the blue energy for 18-36 times, until it starts to radiate out from your kidneys to your ears, eyes, tongue, mouth and nose. Gather the blue mist on your skin, enveloping you with a **blue aura**.

11. The **liver** and gall bladder connect to the green color of the wood element. Kindness replaces anger, which is expelled on breathing out. Do the same as above and create a green aura around you. Exhale the dark, cloudy heat. Inhale the **nourishing green** of the forests. Do 18 to 36 cycles, until the green light has completely filled the liver and starts to radiate out to your eyes, tongue, mouth, nose and ears. Invite the green light to form a **green aura** around you.

12. Smile down to the **sexual organs** and reproductive system. Feel **love and the energy of sexual arousal**, the heart and sexual organs coming to union. Observe how this process transforms the sexual energy into Chi. Channel down orange and red light to the sexual organs. Thank them for their work in keeping you healthy and for giving you life force and creativity.

The Cosmic Star and the Earth Star

At the moment of conception, the two forces yin and yang connect with such a force, that only fractions of a moment later, the two forces explode into nine different energy centers. Seven of them we find in the body and two of them outside the body, forming our Personal Stars.

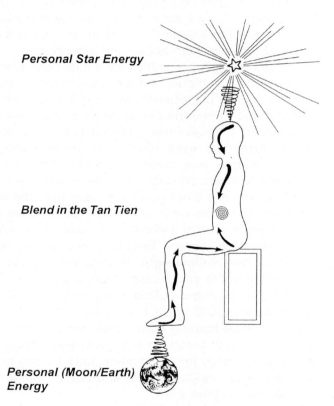

Personal Star Energy

Blend in the Tan Tien

Personal (Moon/Earth) Energy

Fig. 2.3

The two Personal Stars are in fact energy centers connecting the auric field of each individual with the universal forces and the earth forces. In a way one can see the aim of the Taoist Inner Alchemy in bringing these nine forces together, merging them in one force and thus, enabling them to return to the original force, the Wu Chi.

There is a star about 6 inches above your crown and 1 to 3 feet below the soles of your feet, also known as the higher self, guidance, protector, adviser. These stars are our connection to the cosmic force, the universal force and the earth deep below us.

Always make sure your Tan Tien is warm and the sacrum, cranium and mideyebrow are breathing. Be aware of the crown breathing and see a star or a small sun above you. Feel a light beam extend out of the crown and make a connection to the star above you. Keep on breathing until you feel a strong connection. Feel how the star above you is exercising a strong pulling force on your crown. Once you feel the pull on your crown you will also feel a strong pull down from the ground. Be aware of the star above and the earth and universal force below you. Feel that both of them have a strong 'pull' on you.

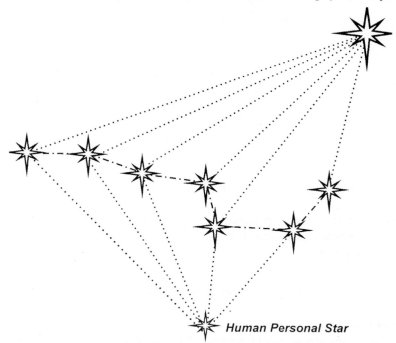

Human Personal Star

Fig. 2.4 North Star, the Big Dipper and Human Personal Star

In Taoism we consider the North Star as emitting a violet light (which is regarded as the highest healing light) and the Big Dipper as emitting a red light.

You can do these meditations sitting, or standing in the Chi Kung posture. The standing position will provide a stronger structure and allow for a better connection with the earth through the feet.

1. Reconfirm the star above you and the earth directly below you.
2. Fix the image of the North Star and the Big Dipper six to nine feet above your crown. See the cup of the Big Dipper filling with the violet light, which gathers Chi from the North Star and the universe.

3. Reach up with your right hand, and hold on to the handle of the Big Dipper. Pour the violet light down to your Personal Star 4 to 6 inches above your head, in order to predigest the energy of the violet light. Then let it flow down to your crown, into the upper Tan Tien, to be processed and flow down to the Heart Center (middle Tan Tien) or to the back of the head down to C-7 (cervical 7) and T-2 (thoracic 2) and down to the palms.

Fig. 2.5

4. Always remember to breathe in slowly so you can process the awareness of the lower Tan Tien. Feel a suction, warmth (Chi) and continue to breathe in and be aware of the suction of the crown, North Star and Big Dipper above you.

Fill the Joints with Chi

The bones have the ability to process cosmic Chi (Chi above and around you) to be used by your body. The joints are also able to store Chi which serves as a cushion between the bones.

1. Be aware of your index fingers and thumbs. Feel Chi enter the fingers and the joints; this will make them tense and stiff. The stiffness and tension come from the Chi filling in the joints and pushing the fingers to become longer. Keep all fingers tense with Chi and slightly raise the index fingers and open the thumbs to the sides. Feel the thumbs tense. Breathe into the fingertips, until you feel the sensation of Chi entering the fingers. Continue to breathe in the Chi and the stiff feeling will go from the fingers to the wrist, elbow and shoulder joints, making the whole area tense and stiff, so the fingers and the arms become one piece. Chi will gradually fill every joint of the body and make the whole body become one piece.

2. Be aware of the big toes, breathe into the toes and feel the toes grow longer. When the Chi fills the joints, the big toes become tense and stiff. Gradually it will fill the other toes and the feet and come up to the ankles, knees, femur bones and hips, until it reaches the sacrum and the spine. A sensation of numbness or an electric charge will start to flow up your legs. The legs and the spine become one piece.

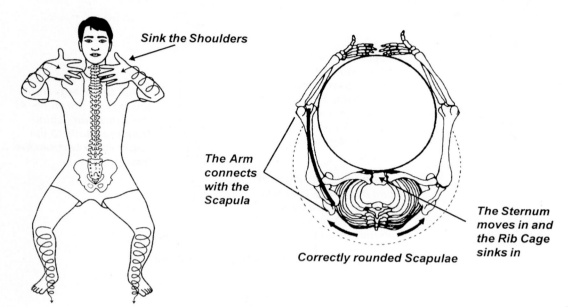

Sink the Shoulders

The Arm connects with the Scapula

The Sternum moves in and the Rib Cage sinks in

Correctly rounded Scapulae

Fig. 2.6 Bone Structure

Bone Breathing and Marrow Washing

Bone Breathing is one of the main practices of the Cosmic Healing Chi Kung practice. This is a method of drawing external Chi through the skin into the bones to help regrow and replenish the bone marrow, thusly assisting in the production of white blood cells. Sending Chi into the bones will therefore enhance the immune system. This process also helps to clean out fat in the bone marrow ("Washing the Marrow"), one of the main causes of osteoporosis (brittleness of the bones). Tension in the muscles close to the bones is decreased so Chi and blood can flow into them easily, and the bones themselves become strong.

The Bone Breathing process uses the mind and the eyes to absorb Chi into the bones. The better your Bone Breathing is, the better your Cosmic Healing Chi Kung practice will be. Mind and eyes are also used immediately after the exercise to gather the energy at the navel. Once you have it, when you move your hand, the energy will follow easily. You will be able to absorb external Chi effortlessly, so you will not need to use your own energy in your healing work.

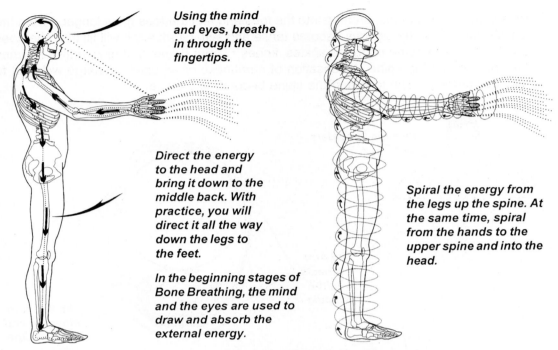

Using the mind and eyes, breathe in through the fingertips.

Direct the energy to the head and bring it down to the middle back. With practice, you will direct it all the way down the legs to the feet.

In the beginning stages of Bone Breathing, the mind and the eyes are used to draw and absorb the external energy.

Spiral the energy from the legs up the spine. At the same time, spiral from the hands to the upper spine and into the head.

Fig. 2.7 Bone Breathing through the Fingers

Bone Breathing

There are several variations in the Bone Breathing and Marrow Washing process. Here we will introduce you to the first type of Bone Breathing, inhaling and exhaling Chi through the skin and packing it into the bones. In this method, you imagine that your bones are like hollow bamboo tubes and that you are breathing and drawing the Chi into them.

Bone Breathing is practiced in a three-stage process. Let your breathing follow a normal pace. Do not strain or hold your breath too long.·

1. You can do this practice in the sitting position or in the Embracing the Tree posture (or any other Iron Shirt Chi Kung posture). You will use your mind and eye power to breathe in a short breath and at the same time feel suction. Suck the Chi of the atmosphere into your hands, eventually expand to the universe, breathe in a few times more. Use a combination of mind-eye-heart power (Yi) to suck the Chi from the atmosphere into your hands, while taking small sips of breath. **Smile.** Once you can clearly feel the increase of Chi-pressure in your hands, you extend the feeling throughout your arms, having the whole skin surface of the arms breathing in the Chi. Feel the skin hold Chi pressure.

2. Inhale one more deep breath and lightly contract the arm muscles to squeeze the Chi into the bones, hold for a while, condensing the Chi into the marrow of your bones. Exhale and at the same time, feel a distinct heaviness in the bone, meaning that the

Chi has been condensed and packed into the bones. Eventually you will use more mind power (mind/eyes/heart power) and less muscle and use soft breathing, to draw the force into the bones. Do this 6 to 9 times; rest and feel the Chi having been condensed into the bones.

3. Proceed in the same way, breathing in progressively through the bones of the forearms, upper arms, scapula, collarbone, sternum and ribs. You may feel a different sensation as you breathe in each area (in some areas the feeling is cool, in others warm or tingling, depending on the bone structure and the quality of the marrow).

4. Inhale and exhale in the same way through the legs and then, in a step-by-step progression, inhale up through the calf bones, thighbones, pelvis, coccyx and sacrum and up the spinal column to the C-7 vertebra.

5. Finally breathe in through the arms and legs simultaneously. Combine their energy as it flows up past C-7 and up through the neck and into the skull. Breathe in this way for at least nine breaths. Conclude by collecting energy at the navel.

Marrow Washing

You can wash your bone marrow with earth force, heavenly force, or with cosmic force. This energy helps to cleanse and rejuvenate the bone marrow.

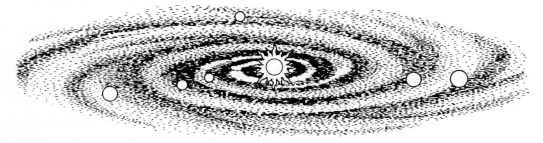

Fig. 2.8 Star and the Direction of Spiral

Heavenly Force Marrow Washing with Violet Light

1. Men place the left palm on the top of the head and cover with the right palm. Be aware of your Personal Star above. Slightly press the palms and spiral in a clockwise direction, meaning to spiral from the front to the right ear, to the back and the left ear for 9 times; rest and feel the increased Chi pressure in the crown. Do 3 sets.

2. Women place the right palm on the top of the head and cover with the left palm. Be aware of your Personal Star above you. Press the palms lightly and spiral in a counter clockwise direction, meaning to spiral from the front to the left ear, to the back and the right ear for 9 times. Rest and feel the increased Chi pressure in the crown. Do 3 sets.

3. **Smile.** Raise the arms, palms facing toward heaven and scoop the galactic Chi into a ball above your head. This Chi ball contains the North Star and the Big Dipper. See the Dipper cup fill with violet energy. Imagine you reach out your arms to hold the Dipper handle and pour the violet liquid over your crown. It will feel as if there is a numbness

descending down. Your palms face down now to empty Chi and the whole galaxy down into your crown. You may perceive this energy as a violet amethyst and red light frequency.

Fig. 2.9 Your Hands scoop up the whole Universe through the North Star and the Big Dipper.

4. Guide this sensation down to your skull, deep into your brain, sternum, cervical vertebrae, thoracic vertebrae, lumbar vertebrae and down through your legs. Feel it penetrating and enlivening your bones, deep into the bone marrow, washing, cleansing, energizing.

   This liquid-like Chi spills all the way down to your feet. Feel it connecting with the earth through the soles of your feet; be aware of the bubbling springs (the K1 point of the kidney meridian) breathing and pulsating.

Fig 2.10 Earth Force Marrow Washing Yellow Light

1. Touch your navel with the fingers of your hand. Focus on the door of life and let the fire activate in the Tan Tien and kidneys. Chi will rise up to the brain.
2. Move your hands down touching your femur bones, feel your hands penetrate into the bones and into the bone marrow. It will feel like an electric shock, or tingling is moving all the way down through the bones of the legs and down to the soles of your feet.
3. Slowly move your fingers down touching the bones and the bone marrow until you are squatting with the heels touching the earth. Move your intention down through the earth to touch the universe on the other side. Raise your sacrum up and picture yellow light coming up from the earth and the other side of the universe, focus on the lower Tan Tien and feel it fill with Chi. Do this three times.

Fig. 2.11 The Hands circle to Gather Earth Chi in Squatting Position.

4. Palms face down to the earth. **Smile**. Be aware of the galaxy and the yellow light, make three to six circles to gather the Chi below. Gather the yellow Chi to touch your heels and feel the yellow Chi rise up the leg bones. Feel it bubbling, like electric currents running up through the bones of your feet, tibia and fibula, femur, pelvis and spine. While touching your bones and bone marrow with your fingers, slide your hands along the whole route on the back of the legs, slowly coming all the way up to touch the coccyx and the sacrum. Concentrate on your Sexual Center so the energy will flow and spread out to the sexual organs. Go back to the navel and gather the Chi into your Tan Tien.

The Source of Chi and Color

There are different sources of Chi in the universe. Cosmic (air), nature, earth and human to name a few. In humans, each part of the body has a different kind of energy and these energies correlate directly with the universe and nature. Each part of our body, organs and glands, can produce, receive, transform and emit different types of Chi.

Earth Chi

The earth Chi penetrates into and out of the ground and extends several inches away from it. It is dense and more closely packed than some other forms of energy. It is usually more dense than cosmic Chi. We can easily see this earth Chi by staring for a few minutes before sunset, at the horizon and the line that appears just above it. You can see the density and movement of the earth Chi as it interacts with cosmic Chi. With practice you will gradually see the earth Chi just a few inches away from the ground.

Earth Chi contains yellow and some white Chi. Earth and cosmic Chi, when combined, have a very powerful healing reaction in the body. It is very balancing and mild. In healing we always use **white Chi to dilute** and tone down the more intense colors. Some colors are too powerful, overactive or 'heaty' if used by themselves. The body will absorb other sources of Chi much more easily when properly diluted with white Chi. **A very effective mixture is 70% white Chi and 30% color.**

Simple Practice:
During and after sunrise (and before sunset) look at the edge of the sky and the earth. Stand still and extend your palms toward the sun, **smile** and absorb the colors in to you.

Human and Nature Chi

This Chi is derived from all the things we can see on the earth. In Cosmic Healing, we use energy from the mountains, lakes, oceans, forests, caves, valleys, rocks and precious stones. The Taoists classify the elements into five forces: earth, metal, water, wood and fire. There are five elements in our body, in nature, in the cosmos and in the universe.

According to Taoist tradition, once we make the connection to ourselves and control our internal bodily elements, we will quickly make connections to nature and the universal forces and employ them easily.

Solar Chi

Before sunrise or sunset there is more white Chi in the air which we can use abundantly for health and healing. White Chi affects the lungs and the large intestine, so we direct this Chi to these organs. This will generate further Chi to maintain our daily activities. White contains all the colors of the rainbow or spectrum.

Sun Essence

The best time for practice with the sun is at sunrise and sunset, when its glare is not too strong for the eyes. The sun spectrum from sunrise to 9 a.m. is violet, and can be used for all organs, especially for spiritual work. You can select any color that you need.

9-11 a.m. is blue and can be used to strengthen the kidneys.

11 a.m.-1 p.m. is green for the liver.

1-3 p.m. is orange for sexual energy.

3-5 p.m. is red for the heart.

Seasonal Sun Practice

You can **emphasize** practice of the sun 'spectrum' inside the organ that corresponds to the season and its color;

Winter in the kidneys, blue.

Spring in the liver, green.

Summer in the heart, red.

Fall in the lungs, white.

Indian summer in the spleen, yellow.

Absorbing the Breath of the Sun in the Four Seasons

In Spring, absorb the orange Chi of the sun *before* it sets. In fall, absorb the orange twilight Chi of the sun *after* it has set. In Winter, absorb the white vapors of midnight (sun shining on the moon). In Summer, absorb the perfect clarity of the meridional sun of midday (protect the eyes during midday sun absorption). Breathe each in deeply.

These four types of breath, in addition to the blue breath of heaven and the yellow breath of the earth, are called the **six breaths.**

Sun Practice

1. Practice with the sun during and after sunrise.
2. Start with the Inner Smile, 'Warm the Stove' and make the navel warm.
3. Be aware of the mideyebrow. **Smile** into your eyes. Make your eyes cool and soft.
4. Open your eyes, look at the sun and keep on blinking the eyes. Close your eyes for a while. The eyes should be facing the sun. (You might see a red and yellowish color). Select the yellow and breathe it in through the crown and mid-eyebrow and into the nose, eyes and mouth (mouth closed, but feel the color penetrate into it). Feel the bones in your skull, the brain and the bone marrow. Absorb the yellow spectrum to wash and help grow healthy marrow. Let this ray penetrate down to the neck. Some might feel numbness, like a wave penetrating deep into the bone marrow and each cell of the body.
5. Let this ray go down to the sternum and the rib cage and feel it activate the thymus gland. This will help to strengthen the immune system.

6. Let the color flow down to the spine and feel numbness, tingling, or warmth in the interior of the bones. This feeling may spread out to the organs. Let it go down to the hips and sacrum. Feel that the bones and the bone marrow have been activated and let the Chi descend to the bones of the legs and feet.

    The sun practice can produce the effect of a cosmic baptism. Feel the sun's ray baptize your whole body.
7. Rest and let the body absorb all these cosmic nutrients.
8. After you practice, look at the sun; single out the colors and picture the organs and see the organs glow with their relevant color.

Follow with the Seasonal Sun Practice (previous page) for the relevant time of year. During fall, picture the white color in the lungs. Look at the sun, blink the eyes, then close the eyes; select the white color and breathe into the lungs.

    Winter into the kidneys, blue rays.
    Spring into the liver, green rays.
    Summer into the heart, red rays.
    Indian Summer into the spleen, yellow rays.

Sun Essence Captured in Water

The essence of the sun is captured in water by exposing the water to sun from sunrise to 9 a.m. This is for absorption of violet, which can be used for all organs and especially for spiritual work. The time from 9-11 a.m. is for the absorption of blue and can be used to strengthen the kidneys; 11 a.m. - 1 p.m. green for liver; 1 - 3 p.m. is orange for sexual energy; 3 - 5 p.m. is red for the heart.

    A special water can be made on the first fifteen days of the month in which the sun comes to the Golden Door. This water is called "Mineral Light Mother of Waters".

    To capture this sun essence, put purified rain or spring water in a sterilized bottle out in sunlight during the corresponding phase of the spectrum for one or more days.

    You can drink the water, or make herb tea or mix with food or medicine.

Solstice and Equinox

Taoists believe that the sun stops in its movement on the first day of each season. The moon stops on the days of the equinoxes and solstices. These stops are called "Doors". It is the "Golden Door" in the spring. This is the door of access to the sun. In Autumn it is the "Eastern Well", this is the door of access to the moon. The next stage is "Universal Yang" in the middle of summer when the sun culminates. "Great Cold" is the culmination of the moon in winter.

    Symbolically, it is thought that the practitioner goes to be received by the Lord that grants the fruits of immortality. Gathering the sun essence at the "Golden Door" is done on the 3rd, 9th, 17th, 21st and 25th of the month in which the sun enters at the Golden Door. The exact same practice is done for the moon when it reaches her door. The days for gathering the moon essence are the 3rd, 15th and 25th.

Healing Colors

Blue Chi

Blue like Yin, water energy, has a cooling and inhibiting effect, (opposite to red, which has a strengthening and stimulating effect). When we draw energy down, some peoples' bodies can't adjust to it immediately, so using blue Chi is always good.

'Water blue' is the one element that always brings harmony and does not cause any harm.

Blue has a cooling , soothing and mildly anesthetic effect, so it can reduce pain and inflammation.

Blue can help make the blood clot, thus it is beneficial for stopping bleeding.

Blue brings down fevers.

Blue can help induce rest and sleep.

Blue "washes" away dark, negative Chi.

Green Chi

Green Chi is mild and safe. Green Chi is used in cleansing and decongesting disease in the body. It has a 'loosening' effect on the ailment. Once loose, you can use the orange Chi to expel the disease. Negative energy can then be removed by localized sweeping, either through the arms or through the legs.

If you need to energize the organs, first energize with light green Chi. Darker green and orange Chi can be used for cancers.

One should use green Chi before using orange. When green Chi and light orange are projected simultaneously the effects are multiplied. They can be used for hard and deep deposits.

It is important to use green Chi before using orange, red, or violet.

Light green Chi is used to break down and loosen stubborn diseased energy.

Then light orange Chi is used to expel the loosened diseased energy.

Green Chi flushes infection.

> detoxifies.
> breaks down dead cells.
> helps break down blood clots.
> helps dispel colds and fevers.

White Chi

Air Chi, solar Chi and earth Chi consist of white light. White Chi is the harmonizing Chi. It moderates and redistributes excess Chi generated by other colors, from the area of bodily treatment to other parts of the body, by way of preferential need. For the purposes of healing, it is good to have a blend of 70% white and 30% of the other color.
Experiment with blending white Chi with other forces:
    Project the luminous white to the core with color Chi to the periphery.
    Then reverse and use the color Chi at the core and the white Chi at the periphery.
    Light color Chi mixes well with white Chi.

    When in doubt just use white Chi, especially for infants and babies. Use white for older or weaker people and use blue, green and pale violet for minor ailments. For minor ailments, it is good to use the blue and green and light violet always mixed with white.
    Light white violet or golden Chi for severe ailments.
    White-red has a stimulating and strengthening effect.
    We have a soft violet and a very strong violet in the North Star. You can dilute these colors with white.
    When you want to change to a different color Chi, it is good to flick or shake the hand a few times before energizing with other Chi.

Red Chi

Light red Chi has a strengthening effect. Dark red will weaken the treated part. When using color for healing you will need to project luminous white at the core with light red at the periphery, to strengthen the organs.

A light, whitish red:
    Strengthens the weak organs and affected parts.
    Improves circulation.
    Dilates the blood vessels and air tubes; useful for treating heart and asthmatic patients.
    Reduces excess cold energy.
    Good for treating allergies.
    Expelling or elimination of waste, toxins, germs and diseased energy.
    Reviving unconscious patients and prolonging the life of dying patients.

Avoid the use of dark colors, which may cause an adverse reaction. Dark red Chi should not be used because it can cause inflammation and constriction. It should not be used on venereal ailments because it stimulates the rapid growth of venereal germs.

Orange Chi

If you need to use the orange Chi, you should first use the blue Chi to cool and calm the treated area.

Use light orange mixed with white. Orange is a is a powerful color, so it should be avoided in treating delicate organs such as eyes, brain, heart, spleen and the Spleen Center and the Throat Center.

Orange Chi has a stimulating effect on the large intestine and can affect the bowel movement. The solar plexus and the navel are connected to the small and large intestines so use with caution if you need to use orange on these organs. Avoid use in patients suffering from appendicitis because it might accelerate the rupture of the inflamed appendix.

Orange Chi can also be used to activate, or awaken the consciousness of a dying person. Dark orange and dark green have a destructive effect so they can be used, with extreme care, to treat certain cancers.

Orange Chi:

expels and eliminates waste, toxins, germs and diseased energy,

helps relieve constipation,

aids in menstrual problems,

is used for healing arthritis, cysts, colds, coughs and lung problems.

Yellow Chi

Yellow Chi has a close connection to the nerves, bones and the bone marrow. Yellow is also the color of the spleen. The spleen is involved in the assimilation of food and the appetite. So, when the spleen is balanced, the appetite will be controlled.

Yellow Chi has:

a stimulating effect on the nerves,

helps make the tissues, organs and bones healthy,

is good for broken bones, skin problems and repairing the cells,

has the power of multiplying; growing the nerves and bone marrow.

Ordinary and Luminous Violet Chi

From surrounding Chi; air, earth, solar energy. From the higher self, soul, crown point, North Star and Big Dipper. Divine or soul energy.

This special light has all the properties of the other colors. Luminous violet is much more powerful than ordinary violet Chi.

Many of their divine properties are listed here. Remember, always use the blue or green to prepare the area first.

It has the properties of all types of Chi.

It causes rapid regenerating effects on damaged organs and nerves.

Dark luminous (electric) violet can be used for tumors or cancers.

It develops the crown center, spiritual essence and core.
Good for psychological ailments.
There is more information about this light in Cosmic Healing I.

Internal Organs Chi

This Chi is manufactured by the body daily and is readily available. It is good to mix it with universal or cosmic Chi for healing.

A brief word about detoxifying organs' Chi.

Before we can effectively use organs' Chi, we must be sure that it is healthy. Many of the organs hold excess negative emotional Chi. We call this an emotional link. Many diseases are caused by emotional links. People use psychology to deal with such problems and it can work to a certain level but, the energy tends to jam up in the organs if it is not released.

Commitment is of course necessary for successful practice. If you are teaching, tell your students that the **Inner Smile** should be done every day; also to contract the pelvic floor muscles 9-18 times, until they feel the energy radiating upwards. This will help strengthen the major organs. It is alright to insist that if they don't do the Inner Smile and toning up the body every day, they will not heal. If they do commit to doing some daily practice and they come to you for work on their energy field, you will be able to help. Using Chi, color and mind power helps to improve the organs.

Cosmic Healing works very well with Chi Nei Tsang (Chinese Internal Organs Massage). Cosmic Healing will do what it can. Chi Nei Tsang and the Universal Tao practices will do what they can. You have to allow the practices to take care of themselves, as the **Tao begins to flow through you.** Allow yourself to heal. When you combine the above practices you will open yourself to the forces of nature and the Divine.

The person you are treating should be under the supervision of a medical doctor. Such supervision is especially necessary with serious physical, emotional and mental disorders. The patient should have a balance between the prescribed medicine and the work with the Universal Tao. The doctor should be advised of what we intend to do with the patient.

When working with improving organ health, the major point is to draw in white Chi, breaking down red, orange, yellow, green, blue, and violet; then distribute it to all of the organs.

Ming Men Chi

Yellow, pelvic organs.
Kidney power. Regulates blood pressure and is good for increasing low vitality and aiding back problems. Internal root of the meridian system. Healing for prenatal traumas.

Solar Plexus and Liver Chi

It is very important to use the Inner Smile when using this Chi. The solar plexus is very strongly connected to the liver which is also a very strong emotional center. A lot of emotions (cloudy grey in appearance) get stuck in the solar plexus.

Navel Center Chi

Yellow, some violet - increasing original Chi - helps to circulate Chi in the meridians. Good for small and large intestines, constipation, loose bowels, inability to assimilate food and nutrients and aids in raising overall vitality.

Heart Center Chi

Golden and red Chi. The thymus gland and defense system. Energize the Heart and Lungs Center through the back of the Heart Center. The heart is the seat of compassion.

Throat Center Chi

Green. Thyroid, parathyroid, lymphatic system, sex center, asthma

Mideyebrow

Yellow and violet. Pituitary, endocrine system, eye problems, cancer.

Forehead

Light violet. Pineal, nervous system, cosmic consciousness.

Crown Center

Violet and golden. Entry point of Divine energy.

Spleen Chi

Yellow. The spleen connects to the solar plexus and the navel. It is the major center that connects to all the organs. Holding solar energy or a white ball at the solar plexus will help distribute Chi to all the organs.

If the solar plexus gets clogged, the liver and spleen will be blocked as well. The spleen is linked with the 'Door of Life' (point opposite navel on the back) and the navel.

The spleen (located at the left side under the rib cage) can take in the white Chi and absorb it directly through the front or back, the spleen center or the navel area. The Chi will be broken down into color and distributed to other centers and to the organs.

A dirty spleen center can lower immunity, create dirty blood, bone ailments, arthritis and rheumatism.

Basic technique to improve health, reduce tension and retard aging.

Green or blue light mixed with white. Localized sweeping of the front of the solar plexus 30 times counterclockwise, guiding dirty Chi to leave the organs. In other words; counter-clockwise sweeping motions to move energy.

Perform a localized sweep with blue in the solar plexus, liver, stomach and pancreas.
Energize crown, forehead, back of head, left and right brain with white.
Sweep front and back of heart and lungs with white.
Sweep front and back of spleen, spine, navel, lower abdomen, kidneys with white.
Sweep the sexual center with white.
Sweep the base of sacrum with white.
Sweep the arms and hands with white.
Sweep the legs and feet with white.

To Stabilize:
After energizing weak people, use light whitish blue and tell them not to take a shower or bath for 24 hours.

Eye Problems

Use green and yellow.

Constipation

Use yellow and orange for the large intestines. Diaphragm, liver, pancreas, stomach, heart lungs. Energize the pancreas through the back of the solar plexus. When the intestines are exhausted, they can be revitalized at the solar plexus center.

> ## Use Compassion, Love, Kindness

Microcosmic Orbit

The Microcosmic Orbit Meditation awakens, circulates and directs Chi through the Governing Channel, which ascends from the base of the spine up to the head and the Functional or Conception Channel, which runs from the tip of the tongue down the middle of the torso to the perineum. Dedicated practice of this ancient esoteric method eliminates stress and nervous tension, energizes the internal organs, restores health to damaged tissue, and builds a strong sense of personal well-being.

The Microcosmic Orbit is the foundation of Cosmic Healing practice. Each new practice is dependent upon the quality of your meditations and your ability to perfect the Microcosmic Orbit. In order to master Cosmic Healing, one must practice meditation daily.

The meditations in the Microcosmic Orbit 'system' also strengthen the Original Chi and teach you the basics of circulating energy. This enables the palms, the soles of the feet, the mid-eyebrow point and the crown to open. These specific locations are the major points where energy can be absorbed, condensed and transformed into fresh new life force.

Focus on the lower Tan Tien (the area where the Original Chi is stored, between the navel, kidneys and sexual organs). Feel the pulsing in this area, observe whether this area feels tense or relaxed, cool or warm, expansive or contracting. Notice any sensations of Chi: tingling, heat, expansiveness, pulsing, electricity or magnetism. Allow these to grow and expand. Then let this energy flow out to the Navel Center.

Use your intention (mind-eye-power) to spiral in the point and guide and move the Chi. Let the energy flow down to the Sexual Center (the Ovarian or Sperm Palace).

Move the energy from the Sexual Center to the perineum and down to the soles of the feet.

Draw the energy up from the soles to the perineum and to the sacrum.

Draw the energy up from the sacrum to the Door of Life (the point in the spine opposite the navel).

Draw the energy up to the mid-spine point (T11 vertebra).

Draw the energy up to the base of the skull (Jade Pillow).

Draw the energy up to the crown.

Move the energy down from the crown to the mid-eyebrow point.

Touch the tip of your tongue to your upper palate; press and release a few times; then rest and lightly touch the tongue to the palate, sensing the electricity or tingling feeling of the energy flowing in to the tongue. Move the energy down from the mid-eyebrow to where the tip of your tongue and palate meet.

Move the energy down from the palate through your tongue to the Throat Center.

Move the energy down from the throat to the Heart Center.

Bring the energy down from the heart to the solar plexus. Feel a small sun shining out.

Bring the energy back down to the navel.

Continue to circulate your energy through this entire sequence of points at least nine times. Once the pathways are open, you can let your energy flow continuously like a stream or river, without stopping at each point.

Conclude when you wish, by collecting energy at the navel.

Men: Cover your navel with both palms, left hand over right. Collect and mentally spiral the energy outward from the navel 36 times clockwise and then inward 24 times counter-clockwise.

Women: Cover your navel with both palms, right hand over left. Collect and mentally spiral the energy outward from the navel 36 times counterclockwise and then inward 24 times clockwise.

For more details of this practice please see the book, *'Awaken Healing Light'*
by Mantak Chia.

Cosmic Inner Smile and the Six Healing Sounds

These are very important practices to make the connection between the organs, colors and the good virtue energy in each organ. The colors will help you to make the connection to the cosmic and universal healing power.

Red from heart
White from lungs
Yellow from the spleen
Blue from the kidneys
Green from the liver

Each organ has its own vital color and will radiate this color in abundance, as an aura for vitality, protection and healing. These colors are connected to the universe. Over a period of time, the power of each healing sound will help enhance the universal connection. Each sound will provide different healing power. The practices also help balance, refine and transform negative sick energy back to positive vital energy.

Iron Shirt Chi Kung and Bone Breathing

Iron Shirt Chi Kung and Bone Breathing are standing meditations. These exercises help you to become grounded and build good structure. They help you to take in greater force and connect to the earth force. In turn, this will help draw in the heavenly energy. The practices strengthen the body and enable it to contain a greater energetic charge. These abilities are essential prerequisites for handling increasing amounts of energy.

Iron Shirt Chi Kung also includes the art of Changing the Sinews and Washing the Marrow. Through these subsystems, you learn to absorb, store and discharge large amounts of energy through the tendons and bones. *These practices are outlined in detail in the books, 'Iron Shirt Chi Kung I and Bone Marrow Nei Kung' by Mantak Chia.*

To attain skill in Cosmic Healing, it will help if you practice the meditation above as a minimum requirement. If you already have other Chi Kung or meditation practices they will also be beneficial. Beyond this basic level, the Universal Tao System includes many other intermediate and advanced Chi Kung practices and meditations. The further one advances, the greater one's mastery of Chi.

Your increasing level of skill in the Universal Tao System will reflect immediately in your Cosmic Healing practice. Furthermore, you will discover that you can incorporate many of your Universal Tao practices directly into your practice of Cosmic Healing.

Activating the Six Directions and the Three Fires

This powerful energetic technique allows one to extend the mind, to touch the force, and to draw that energy back into the body.

The Six Directions teaches you how to expand your mind and chi for receiving healing power. By practicing the Six Directions daily this will help you increase your healing and cosmic power. Turn your mind and Chi into the cosmos, multiply them and draw them back.

Direction Below

When you achieve the three minds into one mind and expand into the six directions, press your hands down and start with the low direction. Picture yourself standing on the earth and expand yourself very far away – deep down into the earth. Very, very deep down into the earth. Your hands become very long; your feet become very long — they go all the way down into the earth and out past the galaxy below on the other side.

Push. When you push, connect with the galaxy below — pull and think about your Tan Tien filling with Chi. Push and pull. Push and pull. Fill your Tan Tien with Chi.

     A.   **B.**   **C.**

Fig. 2.12. A. Hands Expand through the Galaxy   **B.** Hands Push Forward and Pull back
C. Smile to the Primordial Chi from Universe back to the Lower Tan Tien.

1. Stand, feet together. Put your hands down, parallel to the ground. Expand your hands very far away and your mind very far away, touching the ground. Continue expanding your hands, feet and your mind very far away beyond the earth below. Go down through the galaxy, way beyond to the primordial force. It's just like you are extending all the way to the primordial force as it was about 30 billion years ago.
2. Push, moving the hands forward six inches only.
3. Pull, moving the hands back by the sides. Think about your Tan Tien and feel Chi coming to the primordial force in your Tan Tien. Smile to your Tan Tien, dark, deep and vast.
4. Push: touch the primordial force in the universe.

Fig. 2.13: A. Primordial Forces Enter the Lower Tan Tien.   **B.** Activate the Tan Tien Fire.
C. Fire Burning Under the Sea.

5. Pull back the dark primordial forces with your hands to your Tan Tien.

    Push and pull: It's just like you go to an empty space – vast. Then you come back to your Tan Tien – also empty, just like the primordial condition before anything existed. That is where all the forces come from. Push and pull 3 – 9 times.

Front Direction and Tan Tien Fire

Next, be aware of the front direction; a huge fireball appears in front of you. Open your palms: scoop up the Chi, scoop up the fire. Bring the fire into your Tan Tien. Activate the Tan Tien Fire.

1. Start with a small dot of light inside you. Expand your awareness to the universe in front of you.
2. Become aware of a big fireball in front of you. Feel your hands become bigger and longer. Scoop up the fireball. You may close your eyes to help your inner sensing.
3. Use the fireball to light the fire in your Tan Ten. Feel the fire burning in the darkness, the 'fire burning under the sea.'

Fig. 2.14 Smile to the Burning Fire.

Back Direction and Kidney Fire

Be aware of the back of the Tan Tien, the Door of Life and the back or rear direction. Extend your mind very far away to the 'back'. Scoop up the fire and light up your 'Kidney Fire'.

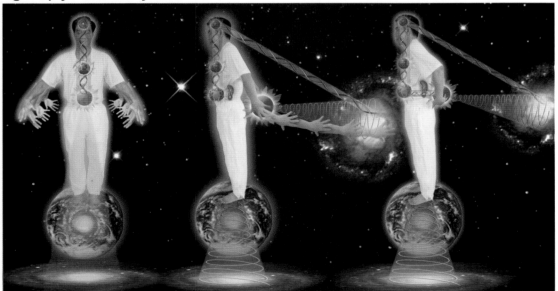

Fig. 2.15 Be aware of the back direction, move the arms toward the universe, Scoop Up the Universal Fire.

1. Expand your awareness all the way to the back. Move the arms toward the universe behind you.
2. Touch the universe; scoop up the fire. Activate the Kidney Fire. Maintain your awareness in the Tan Tien and expand out to the universe. The energetic spiral glows in the Tan Tien. Spiral in the heart, spiral in your crown and spiral in the universe.

Heart Fire

Raise your hands up under your armpits and feel yourself holding the two fireballs. Touch the heart by extending the fingers energetically in from the sides; feel your hands extending into your heart and very far away. Activate the Heart Fire.

Fig. 2.16 Activate the Heart Fire.

1. Move your hands up under your armpits and extend your fingers deep in to your heart and very far away.
2. Tan Tien and the universe: you are connecting to the 'charger,' charging more fire into yourself.
3. Feel your heart soft in the center. Feel the warmth of the fire energy of love, joy and happiness in the heart.
4. Feel the connection with the unconditional love in the universe as you keep your heart consciousness in your Tan Tien and extend your awareness out to the universe.

Sacred Fire *(Chi Fire)*

Connect the Three Fires to combine into one Fire: *Heart to Kidneys to Navel to Heart*.

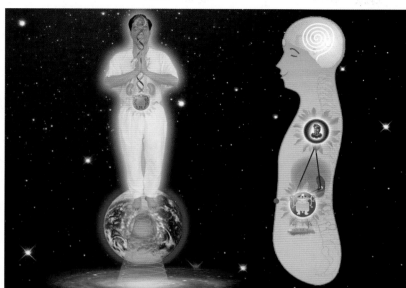

Fig. 2.17 Connect the Three Fires and Sacred Fire.

1. Move your hands together in front of your heart. Hold your hands together in front near the heart and feel the fire burning in there. Connect the Heart Fire to the Kidney Fire and from the kidneys to the Tan Tien Fire near the navel and back up to your heart — connecting them as one triangular Sacred Fire, doubling or tripling their collective power.

Open the Third Eye

Now, extend your hands out to the front, very far away – pushing, pushing, pushing. Turn your palms inward, and extend your middle fingers inward toward your third eye. Picture a crack in the middle of your forehead and pull the crack open. Feel the light from the heavens opening it and feel them shining into your brain.

1. Open your palms. Open your eyes, very dim eyes. Look to the universe. Extend your hands to the front, palms vertical. Extend the arms from the scapulas. Touch the universe.
2. Turn your palms inward and extend your middle fingers inward toward your third eye.

3. Picture a crack in the middle of your forehead and let the heavenly light shine into the brain; pull the crack open and let the light reflect into the organs.

4. Close the third eye. Again, open. Pull: open-open-open. Then, close. With the third eye open, the light from the heavens shines into your brain and reflects down to all your organs. Open and close the third eye 3 - 9 times.

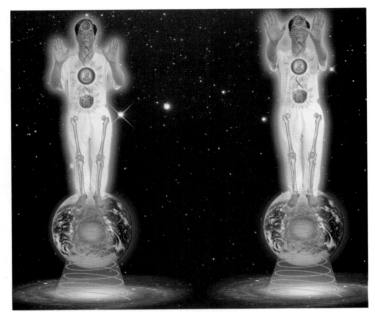

Fig. 2.18 Look as you Touch the Universe in front of you.

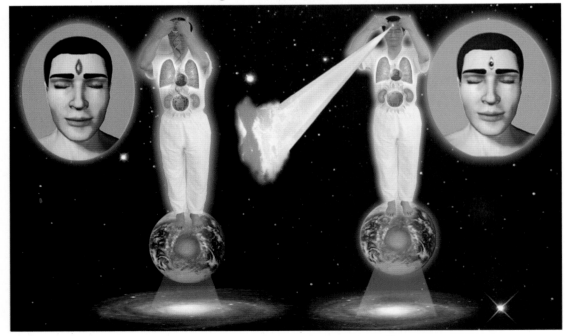

A.   **B.**
Fig. 2.19 A. Close the Third Eye.
B. Pull open the Third Eye and let Heaven's light shine into the Brain.

Front Direction: Push/Pull Master Practice

Now, turn your palms, pushing out. Push. Pull. This is the master practice that is imperative for successful completion. When you first start practicing you should do it at least one hundred times and increase up to 200 times. Push and pull. When you push, you feel your hands extended very far away – very long – reach the sky. Touch the universe.

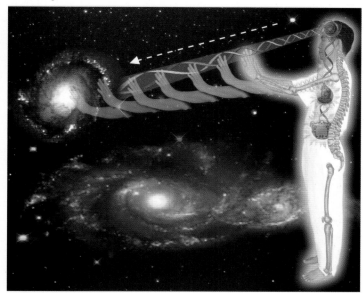

1. Push: Extend your arms and hands to the front, palms vertical. Extend the arms from the scapulas.
   Expand: smiling, smiling, touching the universe – touching the force, touch the cosmic Chi.

Fig. 2.20 Master Practice - Touch the Universe.

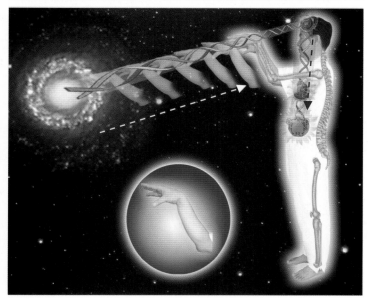

2. Pull. Draw the Chi back to you from the universe. Moving the arms from the scapulas, draw the hands toward your body in a horizontal position.

Fig. 2.21 'Drawing' Universal Chi and Think about your Tan Tien.

Pull. Think and smile to your Tan Tien. Push, very far away to the universe.
Pull. Push: smile, relax and let go, touching the sky, touching the universe.

Fig. 2.22 Let go - Push and
touch the Universe.
Repeat 6, 9 or 18 times.

Left and Right Directions

Now, move your hands to the left and right directions. Pull the Universal energy in. Push; touch the universe. Pull; think about your Tan Tien. Push – all the way, touching-touching-touching the universe.

1. Move your extended
   hands from the front
   horizon to the left and
   right sides.

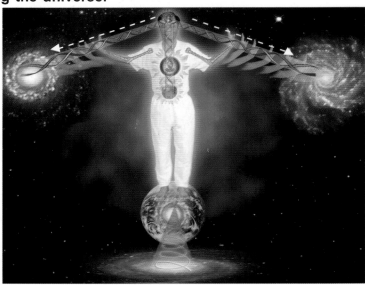

Fig. 2.23 Touch Left and
Right Universe.

2. Pull. Tan Tien: Smile to your Tan Tien. Keep smiling to your Tan Tien.
3. Push to both sides. Expand all the way, touching the universe.

Push/Pull: touching, touching the universe, drawing the Chi into you from both sides.

Repeat 3—6 times.

Fig. 2.24 Pull, just think about your Tan Tien.

Direction Above

Turn your palms up to the universe. Scoop up the Chi. Pour the Chi over your crown and touch your crown. Project the Chi all the way down to the perineum and down through the earth to the universe below. Tan Tien and universe; always feel your Tan Tien spiraling, heart spiraling, crown spiraling and the universe around you spiraling.

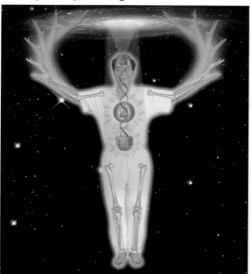
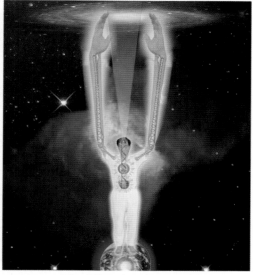

Fig. 2.25 A: Raise the hands above the crown and feel it extend up to heaven.
B: Feel that the hands are big and long and that the bones are hollow.
Fill and pack the bones with Chi.

Raise your hands up to the universe and expand your hands as big as the universe - feel the Chi charge into your bones.

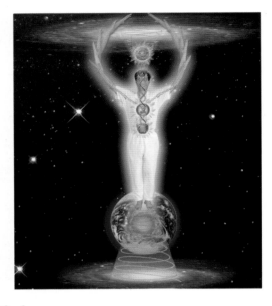

Fig. 2.26 Scoop up the Universal Chi and pour it over the head.

Open the Spine

1. Touch the back-crown point. Pour the Chi all over your crown. Feel your soles and imagine that you feel like there is a waterfall of Chi flowing from your crown all the way down to your soles. Feel your fingers grow long and the Chi penetrate down through your spine to the coccyx. Leave the fingers touchng the back of the crown, to maintain the energetic connection with the coccyx.

Spine

Fig. 2.27 Chi 'Waterfall' Cleansing the Spine.

Turn 'Three Minds into One Mind' at the Lower Tan Tien and expand the awareness to the universe. Let yourself be charged by the universe.

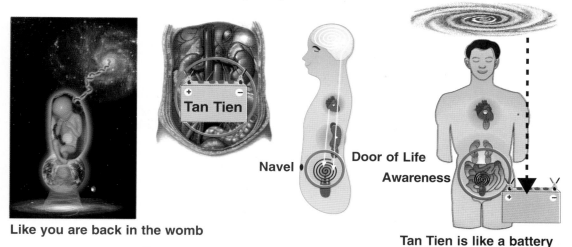

Like you are back in the womb

Tan Tien is like a battery

Fig. 2.28 Universe Charges Tan Tien 'Power'.

Be aware of the Tan Tien and spiral it like Universal energy in motion. Feel the heart center spiraling and the crown spiraling. Be aware of the universe spiraling above, below, front, back, left and right. Let all of the sick energy and the negative forces leave the body and go down into the ground, for Mother Earth to recycle. Extend the Chi from above, all the way down through the earth and the universe below.

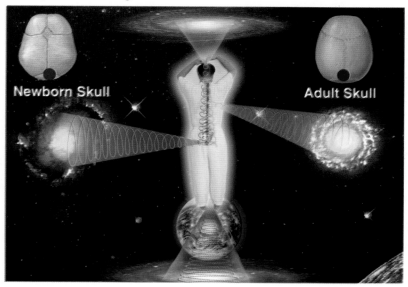

Fig. 2.29 Feel the Lower Tan Tien, heart center and the crown spiraling and feel the Universe around is spiraling and charging the three Tan Tiens.

Open the Middle Channel and Perineum

1. Move to the mid-crown point. Touch the point and project your fingers inwards; deeper, deeper through the middle of your body down to the perineum. Focus on the perineum. Feel the Chi from the universe flow right in to your perineum. Look for one dot of light. Look into the darkness, the vast darkness, the immense darkness: this is the primordial force, a cloudy moving force. Look for a dot of light at the perineum and extend your awareness all the way down through the ground and the universe below.

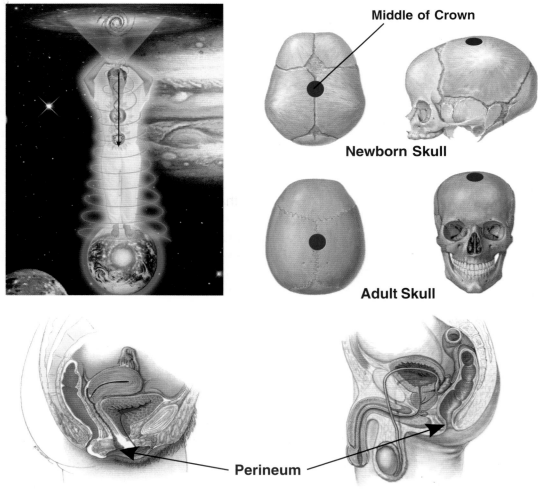

Fig. 2.30 Universal Light Shines from Crown to Perineum.

When finished opening to the six directions and igniting the three fires, gather the Chi in the center and bring this expanded awareness into the healing session.

Tan Tien and the Universe

The expression, 'Tan Tien and the Universe', is a reminder to feel your Tan Tien, heart, mideyebrow and crown spiraling and that you are connected to the universe spiraling in the six directions around you.

1. Establish a Complete Address

You will use your Yi (the three-mind power), to recharge your Chi repeatedly for various purposes. You recharge by connecting to the Universal Chi in the six directions of the universe simultaneously. When you charge a particular area or direct Chi into the body to a particular point, you first establish a connection point for the Chi by placing the hand or fingers at an appropriate location on the surface. This is like giving an address for the Chi to go to. Once the address is established and the Chi starts to go there, leave your hands there.

Then you move your attention to where you want the Chi to go in the body. Feel the Chi connected to and charging the intended location.

2. Charge Tan Tien from Universe

When the address connection is established, be aware of your Tan Tien, heart center, mideyebrow and crown spiraling. Be sure that the conscious mind of the heart is lowered to the Tan Tien and the awareness mind of the abdomen is connected to the mideyebrow crown and out to the universe. Feel them connected to the spiraling energy in the six directions of the universe. Let the universe charge your Tan Tien.

3. Don't Stop at the Address

With your focus in the Tan Tien, the Chi will go from there to the 'address' indicated by your hands and then to the intended location in the body. Don't let Chi stop there, however.

4. Direct Chi out the Opposite Side to Universe

Direct your attention to guide the Chi flow through the body and out the opposite side. The idea is to clear out any blockages and prevent any others from accumulating and also to release sick energy and negative forces down into the earth. Let the Universal Chi flow out through the universe and beyond.

Open the Three Tan Tiens

Move your hands down to the mideyebrow. Touch the mideyebrow. We are going to open the three Tan Tiens, starting with the Upper Tan Tien.

Upper Tan Tien - Mideyebrow

1. Recharge. Remember: Tan Tien – heart consciousness in, awareness out. Spiral – Tan Tien, heart, third eye and crown. Universe – six directions spiraling.

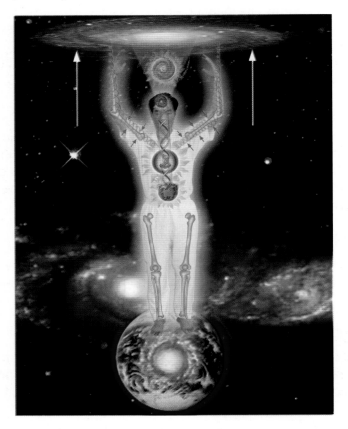

Fig. 2.31 Raise hands and charge the Universe Chi.

2. Move your hands down and touch the mideyebrow. Feel your fingers grow very long (energetically) and penetrate all the way back to the base of the skull. Focus on the back. Remember: Tan Tien and the universe spiraling. With the spiraling, the Chi in the fingers will become hot. It will expand and penetrate out through the back of the head all the way to the universe behind.

Fig 2.32 Fingers touch Mideyebrow and penetrate to the Universe.

Fig 2.33 Tan Tien and the Universe

3. Picture your fingers like laser beams of Chi. 'Tan Tien and Universe': Feel your Tan Tien and the universe spiral and charge your fingers. Move your fingers out from the mideyebrow around the side of the head to the top of the ears. Your fingers are like lasers -cut-cut-cutting open your skull right in the middle, around to the top of the ear, cutting open your Upper Tan Tien. Cut and project your fingers long into the middle of your brain. Spiral your Tan Tien and the universe. Leave your fingers there. Concentrate on your Tan Tien spiraling – your heart, crown, the universe above, below, front, back left and right all spiraling. Your Tan Tien is a big empty space: primordial force; darkness. You can put so much Chi inside there! The Chi penetrates into your brain.

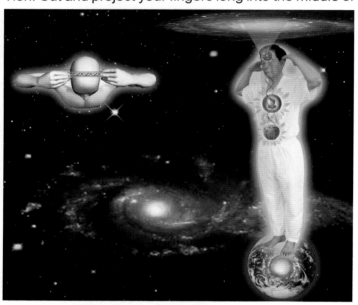

Fig. 2.34 Move the Fingers to the Top of the Ears and feel them Grow Longer. Cut Open the Center of the Skull.

4. Move your hands all the way to the back, cutting to the back of the skull. Touch and feel the upper Tan Tien open.

5. Touch the base of your skull. Focus on the mideyebrow. Feel the Chi flow like a laser beam from back to front and out to the universe in front. Complete the opening process by moving the hands back around to the mideyebrow, cutting as you go.

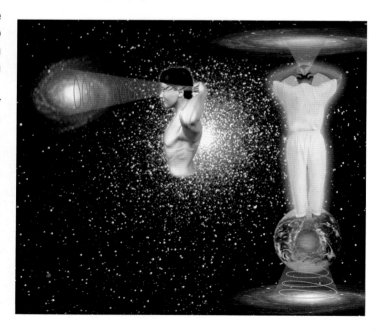

Fig. 2.35 Chi Moves Like a Laser from Front to Back of Skull.

6. Recharge in the universe. Feel your bones and your arms are hollow. Fill and compact them with Chi.
7. Scoop the Universal Chi and pour it down over your crown and all the way down, down to the middle Tan Tien.

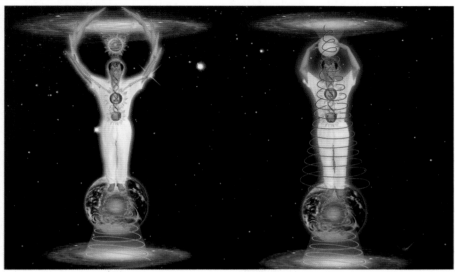

Fig. 2.36 Recharge in the Universe, Scoop and Pour the Chi down to the Middle Tan Tien (Heart Center).

Middle Tan Tien - Heart Center - Conscious Mind

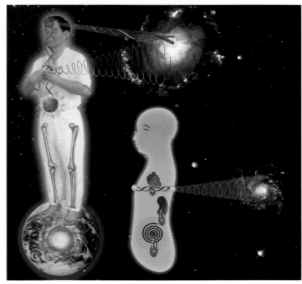

1. Move your hands all the way down to your heart center at the mid-sternum. Touch. Focus on the point opposite the heart, T5/T6, on the spine. Fingers 'long', Chi penetrates into your thymus gland. Light – golden light – penetrates into your thymus. Feel the Chi penetrate through your heart all the way through T5/T6 to the universe behind. 'Tan Tien & the Universe' also feel your Chi Fingers penetrate into the bone and bone marrow and spread out into your rib cage.

Fig. 2.37 Golden Light Enters the Heart, Thymus, Bones, Marrow and Penetrates to the Back and all the Way to the Universe.

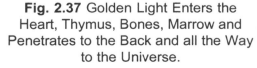

Recharge and cut around to the Armpits

1. Recharge In the universe, pour Chi over the crown down through the body and lower your hands down to the heart center. Touch with the fingertips. Move your hands around under your armpits, extending the Chi like laser beams cutting open this middle Tan Tien. Pause under the armpits as you send the Chi into the center.

Fig. 2.38 Cut Open the Middle Tan Tien by Cutting Around the Armpits.

2. Continue to move your hands around to your back at T5/T6, touch and send the Chi from back to front. Let the beam of Chi penetrate out through the heart center to the universe in front of you. Then, move the hands back around the sides to the front, cutting as you go.

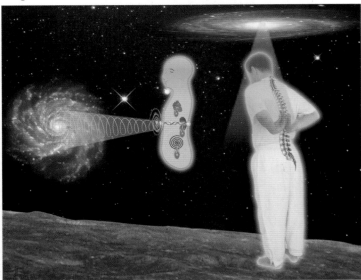

Fig. 2.39 Chi Beam from the Door of Life penetrates the Heart Center in the front.

Lower Tan Tien - Navel - Awareness Mind

1. Recharge with Universal Chi. Tan Tien and universe: Again, raise your hands and charge with the Chi in the universe. Your hands are very big, very long. The bones are hollow and compacted with compressed Universal Chi. Scoop the Chi from above and guide it down. Pour all the way down, down, down, down to the navel. Touch the navel and focus on the Door of Life opposite, on the spine between L2/L3. Touch and feel the Chi penetrate to the Door of Life. Tan Tien and universe. Feel the Chi penetrate through to the back and out to the universe behind.

 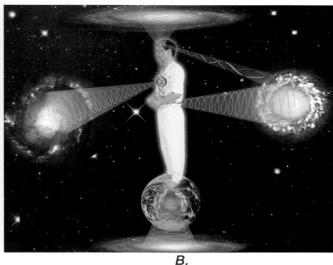

A.   B.

Fig. 2.40 A. Recharge the Lower Tan Tien and Penetrate through to the Door of Life. **B.** Raise the hands up to the Universe & charge with Chi. Bring the Power down to the Lower Tan Tien.

2. Open this lower Tan Tien the same way as for the upper and middle Tan Tiens. Tan Tien and universe – charge more Chi into your hands and let them be like lasers cutting it open. Cut around to the sides. Pause. The fingers of the left and right hand are very long, extended energetically inside. Cut and feel the energy penetrate into the navel and Tan Tien .

Fig. 2.41 'Cut' Open the Lower Tan Tien with Laser Fingers.

3. Continue cutting to the Door of Life. Touch and send the Chi from the Door of Life back to the navel and out to the universe in front.

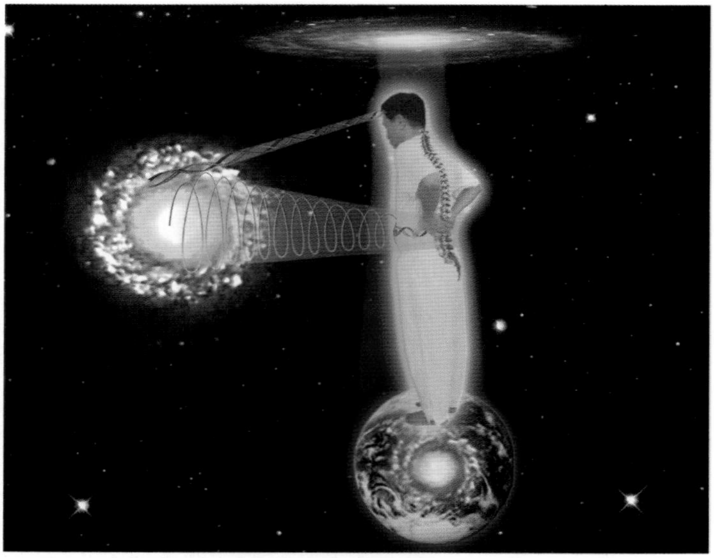

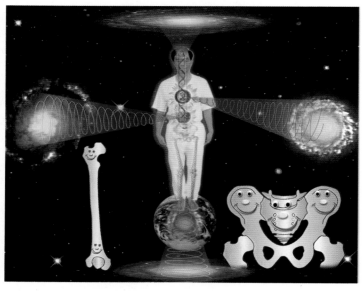

Fig. 2.42 'Cut' Open the Door of Life and Send Chi to the Universe in Front.

4. Move the hands back around the sides to the navel, extending the fingers and "cutting" the Tan Tien open as you go. Touch the navel: Tan Tien and the universe spiraling. Feel more Chi and feel the Tan Tien open.

Activate Chi in the Bones of Hips, Legs and Sacrum

1. Now touch your pelvic bones by energetically extending your fingers from the front area near the hips to the back. Feel Chi penetrate into your pelvic bones: funny, laughing, happy bones.

2. Touch the femur bones. Tan Tien and universe. Charge the fingers. Also, feel the funny, happy, laughing vibration inside the bones and in the bone marrow. Be aware of the Three Tan Tiens. Spiraling from the universe. Spiraling charging your Tan Tien. Charge your hands and your bones.

Fig. 2.43 Touch the Femurs - Happy Laughing Legs!

3. Now we are going to slowly lower the sensation of Chi down through the bones to the earth. Move the hands down the legs as you bend down.
4. Lower yourself all the way down to the ground and sit on your feet. Move the Chi with your hands down to your toes, down through the earth and the universe below.

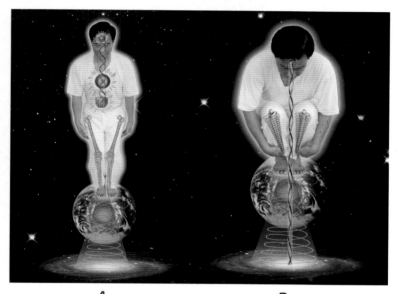

A.   **B.**

Fig. 2.44 A. Sink the Chi into the Earth.   **B.** Lower & Sink the mind & Chi down to the Universe.

5. Raise your sacrum up, keeping your hands at the toes. Smile to your Tan Tien and feel the Chi from the universe rising to fill the Three Tan Tien.

Fig. 2.45 Raise the Sacrum and Smile to the Tan Tien.

6. Lower down again. Lower the Chi down to the earth and the galaxy below.
7. Once more, raise your sacrum up, maintaining hand contact with your feet. Smile to your Tan Tien.
8. For the third time, lower down. Open your palms, gathering the Chi from the earth below. Gather and scoop the Chi.

Fig. 2.46 Gather the Earth Chi.

9. Touch your heels and feel your bones as you slowly rise up. Fill your bones with Chi as you guide it up with your hands.
10. Fill the bones in the upper legs as you move your hands up.

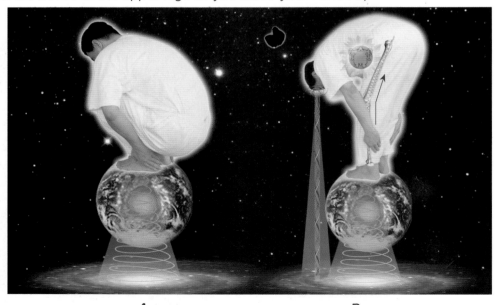

A.   *B.*

Fig. 2.47 A. Fill the Bones with Chi. **B.** Feel your fingers Penetrate into the Bones as you Rise.

11. Feel your bones and fill them with Chi, all the way up to your coccyx. Touch your coccyx. Leave your fingers there and be aware of the Chi gradually feel the Chi rising up to the Tan Tien and the universe. Feel it charge the fingers and the spine.
12. Come up to the sacrum. Tan Tien and the universe.

A.   B.

Fig. 2.48 A. Bring the Chi to the Coccyx.
B. Move your hands up to the Sacrum and feel the Chi Rise up to the Crown.

13. Come up to the 'Door of Life', and then back to the navel. You may sit down to continue the next step in the Cosmic Healing Practice.

Fig. 2.49
Bring the Chi to the Door of Life and let it penetrate to the Navel.

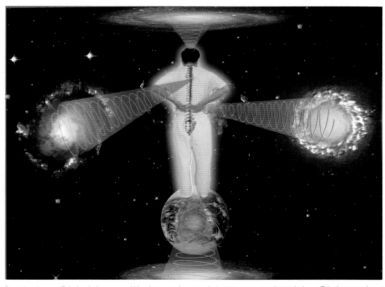

Practice daily until you feel the Chi. You will then be able to apply this Chi to the Healing Sessions.

Sacred Water Practice

Invoke the power of the Sacred Water practice to cleanse and heal the body's sick, toxic or negative energy. **If you are working with a group of people, direct your energy through the energy body overhead and into each person's star, as you guide them through the procedure.**

Outline of Practice:-

I. Hold a glass one quarter full of water in your left hand, folding the middle and the ring fingers into the center of the palm.

II. Hold the glass in front of your body as you point the 'Sword Fingers' of your right hand up to Heaven.

III. Make a request to receive healing energy and feel yourself touch a heavenly pool of sacred water energy. Feel the pool pouring down heavenly water to fill your arm.

IV. Place your fingers on the cup and ask:
Command 1: *"Yin power and good fortune come from the east. Yin power please dissolve all negative energy, all sickness and bad fortune".* Make a cross over the top of the cup.

V. Bring your arm down and point the sword fingers around the inner rim of the glass. Smile as you circle the fingers around the rim.
Command 2: *"By my request. Please carry out the order now."* Repeat this three times, charging the water with Yin Power. Project your thoughts into the water.

VI. Use the thumb and index finger to remove the sick energy from the cup, without touching the water. Do this three times. Talk to the sick cells. Tell them to listen to your command:
Command 3: *"All sick cells please listen: Clear, clean and bright, this Sacred Water will take all the sickness away."*

VII. Repeat the order and visualize yourself removing the sick energy from the cells and returning it to Mother Earth for recycling.

VIII. Hold the cup with both hands near your heart.
Command 4: *"This Sacred Water will give me/you health, wealth and longevity."*
Project love, joy, thankfulness, gratefulness, appreciation and the energy of compassion into the cup.

IX. The Sacred Water will carry the message of the practice to all the cells, where it will remain. If you are practicing in a group, drink the water in unison. If you are working with a student, pass them the glass using both hands.

Step I: Prepare the Hands and Arms to Receive the Universal Chi

Left Hand position Prepare to hold a cup or glass with the left hand by folding the ring and middle finger into the center of the palm. Hold the glass in front of the body.

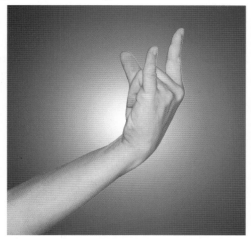 

A.   **B.**
Fig. 2.50 A. Fold Ring and Middle Fingers.   **B.** Hold Glass in front of Body.

Step II: Prepare the Sword Hands to Receive the Universal Chi

Right Hand position Form the right hand into a 'sword hand' by folding the pinkie, ring fingers and thumb into the palm. Straighten and hold the index and middle fingers together and extend them upward.

Fig. 2.51 Prepare to Receive the Universal Chi.

Step III: Fill Your Arm with the Power of the Heavenly Pool

Sense the sword fingers and the arm as being 'long' and 'big' as you raise them towards Heaven. Sense that the middle is hollow and the bottom is sealed at the shoulder. When the mind's attention is focused on merging with the primordial Chi of the Universe, the energy of your thoughts will be multiplied.

As you make your request to the Universe, feel that you are touching a heavenly pool of Sacred Water Energy. Feel that the pool is pouring down like a waterfall to fill the arm. When it is full compact and compress the Sacred Energy into it as much as you can.

Fig. 2.52 Touch the Heavenly Pool.

Step IV: Make the Cross on the Top of the Cup

Put Sword Fingers on top of the Cup. Ask for the Yin Power: **Command 1:** *"Yin Power and good fortune, come from the east. Yin has the power to dissolve all negative energy, all sickness and bad fortune."*
Command 2: Make the cross on the top of the cup and say *"By my request"*.

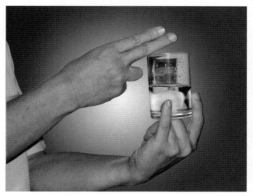 

Fig. 2.53 Fortune come from the East - Yin has the power to dissolve all Negative Energy, all Sickness and Bad Fortune."

Step V: Charge the Water to Transform it into Sacred Water

Bring your arm down and point the sword fingers into the glass of water. Smile and circle the sword fingers around the inner rim of the glass.
Continue to order: *"Please carry out the order now."* Repeat 3 times to charge the water with the Yin Power. As you do this, project a good thought into the water.

Fig. 2.54 "Please carry out the order now." Repeat three times, charging the water with the yin power.

Step VI: Command 3: *"All sick cells please listen : Clear, Clean and Bright, This Sacred Water Will Take all the Sickness Away."*

Give the above command. Use the thumb and index finger to pick up sick energy from the cup, without touching the water. Do this three times.

Fig. 2.55 "All sick cells please listen: Clear, Clean and Bright, this Sacred Water Will Take my/your Sickness Away."

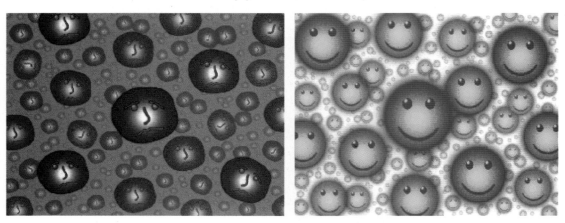

Fig. 2.56

A. Ask for the power to see the cells - If they are toxic and dark, ask for them to be cleaned out.

B. "Clear, Clean and Bright".

Step VII: Let go of the Sick Energy to be transformed by the Earth

As you **repeat** the order, picture yourself removing the sick energy from the cells and discarding it down into the Earth to be transformed and recycled.

Step VIII: Fill the Water with Compassion

Hold the cup with both hands near the heart and project goodness into the water.

Command 4: *"This sacred water will give me/you health, wealth and longevity."*

Project love, joy, thankfulness, gratefulness, appreciation and the energy of compassion into the cup.

Fig. 2.57 Sick Energy return to the Earth. **Fig. 2.58** "This Sacred Water will give you Health, Wealth and Longevity."

Step IX: Drink the Sacred Water

The Sacred Water will carry the message to all the cells. It will keep the message of the Sacred Water practice in all of the cells. Use both hands to pass the Sacred Water to the student you are working with, or drink it yourself and/or in unison with your group. **Feel the water go into all the cells of your body. Feel it removing the sick cells and purifying your body.**

You can also sprinkle it on to any area that requires healing

Fig. 2.59 Drink the Sacred Water.

Chapter III
Taoist Astrology and
the Structure of the Universe

Origin of Astrological Information

Thousands of years ago, people experienced the shimmering stars as their natural connection with heaven. Society was organized in accordance with the laws of the universe and people viewed their relations as a reflection of the configurations of the stars. Human arrogance, the drive for power and a growing disdain for nature led to the vision that the earth was the center of the universe. Instead the earth is our temporary home and is our central point from which we observe the universe.

At the same time, leaders began to rule their countries without being in touch with heaven. A mixture of power, ambition, desire for wealth and religious conditioning led to an increasing disconnection from the natural receptivity to the energy from the universe.

Since then this self-created isolation has been growing and is dominant in present day society. Although there is a longing to reconnect, many healers, therapists and practitioners of meditation or astrology understand the ancient practices with their rational mind but miss the subtle connection.

We should remember that the knowledge with which astrologists work now comes originally from a direct experiential connection with the universe and the understanding that many masters cultivated throughout several thousand years. Many present day astrologists are guided solely by this ancient information.

The question may be raised as to how the early astrologists, who wrote down their experiences and transmitted them, gathered and collected their information? They had no sophisticated equipment like telescopes. Through a combination of observing the universe and relating it to changes in the energy on earth, in nature and human beings and through meditation or spiritual practices, they were able to assimilate their knowledge.

During the Tang dynasty many Taoist masters and students spent their whole lives in Kuans or watchplaces/observatories. The masters had selected these unique locations in nature, based on the presence of strong cosmic energy. Most of the Kuans were located high in the mountains, sometimes in very inaccessible places. The interaction of the strong natural forces with natural crystal antennas (mountains) and the planetary/star observations-meditations formed a perfect platform for the Taoist astral travel and spiritual practices.

These masters clearly saw the cranium as our own bony planetarium. A key realization was to break through the illusion of the separate realities of 'inner' and 'outer'. Their supernatural astrology helped them to realize the universe within the cranium and from there, into the Tan Tien.

Fig. 3.1 Astrologer Casting a Horoscope

In the Taoist view, their highly advanced insights could only come about through the growth of the higher centers and glands which allowed them to perceive and understand the reality of the universe beyond the normal material and visible manifestations.

Of course, astronomy provides us with a great deal of interesting information. It has recently become clearer that astronomy parallels all universal law. We should realize that these laws can be further enhanced with the aid of high powered telescopes. Taoists say "without leaving the room, you can know heaven and earth".

The Newtonian view of the universe which uses a mechanical approach to reality by way of an exclusively rational concept at the expense of our body, our ability to sense and use our intuition and feelings, has gradually and increasingly disconnected us from the realm of the spirit and the living cosmos.

Strangely enough, the more we attempted to know the universe through observation with a telescope, the more we became separated from it's subtle origin.

This is so, as the rational mind tends to move horizontally and may find it difficult to enter into the realm of the spiritual laws. Unless of course it is the rational mind of a spiritually evolved person. Each time an astronomer reaches further into the universe, finding new information, some scientists try to use it in a concept of how the history of nature formed and the universe must be. But these fundamental questions cannot be solved within the realm of time and space. It is good news to see that a growing number of modern scientists are becoming more open to the paradigm that the universe has a time-less and spaceless origin.

"As above, so below". We look at ourselves the same way that we look at the universe, even if we are not concerned about the direct connection between the two. If we try to understand the body, by way of observation with a microscope and chemical analysis, it may help us to see how the laws of energy and Chi manifest in the realm of matter. It may increase our ability to enhance the fundamental questions of life which lead to greater freedom and happiness.

Many scientists who previously subscribed to the Newtonian view now agree to the following: that the essence of the material world are frozen energy waves that *appear* as matter to the external senses.

Many scientists believe that by the year 2030, the computer will be able to take over the complete human brain function. This idea is well accepted in modern science but shows at the same time, the very limited understanding of the true quality of our intelligence and the human mind.

Centuries of religious repression have discouraged people's sense of responsibility for their lives as well as the search for freedom and spiritual independence. Hence, science, astronomy, religion and many other fields of experience can be useful in our search for spiritual achievements. All of these schools of thought merge into one, as they reconnect to our true origin.

Working with planetary and star energies gives us an access to the ground layers of our emotional, social and mental tendencies. The rational mind and emotions, higher mind and spirit are related to the planets and starworld. Star energy and higher mental energy have a higher frequency than planet and rational mind/emotional energy. The separative, rational, more horizontal mind is related to the emotions; the higher mind or universal mind is related to the collective intellgence and our spirit.

More than likely you have observed that it is your emotions and thoughts which hold you back from reaching a balance in your life or progress in your meditation practice, or to focus and connect when you work as a healer.

The planets are far closer to us than the stars and their energy field has a much slower vibration. To give you an idea, the earth is 150 million kilometers away from the sun. Pluto, the planet farthest away from the sun has an orbit of about 6 billion kilometers. The closest star (except for the sun) in our universe is Proxima Centauri at a distance of 4.3 light-years or 270,000 times farther away from the sun (a light year is the distance that the light travels in one year at a speed of 300,000 kilometers per second).

How to use Astrological Information

Ancient peoples believed that under the influence of very specific conditions of stars and planets at the moment of birth, the basic quality of a human being is formed and the personality and tendencies in a person's life are basically fixed. It is important to see this constitutional quality as a strong tendency and not as a fatalistic prediction or inevitable course. This unique quality will indeed influence you for the rest of your life. But it is important to see that this condition works on our body and soul, not on our spirit. The reason for this is because the spirit is eternal. It has and always will exist. It is free from the laws of karma and reincarnation. It is therefore free from the laws governing individual incarnations. For that reason Taoist astrologers say that astrological conditions should not be seen as limitations but rather as directions based on universal influences. It just gives you clear information as to where you come from and how your tendencies may evolve. Since our spirit is timeless and spaceless, we can still move in any direction. An intelligent person moves with the flow or the intelligence of the universe, in order to keep the life-force inside. It is good to remember that you can actually move in the direction you truly wish to move to, always following the truth within your heart. If you decide to join a football game, you are immediately fixed by the rules of the game. If you see all these rules as limitations, you would do better to play another game. **The art of playing the game of life is to see, understand and accept the limits in the material world and learn how to move freely within them, whilst maintaining awareness of your connection with your unlimited spirit.**

Two basic questions to ask when moving to a certain place are: "Where am I now?" When you know the answer; "What is the best way to achieve my goal ?" Through the connection with our spiritual origin and planetary/galactic forces, we can strengthen the weaker points in our energy system and our personality. In this way we can use astrological information as a source of personal growth and not as an excuse for unconscious emotional behavior.

A Brief History of Astrology

Chinese astrology is a very broad subject which contains much information and is highly complicated for the untrained mind. There are many ways of interpreting the universal conditions, which are brought together in different systems with their own specific diagrams and calculation methods.

In the ancient Taoist literature much attention is given to the subject of "astrology". The 18th century Imperial encyclopedia has 2500 chapters on astrology! What we wish to do in this book is to make you aware of the nature and origin of this wisdom and how it relates to spiritual practices and the laws of the universe.

In most Chinese astrological systems it is mentioned that between 4000 and 5000 years ago, the stars and planets were perfectly situated. At the moment it looks like no one can really describe what that means from a pragmatic point of view. What is clear is that this period may have seen a unique universal condition. From that point on, Chinese astrologers have counted the years, months and days and calculated movements and observed the sky. Noio, the Great Minister of the Yellow Emperor Hwang Ti set the beginning of the first 60 year cycle at 2637 B.C. (according to stems and branches) which means we are in the 78th sexagenary cycle now.

Most sources claim that Chinese astrology developed wholly independently from other cultures and traditions, but this is probably not the case. If we compare Chinese, Mayan and old European calendars and zodiacs and also the language and architecture we find parallels that simply cannot be accidental. It is clear that all these cultures were shaped by the same information source. The advanced spiritual development of these different cultures allowed them to translate information from the same source in the form of an astrological system reflecting the order of the universe. This translation happened in coordination with their specific location on the planet.

As you will see in the following overview, people all over the world were already observing the stars long before the start of the Chinese calendar 2637 B.C.

Although there is still discussion on the subject, the famous Egyptologist, Schwaller de Lubicz states that the Egyptian calendar has its starting point about 4240 B.C. This calendar was based on astronomical observations made during a period more than 6000 years ago.

Also in Egyptian civilization astronomy/astrology was used to crystallize the universal laws into human life. The great pyramid was built at approximately 2170 B.C. One of its functions was to serve as an astronomical observatory. The entire geometry of the pyramid was based upon astronomical positions and movements. Notes of astronomical observations from the Sumerian culture (3000 B.C.) have also been found. Different cultures describe the destruction of civilization about 12,000 years ago, under influence of the star Vega in the constellation of Lyra. An earth axis shift occurred and big floods destroyed civilizations.

Chinese astrology probably has its own roots but was later greatly influenced by Indian (Hindu) and old Babylonian astrology. The year 10,000 B.C. appears to have been a critical point in astrological history. Archeological findings in Europe, South America,

Africa and Asia prove the existence of a highly developed civilization that was strongly influenced by astronomical and astrological knowledge.

In a museum in Peru, a rock shows the engraving of a human figure looking through a telescope to the sky. This piece of art is estimated to be more than 30,000 years old. This is just one of the many archeological treasures that shows that there must have been other cultures before our culture was born less than 1,000 years ago.

The Greek historian Solon claimed that astronomical observations and calculations were made nine thousand years B.C. (or 11,000 years ago).

Oracle bones from the Shang dynasty (17th to 11th century B.C.) mention astronomical observations of stars more than 4000 years ago, which were then interpreted as being lucky or unlucky. In many parts of the 9 Chinese Classics and certainly in the 5 canons or "Ching books" astronomical/astrological observations are described as coming from this same period.

Differences between Chinese and Western Astrology

The main differences between Chinese and western astrology are their reference points. In western astrology, stellar positions are found and calculated in the ecliptic. The ecliptic is the trajectory the sun apparently makes around the earth, through the Milky Way. The plane of the ecliptic is inclined at an angle of 23 ½ degrees to the plane of the equator. The ecliptic is also known by Chinese astrologers as the yellow route, but they also work with the North Star as the central reference point in the sky and the celestial equator or red route as the base line. In this context the lunar zodiac is used where the moon cycle around the earth (28 days) is divided into parts of 1 day (thus, 28 segments). This is also related with the 28 years it takes Saturn to turn around the sun. The Chinese zodiac or 12 animal cycle also refers to the 12 years it takes planet Jupiter to move around the sun.

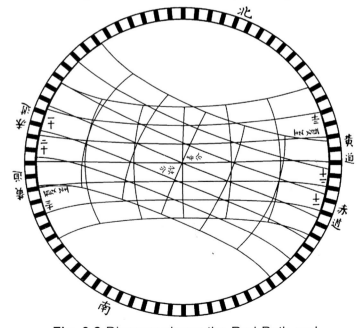

Fig. 3.2 Diagram shows the Red Path and Yellow Path (the celestial equator and the ecliptic).

The animal names used in Chinese astrology came to China from India. They were based on the legend of the Buddha. He was visited by 12 animals that came to say goodbye to him before he left the earth.

Before this, the earthly branches, in combination with the older decimal system of the 10 heavenly stems, was used. The combination of stems (10 or two times five) and branches (12) (gives a series of 60 based on the twelve animals and the five elements) was used to count the years and days and was also called 10 mothers and 12 children. Research shows the strongest difference between modern western and traditional Chinese astrology is the focus on the North Star as the 'Heavenly Gate'. This shows the direct relationship with the Taoist spiritual practices. Chinese astrology and direct astronomical observations have always been closely related. They made observations constantly and based many of their calculations directly upon them. The appearance and movement of a planet or star as well as its brightness, aura and shades were closely studied. Some Chinese Emperors had a 24 hour a day observation crew. In this way all signs from the universe were picked up and used to make personal and political decisions. Many stars and planets were connected to gods, emperors or sages. Changes in the expressions of heavenly bodies were seen as direct signs from the divine world.

Although they had no astronomical tools, in their own terms, Taoist astronomers knew about supernovae (exploding stars), black holes (imploding stars), pulsars and quasars.

Chinese astrology is based on direct observation of the sky and it is used in this book as the information bridge to universal energy.

Many astrologists all over the world, focus on their tables and books, only looking down, instead of connecting with the universe. Even in China, the traditional art of astrology is hard to find these days. It has been taken over by western astrology or other methods of prediction. As Taoist Ming Shu stated, "very few are still combining their astrological calculations with spiritual practice and with observing the sky." This, of course, gives less depth to their work.

The Zodiac band extends above and below the plane of the ecliptic. The Zodiac with its 12 signs is known in many different cultures.

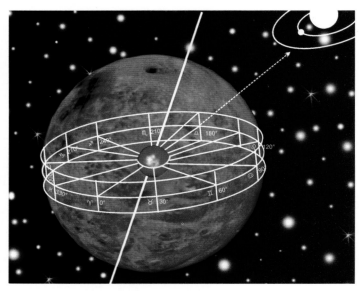

Fig. 3.3 Western Zodiac, Zodiac Band and Plane of Eliptic

Fig. 3.4 Lunar Zodiac

Seven Days of the Week	Related Planets	Constellations			
		East	North	West	South
Sunday	Sun	Fang Room	Hsu Void	Mao Pleiades	Niao Bird
Monday	Moon	Hsin Heart	Wei Danger	Pi Net	Chang Drawn Bow
Tuesday	Mars	Wei Tall	Shih House	Tsui Beak	I Wings
Wednesday	Mercury	Chi Basket	Pi Wall	Shen Orion	Chen Board
Thursday	Jupiter	Chio Horn	Tou Ladle	K'uei Astride	Tung Well
Friday	Venus	K'ang Neck	Niu Ox Boy	Lou Mound	Kuzi Ghosts
Saturday	Saturn	Ti Base	Nu Maiden	Wei Stomach	Liu Willow

The 28 days of the Lunar Zodiac in relation to the 5 Palaces around the North Star, are the 28 segments. The Moon will rotate in each palace during seven days. This period is connected with the seven days of the week. This brings a cycle of the seven planets during the days of the week in the 28 constellations. Specific influence of the sun (moon + 5 planets) and the 28 constellations (4 x 7) each of the 7 days of the week.

Although much more information is recorded and transmitted in China compared to most other civilizations, the real meaning of many methods is very rare to find. The system of stems and branches is a good example of this. Today this system is used on computers and in the form of diagrams, by many practitioners of Chinese medicine all over the world, but very few of them know what the system really means and where it comes from.

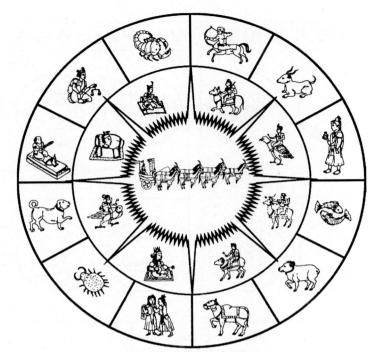

Fig. 3.5 Hindu Zodiac

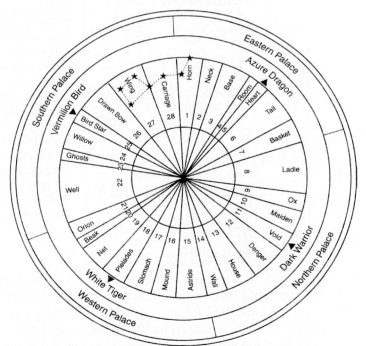

Fig. 3.6 Star Palaces and Constellations

Chinese Astrology and the Laws of the Universe

As human beings we are the highest manifestation of the Cosmic light which has its origin directly in the Tao, the oneness. The life we lead now originated from this source. From this one unlimited intelligence a process of densifying/materialization or multiplication has led to your individual incarnation or manifestation in the physical realm. Taoist philosophy describes this process as 'the one giving birth to the two'. The interaction between the two, further differentiates into the world of phenomena. To connect to the spiritualizing spiral of true intelligence that we are, will strengthen the connection to the Tao. This process will deepen through astronomical information (observation) and meditation (explained further, later in this book).

In Chinese cosmology and philosophy the world of duality yin/yang, gives birth to the triple unity. This triple unity we find in the three basic energies in the universe (universal, cosmic and earth) and the interaction between heaven, man and earth. In the body, the interaction of heaven and earth forces (two) gives birth to the three Tan Tiens.

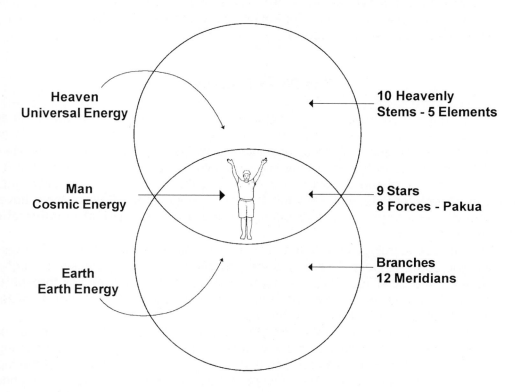

Heaven
Universal Energy

10 Heavenly
Stems - 5 Elements

Man
Cosmic Energy

9 Stars
8 Forces - Pakua

Earth
Earth Energy

Branches
12 Meridians

Fig. 3.7
Interaction of Man with the Realms of Heaven and Earth,
the Pakua and the Stems and Branches

These three realms contain the main principles applied in Chinese philosophy and astrology. The ten heavenly stems are based on the yin and yang aspect of the five elements (related to yin/yang senses/organs/systems). The I Ching and its internal principle of the pakua or eight forces relates to the eight extraordinary meridians in the body. This more prenatal meridian system is nurtured by the eight planets (the sun and moon form the central aspect) and the eight related star essences. The principles of the pakua are also found in the Taoist 9 star astrology (8 forces + the central Tai Chi = 9). The North Star and Big Dipper energy are essential to the whole Taoist practice. Taoist masters observed that in the central star palace, 9 major energy points clearly reflect the changing energy quality of the universe and of our planet. These 9 points are the 7 stars of the Big Dipper, the light or yang star, Polaris and the light of the yin star, Vega.

The 12 earthly branches are in relationship with the earthly forces and also the 12 main acupuncture channels.

The heavenly stems have a high frequency energy - related to realm of cosmic law and Universal energy. The earthly branches have a lower frequency, related to the earth energy and the surroundings of the earth in the 12 different directions.

The principles of the five elements, the pakua and, to a lesser degree, the related stems and branches, are fundamental for the planetary and stellar meditations. We will go deeper into these topics as we progress.

The Five Elements

Every part of Chinese philosophy is connected with the five elements. The law of Yin and Yang, Five Elements and Pakua (eight forces) come from the unmanifested world and control the whole world of phenomena, including the world of stars and planets and life on earth. Written evidence of the use of the five elements has been found around 300 B.C. although they were certainly known and used before that time. Much confusion arises between the Greek four elements and the Chinese five elements. Both of them have a clear underlying philosophy. **The five basic planets are the physical manifestation of the five elements.**

Ancient Chinese astrology divides the sky into five palaces, also called the five cardinal points. The earth, or Central Palace, is the part of the sky which is visible throughout the whole year. The other four Palaces can be located as the earth moves through the four seasons during its annual rotation around the sun. Each of the outer 4 palaces covers an area of about 90 degrees in the sky.

The one (circle) gives birth to the two (Tai Chi), from there we find the three (e.g, heaven, earth and man), a further differentiation leads us to the pakua. Inside these eight trigrams we find the five elements (see figs 3.10 and 3.11). The combination of the eight trigrams gives us the 64 trigrams. This concept of the order of the universe and an understanding of these laws was traditionally necessary to be able to work with Chinese astrology.

The pakua can be looked at in different ways. In a common form the five elements are located as follows: earth as the center, south on top, north below, east left, west right. If the observers look to the south, following the main trajectory of the sun they see the chart as shown below.

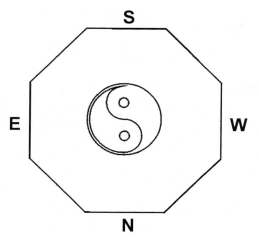

Fig. 3.8

But if we move southward with the direction of the sun and look from that position to heaven then north would be on top, south bottom, east left, west right. The way the pakua is presented shows the point of view of the observer.

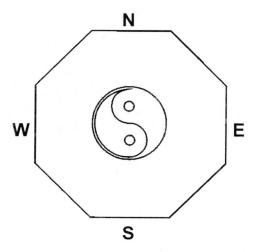

Fig. 3.9

The most commonly applied system of using the five elements according to the seasons is with the earth element (Indian Summer) coming after the fire element (summer) (See fig. 3.10). Another less popular method uses the earth in its central aspect and places a short earth period in between every season (See fig. 3.11).

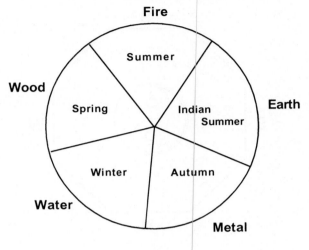

Fig. 3.10
Most common way of using the 5 elements in the year's cycle:
5 periods of 72 days each (the Astrological Year counted 360 days).

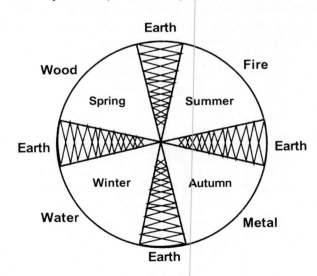

Fig. 3.11
Earth element seen as the changing and balancing point between the seasons.

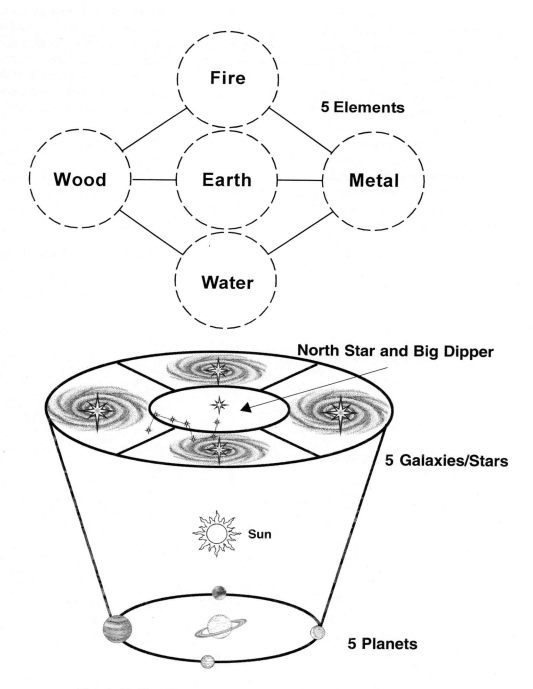

Fig. 3.12 Five Elements through the Universe

The dominance of one of the five elements in a person's basic energy will give a charge to the person's quality and way of living. Of course, all of us have some of all five elements but according to the year/month/day and in some systems also the hour/minute at the moment of birth, one of the five elements will be stronger than the other four. As mentioned before there are many different systems, all using different methods to make calculations. Most of them work well if we understand their point of view and if we use them as a 'whole'. Mixing different astrological systems tends to create much confusion.

The most typical positive or creative qualities of the different elements are:
Wood: Practical, creative, casual.
Fire: Lively, talkative, quick.
Earth: Stable, reliable, conservative, primitive.
Metal: Vigorous, progressive, determined, calculated.
Water: Contemplative, attentive, communicative, adjustable.

(For a better understanding of this topic, read: "Fusion of the Five Elements I", by Mantak Chia)

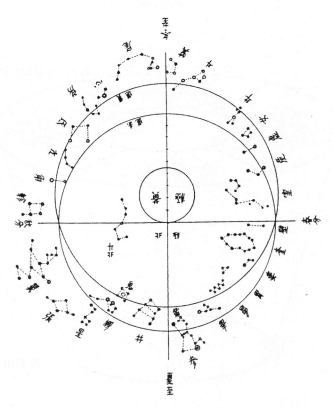

Fig. 3.13 North Star - Big Dipper - 28 Constellations

The Pakua - The Eight Forces

The pakua (or eight forces) were first described by Fu Hsi as a sign from heaven brought in the form of stripes on the back of a turtle. The I Ching or book of changes is based on the pakua. The combination of the eight directions gives birth to the 64 hexagrams also used in **I Ching** astrology. The eight directions and the center form the nine palaces used in the Chiu Kung Ming Li or Nine star astrology and also in the Lo-Pan, the basic tool of Chinese geomancy and in Feng Shui. The Lo Shu or magic square found its origin in the Lo Map and is used for prediction.

The eight different signs come from the combinations between the yin ▬ ▬ and the yang ▬▬ .

First there was Tai Ji (extremity) ▬▬ ; this produced the two poles ▬ ▬ yin and ▬▬ yang; the two poles yielded four phases, the four strengths: Greater Yang (Tai Yang), Lesser Yang (Shao Yang), Greater Yin (Tai Yin), and Lesser Yin (Shao Yin). The four phases yield the eight trigrams.

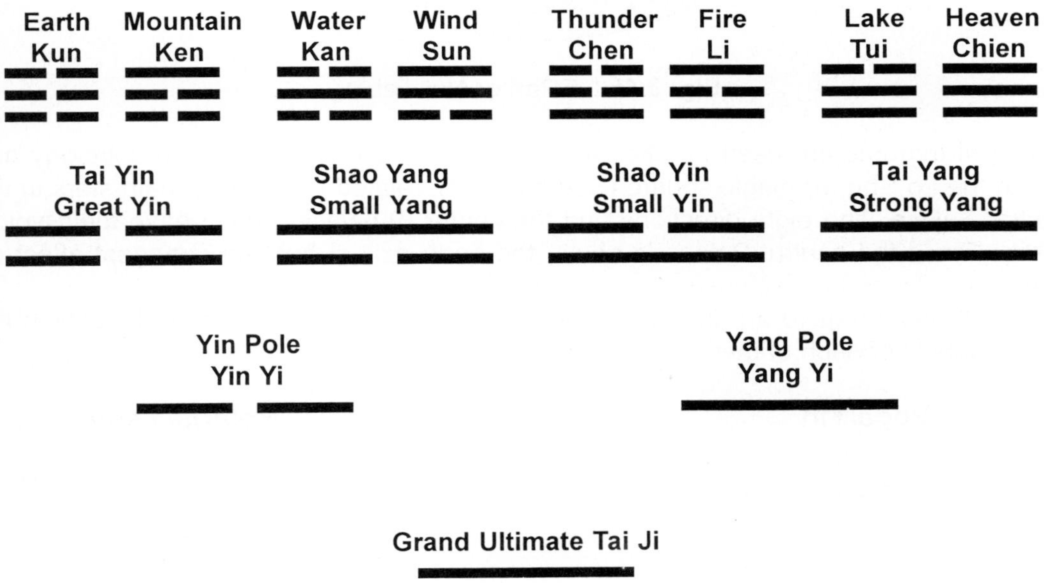

Earth Kun	Mountain Ken	Water Kan	Wind Sun	Thunder Chen	Fire Li	Lake Tui	Heaven Chien

Tai Yin Great Yin	Shao Yang Small Yang	Shao Yin Small Yin	Tai Yang Strong Yang

Yin Pole Yin Yi	Yang Pole Yang Yi

Grand Ultimate Tai Ji

Fig. 3.14 The eight trigrams are divided from Tai Ji.

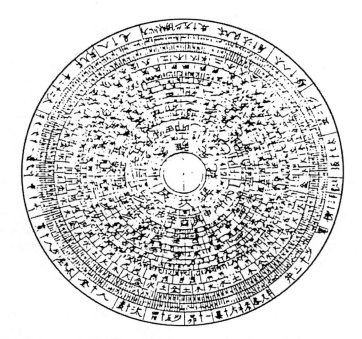

Fig. 3.15 Lo-Pan or Net Tablet.

The eight trigrams are used in different forms of Chinese and Japanese astrology and also in the Lo Shu, or magic square (See fig. 3.17), related to the nine main stars in the Central Palace. The eight directions and the center (9 palaces) each have their typical quality. Since the central Palace is above the earth axis, it has the strongest effect on human energy and consciousness.

Taoist masters gave a name and a number to each of the nine stars describing the unique quality of each of them.

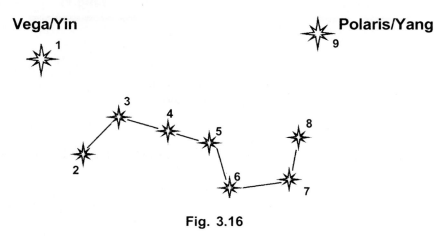

Fig. 3.16

According to the time of birth, each of us is more or less influenced by one of the nine stars with its unique quality based on the five elements and the trigrams. During our lives we keep this basic quality but with time we will move with our numbers to other positions in the magic square (called the houses) each with its unique influence on us. While being influenced we are initiated into life's other possibilities.

4	9	2
3	5	7
8	1	6

Fig. 3.17

Your numbers are situated in the different palaces and will show you the Universal quality that is influencing you the most at that specific moment.

The typical qualities of the Nine Palaces are:

Chen 3	Thunder, the arousing, the new impulse, exciting.
Sun 4	Wind, the penetrating, gentleness.
Li 9	Fire, clarity, conscious, independent.
Kun 2	Earth, the receptive, trust, confidence, openness.
Tui 7	Lake, joyfulness, fullness, satisfaction.
Chien 6	Heaven, the creative, energetic, strong, light.
Kan 1	Water, prudence, dangerous, unreliable.
Ken 8	Mountain, keeping still, stability, rest.
Chung 5	Female trigram, Kun, black earth, the receptive.
	Male trigram, Ken, mountain, keeping still.

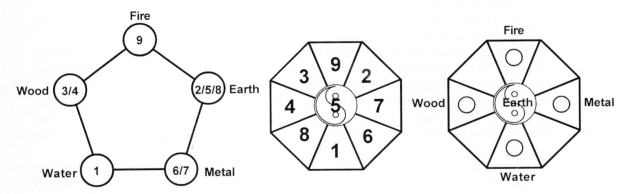

Fig. 3.18 Numerology in the Pakua and the Five elements.

The five elements and eight trigrams are deeply interwoven into Chinese philosophy and astrology. The eight trigrams can be seen as a further derivation of the five elements or from the four directions to the eight directions.

The symbolism in the eight trigrams is used in two different ways. One of them is called "the preheavenly pakua" according to the legendary Fu Hsi, named during the age of the five rulers (2852 B.C.). The other is the "postheavenly pakua" originally coming from King Wen of the Chou Dynasty (1122 B.C.) in his book called Yixici (YI 's related metrical composition) or Yi Da Zhnan (great biography of Yi). This is the first written explanation of the relationship between the preheavenly and postheavenly pakua. The preheavenly state is related to the time before the earth was formed, when everything was chaotic, like a cloud or mist. Nothing could be differentiated (state of Wu Chi).

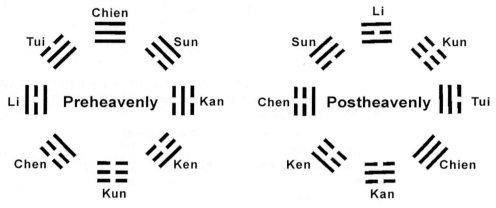

Fig. 3.19 Preheavenly and Postheavenly Pakuas

The preheavenly state can also be seen as the period before the time that the earth started to materialize and heaven and earth began to separate (The Tai Chi or grand ultimate state). The postheavenly state begins at the time when heaven and earth were clearly distinguishable and the yin and yang pole were generated.

In human life the preheavenly and postheavenly states are separated by birth or the moment the baby can see the light, or the sky.

The goal of the Universal Tao practice is to unify the pre-and postheavenly states of being. The quality of the preheavenly state is the basic energy of the newborn baby, totally soft, natural and filled with its mother's essence, Chi and blood.

As well as this, intuition, flexibility, softness, tenderness and creativity are components of this preheavenly or virgin child state. In the Taoist Fusion and Kan and Li practice five virgin children are pictured to store and crystallize the pure virtue energy from the five elements.

Through the Universal Tao practices, the vital essences remain in the body until old age. The practitioner remains flexible, strong, and full of virtue. The unification of 'pre' and 'postheaven' is reached by first "training the postheaven to remedy the preheaven" and then "training the postheaven to return to preheaven". In the unified state the body and mind become one, in accordance with the heavenly principles.

Fig. 3.20

In the art of Pakua Chuan (an internal martial art) the practitioner walks a circular path, stepping one by one through the different Kuas (directions) and then spiraling from one to another. In this way the embryonic formation is repeated and the deep cellular memory inside the DNA is activated. The Microcosmic Orbit has the same life spiral and intelligence inside as the DNA. Walking and spiraling in the Pakua Chuan way is recreating your life process on a deep level.

Through meditation and exercises, the preheavenly mind will start to guide the postheavenly body so that the body will gradually turn into its preheavenly state.

The Ten Stems and Twelve Branches

As described before the ten heavenly stems are the yin/yang poles of each of the five elements, while the twelve earthly branches are related to the twelve sections of the earth's rotation field projected in the star world.

The 60 years of the stems and branches 'cycle' happens in correlation with the Jupiter/Saturn conjunction.

The whole system describes geometrical coordinates in time and space, with Polaris as the center point and other celestial bodies as references. The ten heavenly stems are often related with the planets and the five palaces in the star world.

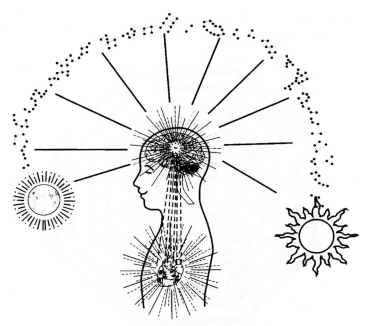

Fig. 3.21 Ten Stems in the Sky

Ten Stems

No.	Name	Transcription	Significance Related		
1	甲	Chia	Yang moving in the East; sprouting.	Fir Tree	} Wood
2	乙	Yi	Plant growing in a crooked way; tendril; twig.	Bamboo	
3	丙	Ping	Growth in southern heart; bloom.	Torch-Flame	} Fire
4	丁	Ting	Vegetation in warm season; summer.	Lamp-Light	
5	戊	Wu	Exuberance; substance of life.	Mountains	} Earth
6	己	Ki	Winter; sleep, hibernation.	Level Ground	
7	庚	Keng	Fullness of crops; the West; autumn harvest.	Weapon	} Metal
8	辛	Sin	Ripened fruit and its flavor; supposed to be metallic.	Cauldron	
9	壬	Jen	Yin at the height of its function; pregnancy.	Willow	} Water
10	癸	Kwei	Water absorbed by earth; Yang preparing for spring.	Unruffled Stream	

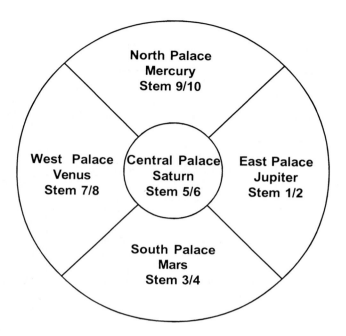

Fig. 3.22 Branches

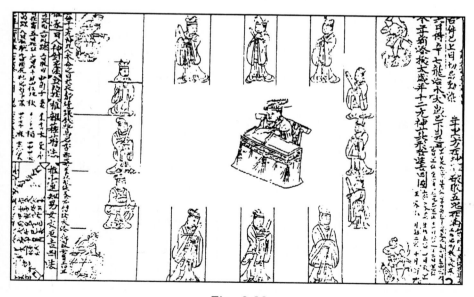

Fig. 3.23
The Deities of the Twelve Branches From a Tun Huang Manuscript Dated AD 978.

Twelve Earthly Branches or Duodenary Cycle / Twelve Animals

				The Twelve Branches			The Twelve Animals	
No.	Name	Tran-scrip-tion	Usual Meaning	Significance in the Duodenary Cycle	Symbol	Element to Which Related	Name	Meaning
1	子	Tze	Child	Regeneration of vegetation	Yang stirring underground	Water	鼠	Rat
2	丑	Chu	Cord	Relaxation; untying a knot	Hand half-opened		牛	Ox
3	寅	Yin	To revere	Awakening of life; plants	Wriggling earthworm	Wood	虎	Tiger
4	卯	Mao	A period of time	Breaking through the soil	Opening a gate		兔	Hare
5	辰	Chen	Vibration	First vegetation; seed-time	Thunderstorm		龍	Dragon
6	巳	Ssu	End	Supremacy of Yang	Snake	Fire	蛇	Serpent
7	午	Wu	To oppose	Yin reasserting itself	Female principle in hidden growth		馬	Horse
8	未	Wei	Not yet	Taste of fruit	Tree in full bloom		羊	Goat
9	申	Shen	To expand	Yin growing strong	Clasped hands	Metal	猴	Monkey
10	酉	Yu	Ripe	Completion	Cider or wine-press		雞	Cock
11	戌	Shu	Guard	Exhaustion	Yang withdraw-ing underground		犬	Dog
12	亥	Hai	Kernel	Kernel or root	Yang in touch with Yin	Water	猪	Boar

The Structure of the Universe
and the Process of Spiritualization

Evolving through the process of spiritualization, our spirit will enter different layers of Universal consciousness. As described in the previous chapter, the universe can be seen as three different realms: one of the pure law, one of Chi and one of the manifestations of law and Chi.

We have all arrived on this planet through a materialization process: a contracting spiral that led us through these three realms into the physical condensed form we have now. From the moment of birth and more so after the physical development has reached its biological peak. The spiritual process, an expanding spiral that projects our spirit into the universe, begins to grow.

When the level of consciousness grows, the intelligence and information network that connects each of us with the source will start to light up more and more; and we will, step by step, experience all the different dimensions of the universe, from our sexual energy to our spiritual origin. In the course of this process, you will find yourself projected into the whole universe.

Of course it is easier to take seven Steps one by one, rather than trying to jump to the 7th at once. The same is true for the spiritual process. We will gradually grow through the 3 realms step by step. The seven meditations in this book will guide you all the way through the manifested world of earth, planets and stars to the world of pure Universal laws.

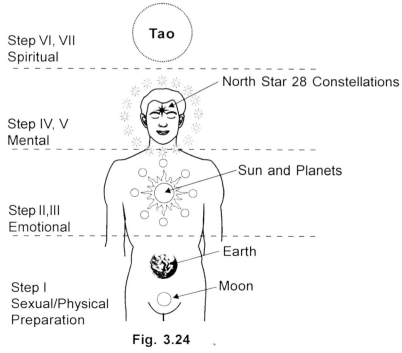

Fig. 3.24

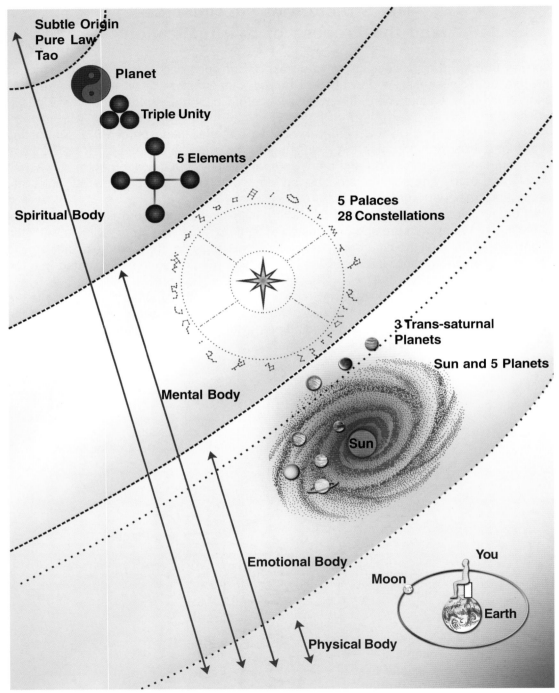

Fig. 3.25 Human Energy in the Universe

Step One: Earth/Sun/Moon Triangle

Before you go on this journey, it is wise to take care of your vehicle. You will need a healthy and strong body and put on your safety belt. This is the rooting or the connection with the earth.

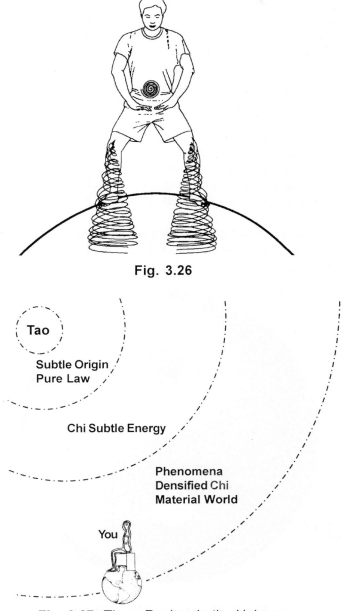

Fig. 3.26

Tao

Subtle Origin
Pure Law

Chi Subtle Energy

Phenomena
Densified Chi
Material World

You

Fig. 3.27 Three Realms in the Universe

Now you need to learn to control, transform and use your sexual energy. Sexual energy is connected to the moon. The sun and the moon energies are easily experienced because we can see and feel them with our earthly senses. Most people do not consciously experience the effects of the moon. We cannot touch it like the earth or feel its radiant energy as easily as the heat from the sun.

The goal of our meditative practices is to tune into the energy frequencies and awareness field of the planets and stars and integrate these into our physical body. The moon is an important step in the development of our universal awareness because the moon meditation triggers deeply hidden layers of the unconscious mind connected with our sexual potential.

Our connection with the moon will help us to become profoundly aware of our sexual essence to which we cannot relate with our ordinary mind.

Through moon and sun meditations, the sexual essence which is stored deep inside the sexual organs and kidneys, becomes available and transforms from Jing into Shen, shifting unconsciousness into consciousness.

When we suppress or have no control over our sexual energy, the earth energy will be insufficient for us to keep balance and be stable enough to advance in the spiritual process. Unconsciously or consciously a part of us may be blocked by sexual frustration and its associated emotions.

All people in the modern world have a layer of heaviness and negativity on the level of their sexuality. This is based on the social/collective conditioning during many centuries of religious and scientific control.

Sun, Love, Consciousness

Moon, Sexual Energy, Unconsciousness

Fig. 3.28 Sun and Moon Balance

Once you have built up a strong center in the lower Tan Tien and are enjoying a good connection with the earth and have achieved control over your sexual energy, you can begin expanding your awareness field.

The Universal Tao practices lead you step by step through these levels. Without these preparations, the effects of your planetary and stellar meditations will be limited as you lack the power to attract, absorb and integrate the energy in your physical body.

Note

If you have not done any Universal Tao practices, you can also do the planetary/stellar meditations. In this case however, you have to build up your physical body/lower Tan Tien and the star/planet connection simultaneously. Keep this balance. Build up regularly, but slowly.

The centering, rooting and cultivation process of the physical body and the sexual energy should be continuously developed because we also expand into and grow further with the universe. In this way you become like a big tree with long and deep roots and you grow the ability to lead information from the universe down into the earthly realm and into your physical body.

The picture (see Fig. 25) "Human energy in the universe" reflects how we can find ourselves back in the universal picture.

(See fig. 3.28)

The cool moon energy in the lower body is balanced by the contact with the warm sun energy in the upper body. The sun will help us to open the heart center and feel connected to nature, the universe and other people. The sun is the central point of the solar system and governs a higher awareness than the other planets. The sun is a star in the planet world and a gate out of the planetary emotional and rational mind layer into the realm of the higher mind and the spirit.

The sun and the moon need to be balanced inside to create peace between the love and sex energy, the conscious and unconscious.

Steps Two and Three

Step two in our universal awareness journey leads us deeper into our solar system. To the sun and the five basic planets. The five basic planets are a materialized form of the energy of the five elements. In the planetary world we find the sources of our collective emotional and lower mental tendencies.

First we connect with the sun and the five basic planets (Mars, Saturn, Venus, Mercury, Jupiter). We integrate their specific frequencies and their qualities/virtues and connect to these energies. The practice described in this book deals with the first five steps.

In step three we expand further out to the border of our solar system into the three planets beyond Saturn (Uranus, Neptune and Pluto). These three planets represent the part of the emotional social consciousness that has recently (the last centuries) formed along with the development of society and social awareness.

According to the Taoist tradition, the five planets can be placed in the cycle of the five elements. If we add the three trans-saturnal planets, we can link them up with these five and use them in the eight directions of the pakua (the eight-sided form). Since Chinese astrologists did not originally know about the three trans-saturnal planets, the use of the eight planets must have been introduced in this century.

Although some Chinese astrologers claim that the trans-saturnal planets were known long before their discovery in the west, we could not find any reference of astronomical/ astrological use of these planets in the old Chinese literature. Some additional planets that are used in China and known as 'counter planets' are instead energetic formations (not materialized). These same principles are also found in the Hindu and Aboriginal tradition.

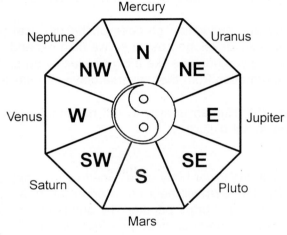

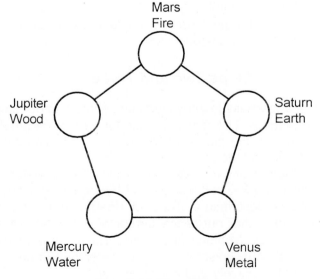

Fig. 3.29 Five Elements

Step Four

This step leads us to the world of the stars, star clouds and milky ways. This represents a finer quality of energy that is related to the higher world of the mind and the spirit. Taoist masters observed several thousand of years ago that the North Star always keeps its position while the 28 constellations turn around it.

For this reason Taoists have always seen the North Star as the center of the star world and also as the gate to the spiritual realm and the Tao. In the planetary and stellar meditation, we first connect with the North Star. In this way we deeply penetrate into the star world. Then connections with galaxies are established that are related to the five Palaces/elements.

Astrological studies of the 12 or 28 constellations combined with intensive meditation on the individual qualities of these signs can deepen our connection with the star world and can greatly accelerate our spiritual advancement. This is, however, a quite advanced and complex practice.

Step Five

We will combine the two most extreme poles in the star world: the ultra yang force of a quasar, with the ultra yin force of a black hole. We will use an uplifting spiral of these two to project an awareness in the pure yang unmanifested world.

Step Six

Here we go beyond the realm of phenomena and the realm of Chi into the realm of the spiritual laws, five elements, the triple unity, polarity and the pure law.

Step Seven

Figure 3.25 on the structure of the universe shows different layers in the universe and how to find them in the body.

The energy core of these different layers are all lined up on the Central Thrusting Channel that is located in the center between the perineum and the crown point. Step seven is what we call 'being and living the source continuously - in a state of absolute freedom'. We could also call this level zero because all separation will end in this state.

The connection and integration of the essence of these core points into our body will automatically raise our energy and awareness level and in this way trigger the connection with more subtle universal frequencies. In this way your body and the universe are becoming one. All your actions and your presence become an effortless reflection of the Tao itself.

Each of the seven steps described above is accompanied by major changes in all aspects of the practitioner's life.

Chapter IV
Astronomical Overview

How to use the Astronomical Information in this Book

Astronomy is a valuable tool to understand and cultivate our relationship with the material universe. The accumulation of astronomical knowledge does, of course, not guarantee a higher energy and awareness level. The information presented may help you create a direct experiential link between where you are living now on the earth and the heavenly energies of planets and stars. Only when this direct, experiential contact is made, can the study of and meditation on the universe improve your quality of life.

In this chapter, we will summarize some basic astronomical facts. They are meant to increase your understanding of the world of stars and planets. If we study some basic astronomy and use it to expand our awareness, our intellectual mind will be more satisfied and will be able to function as a vehicle that can travel beyond time and space. Together with the accompanying pictures it is presented to give you some specific connection points during the meditations. After you have studied the information, simply put the picture in front of you and take it in deeply. Empty the mind of all other activity.

Then close your eyes, expand your awareness and travel with your intention in space. Be aware that the physical objects you are connecting to are just the materialized centers of an energy field or belt. It is the frequency and the energy in the belt that you are tuning into. So, relax.

Keep your hands on the Tan Tien and keep the energy deep inside. Repeat this process 4 to 5 times until you start to feel the connection. Use the meditation techniques as described in chapter XI.

Formation of the Solar System

Planet earth is a small planet that has an annual cycle around a middle-sized star, the sun. There are nine planets in our solar system. Together with the planetoids, satellites, comets, meteors and some gas and dust formations, they form our solar system.

The sun is 10 times as big as the biggest planet in our solar system, which is Jupiter and more than 100 times larger than the earth. Since the mass of the sun is 330,000 times greater than the earth, its gravitational force holds the earth in a fixed yearly cycle. Many believe the birth of the solar system was introduced by the implosion of a cloud of gas and dust. The reason for this implosion is still a mystery, but meteor analyses shows that an exploding star or supernova might have caused this.

Our solar system started its materialization process about 4.5 to 5 billion years ago. Around that time, a cloud charged with cosmic dust gathered at the edge of the Milky Way. The centripetal force in the cloud caused the formation of a more dense center. This created heat, which speeded up the rotational force and flattened the form. After millions of years the immense gathering of energy in the center caused a nuclear reaction and self-inflammation. At other places in this cloud smaller concentrations of gas and cosmic dust gathered as a result of the lower density. They did not inflame but materialized.

The specific place and orbit of each planet in our solar system is located at the balance point between the rotation force/ centrifugal force and the gravitational force / centripetal force both in relation to the sun.

The planets closer to the sun were baked and became very hard because the gases were dispersed by the heat and the ion/electron wind sent into the universe by the sun. Further out from the sun, the temperature is much lower. The planets there materialized into big balls of fluid gas with a vast center, often with a crust of frozen substance.

Expansion and Contraction of the Solar System

Astronomical studies tell us that there are billions of milky ways in the universe and that there are also billions of stars in most of these milky ways. Our solar system travels through the universe at a speed of about 300 km/sec. Even at this speed it takes about 230 million years for our solar system to make a complete cycle through the Milky Way. During such a cycle or what is called a galactic year, the solar system is not always at the same distance from the center of the Milky Way.

When the solar system is closer to the center this is called the galactic summer. Our solar system responds to the stronger contractive force at this point in the galactic year. The planets come closer to the sun in this period, the atmosphere heats up and greatly enhances the size of the flora and fauna. When the solar system is further away from the center of the milky way, the solar system expands, so a greater distance arises between the earth and the sun. This creates lower temperatures and plants and animal species will be smaller (more arctic).

It is generally believed that the first life forms on earth appeared some 3.2 billion years ago. This means that the earth moved about 13 cycles in the milky way.

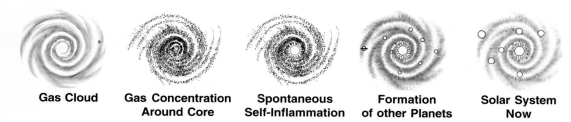

| Gas Cloud | Gas Concentration Around Core | Spontaneous Self-Inflammation | Formation of other Planets | Solar System Now |

Fig. 4.1 Formation of our Solar System

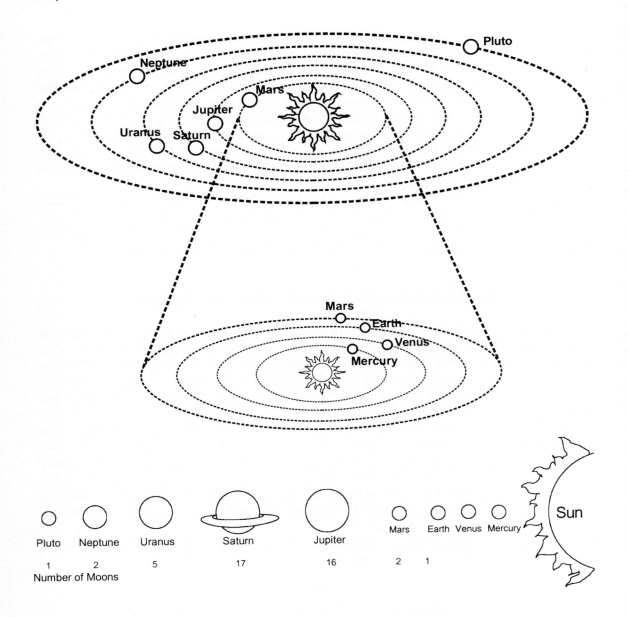

Fig. 4.2 Overview of the Solar System

Overview of the Planets in Our Solar System

Earth

Fig. 4.3

Planet earth is a blue planet with a moderately humid climate and a lightly unstable surface, 70% of which is covered by water. Its atmosphere consists mainly of nitrogen and oxygen. Under the 32km (approximately) thick earth crust we find a 3000 km thick inner mantle. The core of the earth is a moving sea of liquid nickel and iron, which creates a strong electromagnetic field. It rotates around its axis in one day and around the sun in one year.

Moon

Fig. 4.4

The moon is, in fact, not a planet but a satellite of the earth.

Since the moon has no protective atmosphere it has been bombarded out in space for the last 800 million years. The craters that we can see from the earth are 'scars' of this activity, their presence enabled by the absence of erosion. Stones have been found that are more than 4 billion years old, the same age as the solar system. The origin of the moon in relation to the earth is still a mystery. Its rotational speeds around its axis and around the earth are about equal; 28 days. For this reason we always see the same side of the moon. Temperature extremes vary between + 127 °C and - 173 °C.

Sun

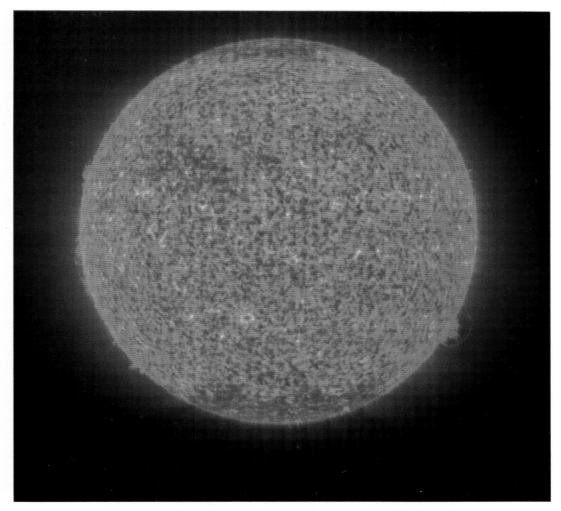

Fig. 4.5

The sun is the giant of our solar system, with a bigger mass than all planets put together. Compared to other stars it is small to medium sized. It is the main light source in our solar system and in this way generates life on our planet. Its main components are hydrogen and helium. The sun radiates enormous amounts of light particles and radioactivity. It turns around its axis in 246 days. The temperature in the center of the sun is about 15 million °C.

Each second the sun radiates more energy than man has used since the beginning of civilization.

Mercury

Fig. 4.6

Mercury is like a giant cinder with a strong pockmarked surface.

Its proximity to the sun has caused its atmosphere to be burned away completely. On the sunny side the temperature rises to 430 °C, on the dark side it drops to - 170 °C. It turns around the sun in 88 days and has a rotational speed around its axis of 58.6 days. The marked surface may also be the effect of shrinkage.

Venus

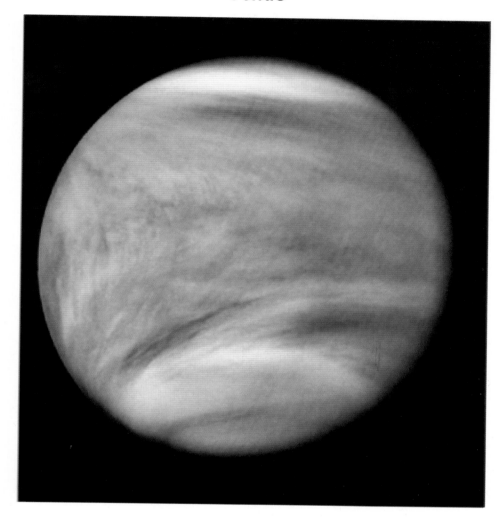

Fig. 4.7

In the past, Venus was called the 'clear morning star' or by others the 'clear evening star'. The reason for this is that when viewed from the earth it swings across our 'planetary view' over a period of about sixteen months. For about eight months it is clear in the morning and the other eight months it is clear in the evening. Its surface is covered under a thick atmosphere where temperature rises to 500 °C. The atmosphere allows sunlight in but not out, which causes a greenhouse effect. A constant acid rain (carbon dioxide and sulfuric acid) falls form the clouds. It turns around the sun in 225 days and around its axis in 243 days. The pressure of its atmosphere is about 90 times greater than that of earth.

Mars

Fig. 4.8

The red planet is a giant sand desert where huge storms occur regularly. It also has ice caps on the poles just like the earth and several giant volcanoes. The highest one is 2 ½ times as high as the Mount Everest.

It has a thin, pink atmosphere and a deep red surface. Temperatures are between + 20 and - 140°C. It rotates around the sun in 687 days. A Martian day also takes about 24 hours. It may have had water on its surface in the past and a denser atmosphere.

Jupiter

Fig. 4.9

The largest planet in the solar system with a diameter nine times greater than the earth. Because of it's constant light during the night, the Greeks called the planet the supreme god. Giant storms with speeds of 350 km/h, lash the dust from the surface up to 25k.m. high. The atmosphere mainly contains hydrogen. Just like the sun, its composition is 9 parts hydrogen, 1 part helium. Because of its smaller mass, it never self-ignited, keeping its temperatures much lower (between + 25 and – 150°C). The center is about 20,000°C. If its mass was 50 times bigger, we would have had two stars in our solar system creating a completely different environment. Jupiter has 16 satellites.

Saturn

Fig. 4.10

This pale yellow giant looks a little like Jupiter. It has the same 3-layer atmosphere and huge storms (speeds of more than 1500 km/h have been measured). It is surrounded by thousands of rings (containing ice and rocks), making it look like an old gramophone record. The temperatures on its surface are around -150°C. It is the lightest planet in our solar system. If we could drop it in water it would float. Seventeen satellites have been discovered around Saturn.

The Three Trans–Saturnal Planets

Uranus

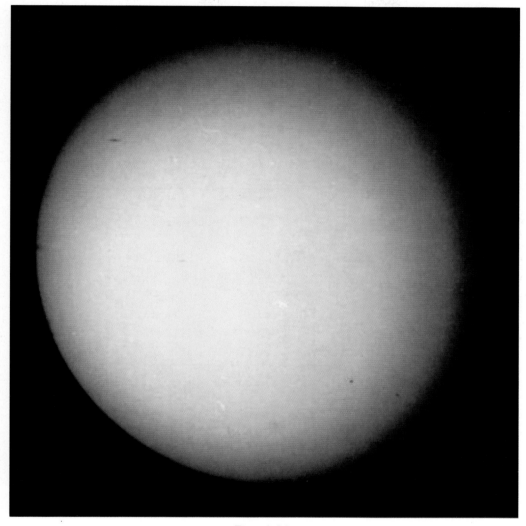

Fig. 4.11

Uranus is the only planet which lies on its side as it revolves around the sun. It is invisible to the naked eye and was unknown until 1781. The astronomer William Henschel discovered it with the use of a telescope. According to scientific models, the outer layer would consist of hydrogen and helium covering a mantle of fluid frozen methane, ammonia and water. Inside would consist of a stony center of metals and silicate. The temperature would be around − 215 °C. It has a diffuse belt of rings and 15 satellites.

Neptune

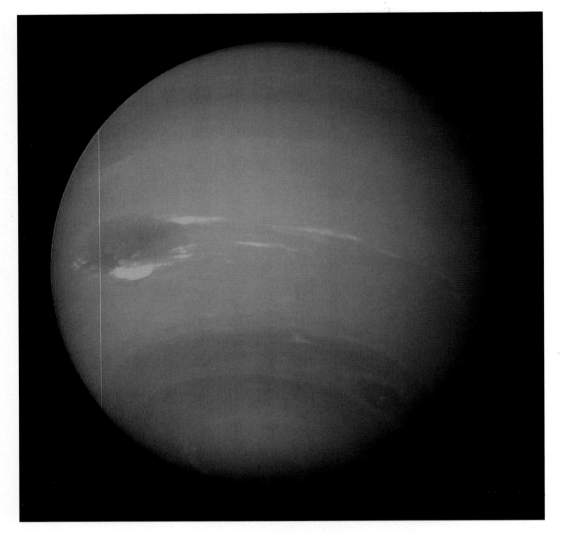

Fig. 4.12

Neptune was first discovered through mathematical calculation before it was ever seen according to the changes in the orbit of Uranus. In 1846, J. Galle discovered Neptune where the mathematicians predicted it to be.

The scientific model developed for Neptune shows a very similar structure and composition to the earth.

Pluto

Fig. 4.13

Clyde Tembough discovered Pluto in 1930. It has an orbit about 6 billion km away from the sun. It has a diameter of about 2300 km (the earth's moon is 3476km) and a mass more than 1/400 of the earth. This frozen stone clump has a thin atmosphere of methane and surface temperatures of − 210 °C. It has an orbital angle of 17°, which is unique in the planetary world. It also has a strong elliptical orbit causing a crossing of the Neptune orbit.

The inner part of the solar system contains four similar, more rocky planets: Mercury, Venus, Earth and Mars. This is followed by an asteroid belt containing millions of irregularly shaped stones. Further out are the four gas/ice giants, Jupiter, Saturn, Uranus and Neptune. Pluto is the farthest planet out in our solar system. It is a very 'small' frozen rock which might previously have been a satellite of Neptune. Many astrologists and astronomers talk about a 10th planet being further out in the solar system. This planet would have a mass twice to five times greater than the earth. This would explain the changes in the orbits of the outer planets. Since Pluto's mass is very small, another planet is probably causing this effect. The angle of the 10th planet's orbit would probably be about 75°.

The planetary field is the central area in our solar system. It is a very little part of the solar system. The cometary field is estimated to be 3850 times bigger than the planetary field. The outer edge our solar system almost touches other solar systems. The nearest solar system is Alpha Centauri. All together these solar systems move around the center of the Milky Way at a speed of 300 km/sec. It takes more than 200 million years to finish a complete cycle around the center of our Milky Way.

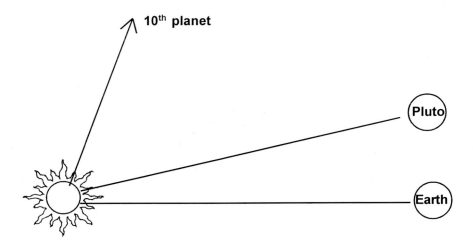

Fig. 4.14 10th 'Unnamed' Planet (Chiron), Pluto, Earth and Sun

It is not accidental that the three outer planets (Uranus, Neptune and Pluto) were only discovered during the last 150 years. As human evolution moves towards the center of the spiral we experience an increasing speed of events (reaching a peak around 2100). This whirlpool of events strongly activates the collective consciousness field. If the body's energy system and the soul connection are not developed, this spiral and the trans-saturnal planets can create a great deal of confusion, exhaustion and mental and emotional imbalance.

But, if we can integrate these forces they will trigger unique human abilities at the level of mind and spirit and the collective social consciousness.

In 1977 a large asteroid like planet was discovered. It has its orbit at its closest point (to the sun) between Saturn and Uranus and at its farthest point far beyond the orbit of Pluto. In this way this planet connects the personal planets with the trans-saturnal planets which are related to the collective consciousness. Astronomers named it Chiron, which is the name of a Greek mythological figure being half-human/half-horse. It is a symbol for healing. Also, since 1977 healing arts have rapidly developed and spread on our planet.

As time goes by, more universal knowledge will be gained, always being connected to related changes in the personal and collective consciousness.

Stars and Galaxies

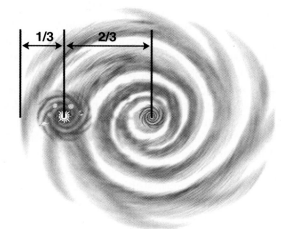

Fig. 4.15 Our Solar System in the Milky Way

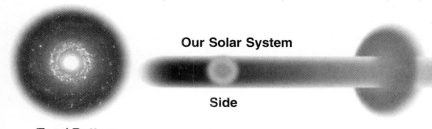

Our Solar System

Side

Top / Bottom   **Fig. 4.16** Shape of the Milky Way

Images taken recently through the Hubble space telescope show the different stages in the birth process of stars. These pictures show that powerful energy, ultraviolet radiation and high speed gas clouds unleashed by adult stars are triggering the birth of new stars in the surroundings. Ultraviolet light emitted by the neighbor stars energizes the clouds. Inside these huge interstellar gas columns, the density can become so high that gravity takes over and causes the gas cloud to collapse and split into smaller clumps or gas eggs. When compression continues a nuclear fusion will ignite their cores so that they become fledgling stars.

The pressure and temperature in the cloud will rise to a point where nuclear reactions arise. After this point is reached, the star will shine for millions of years. A star like the sun, can live for over 10 billion years. Bigger stars are often burned out after 20 billion years. Generally speaking, we can say that the younger stars have violet/blue colors, the middle aged ones are yellowish, the older ones are red-brown and the oldest are black. As the star gets older it might turn into a white dwarf through a lack of fuel, or into a supernova through explosion, or into a black hole through implosion. According to the estimated age of many stars, it is clear that our Milky Way must be over 12 billion years old.

Earth is about 1/3 of the way from the outside border in our galaxy. The galaxy has a diameter of about 100,000 light years and contains about 100 billion stars. The biggest concentration of stars is found in the central area. There are billions of other galaxies in the universe. These galaxies are grouped into clusters and in turn these clusters belong to super clusters. Our galaxy belongs to a group of about 30 other galaxies called "the local group". The closest other big galaxy is the Andromeda nebula. We find this star nebula at a distance of 2,200,000 light years, which means that the pictures we see now were sent out 2.2 million years ago. On a dark clear night, we can see the Andromeda nebula without any binocular or telescope. Some of the stars we are seeing are in fact galaxies composed of billions of stars.

In Taoist astrology the sky is divided in 28 or 64 constellations. Astronomers often use the different distances of the stars in one constellation as proof that there is a connection between the stars in these constellations and in this way they effect the human condition. However, in the unique quality of each constellation, the real distance of the stars is just an aspect that co-creates the magnitude of the star as seen from the earth. The collective angle or direction of influence is what forms the specific group energy and connection between the stars in all constellations.

In the case of Polaris for instance, which is located in the center of the galaxy, it is certainly not the brightest star in the sky.
For the Big Dipper, the five most central stars belong to one star cluster which is at a distance between 59 and 75 light-years (the closest star cluster for us). The outer two stars are at a different distance and move in a different direction.

Different Galactic Forms

There are many different types of galaxies, but they are mostly divided into three main groups.

Fig. 10.17 Spiral Galaxies

Spiral galaxies, like the Milky Way, have a central elliptical region filled with many old stars. Around this center there is a sphere of old stars connected with the outer spiral arms, composed of younger stars and regions of gas and dust where stars are still born.

Fig. 10.18 Elliptical Galaxies

Elliptical galaxies contain very few young stars or gas and dust. They are mainly composed of older groupings of stars. Few stars are born here.

Irregular Galaxies

Magellan Cloud

Fig. 10.19

Irregular galaxies without a particular form. One of these is the large Magellan cloud, the companion of our solar system.

About White Dwarfs, Supernovae, Black Holes, Pulsars and Quasars

As a star gets older it might turn into a white dwarf through a lack of fuel. It also can explode and in this way become a supernova, a star that is a bright as about 10 billion suns. The third possibility is implosion into a black hole, a concentration of extreme density and gravity so that according to most scientists no matter, radiation or light can escape from it. Astronomers believe that pulsars are fast rotating neutron stars that radiate light (or sound waves or radioactive waves) through a small beam, so that we can see it every time it is directed towards the earth.

Quasars are the brightest sky objects in the visible universe. They often shine with a brightness of 200 billion suns and are often visible with the bare eye even though they are at a distance of billions of light years.

Fig. 10.20 Supernova

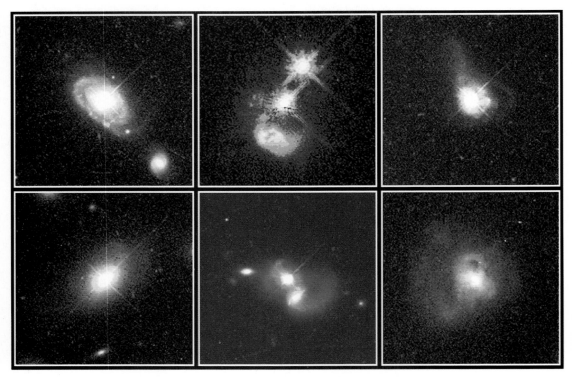

Fig. 10.21 Quasars

Chapter V
Taoist Star Practices and their Effect on Human Awareness

Ancient practices viewed the stars as having a material manifestation. The manifestation of the stars in brilliance, pulsation and color shows the constant interaction of these two forces. Stars were seen as the embryonic essence but also as a great source of Chi. In the stars we find high concentrations of the vital primal essence. The sun was seen as the fullest form of pure yang energy which then was divided out towards the different stars. Because of their inherent relation to the embryonic essence (like sexual essence in our body), stars were seen as forms of water energy. The expression of bright white light shows the inherent metal energy.

For the Taoists, stars are the places where immortal beings reside. Mostly in the central star palace but also in other locations. Newly born stars demonstrate that a high master has made the transition to heaven. One Han master, Ching Fong, predicted that after his death a new star would show up in Hercules and indeed, a supernova suddenly appeared just after he died.

The North Star and the Big Dipper in the Taoist Practices

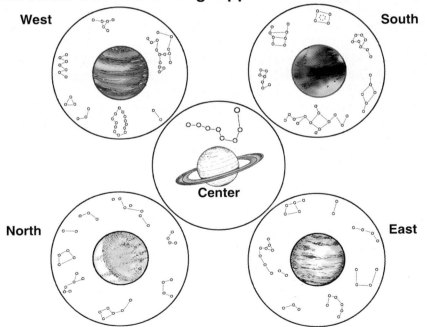

Fig. 5.1 Five Planets, Directions and Constellations

The Taoist masters viewed the North Star and Big Dipper as the greatest celestial sources of power. Their supernatural energy was shown by the name "yang luminosity". The North Star has been used by many enlightened Taoist masters as a gate to the Tao. This North Star gate was used during the meditation practices and finally at the moment of dying. Other spiritual systems use other connection points or gates into the sky.

The Chinese Emperor was seen as a heavenly child. Many stars around the North Star have the name of an Emperor or one of his family members. The great one (Emperor) was often depicted with the Big Dipper in one hand and the North Star in his other hand.

Because of the wobbling of the earth axis in a cycle of 25,800 years, different stars will get aligned over the earth axis. This means that different stars will take the position of the North Star.

In some years ahead there will be a new "North Star"; it will be Vega again. From 1000 to 500 B.C. it was the star Kochab; during the time the Egyptian pyramids were being build it was Dra Thuban; about 13,000 years ago it was Vega (in Lyra). During the Ming Dynasty it was Tian Shu in the Big Dipper. Tian Shu is also the name for 'ST 25' the acupuncture point to either side of the umbilicus.

A name that is generally used for Pole stars is Zhong Ji - 'Center of Heaven', which means, "The best place in heaven" or Tai Yi "The great one". Zhong Ji also relates to the acupuncture point 'CV 3' and Tai Chi with 'ST 23' showing the connection between the body's meridian system in the Tan Tien area and the Taoist gate to the Universal light. Also the name 'Pivot of Heaven' was used. This same name was also used for Dubne, in the Big Dipper. The function of the North Star is to emit the essence, the embryonic energy flow.

The North Star has a close connection to the seven stars of the Big Dipper. The North Star is found at about 5 times the distance of the line projected from 6th and 7th Big Dipper stars. Traditionally the Big Dipper/North Star axis was used to determine the season. he North Star/Big Dipper axis is moving through the four palaces or regulating the four countrysides during the four seasons or one year.

The Dipper is the carriage of the North Star. When the spiritual essence of the Tai Yi spills over, the Dipper lets its essence fall through its seven bright gates of celestial power.

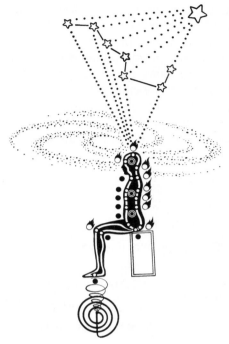

Fig. 5.2

In the Taoist advanced practices the North Star and Big Dipper energies are connected with the different bones of the skull.

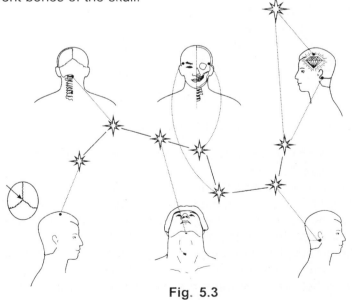

Fig. 5.3

In this way the connection with the Universal Light is deeply integrated in the brain and the glands within the skull (Crystal Room/Palace, see Fig 5.5). Each of the stars has a connection with the lower planetary world (five planets, sun and moon) and with the higher vibrational world of the five elements and the pakua. According to the oracle texts of the Han Dynasty, each of the Big Dipper stars has a unique earthly manifestation in the animal and plant kingdom. The seven star principle is not unique to the Big Dipper. It can also be found back in the Pleiades, the Vermilion Bird and other constellations.

In one type of Taoist astrology the numbers 1 to 9 and the 9 energies of the pakua (8 directions and the center) were used as a form of numerology connected to the seven stars of the Big Dipper, Polaris and Vega.

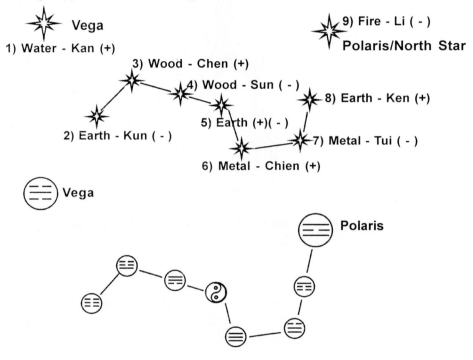

Fig. 5.4 Big Dipper

Since the star Vega, related to number 1 was known as a star related to destruction, it was not connected to the Crystal Room.

In Taoism, the nine stars of the true Dipper are used. There are the seven familiar ones and two hidden or invisible ones. According to one source these stars hold the embryonic essence (Ching) and actualizing spirit (Shen). One T'ang practice which is still used these days in China is the practice through the nine stars of the Dipper while visualizing the star Alcor and holding the breath. Just as the principle of counter planets in Chinese astrology and the modern astronomical theory that quasars and black holes might be functioning together, some Taoists believed that there are nine black stars underlying the nine Big Dipper stars.

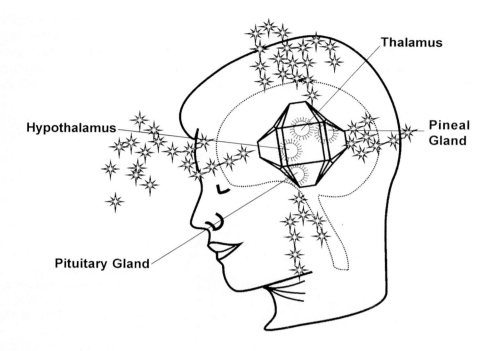

Fig. 5.5 Crystal Palace

In the Universal Tao meditation practices, we use the combined energy of the North Star and the Big Dipper to connect with the Universal Light.

The Big Dipper light (red) is absorbed by the thalamus hypothalamus while the North Star (violet) relates to the pineal gland. The pineal gland is our internal compass, while the North Star is our external compass. Taoist masters believed that if the North Star was able to keep all the constellations in orbit, its size and mass would be enormous.

In Taoist cosmology, 28 constellations are ordered around the North Star and the Big Dipper.

In each of the 28 days of the moon cycle one of the constellations reaches its maximum influence.

The special magnetic field of moon and earth energies combined together, attracts these fine star energies creating a special spiritual condition on our planet.

Besides the 28 constellations around the North Star there are billions of milky ways each with billions of stars in their universe. All these stars have a direct connection with the billions of cells in our body, where at the moment of fertilization and birth a specific position gives you a unique charge and direction in life.

Through meditation practices and by way of integrating new insights and this higher awareness into your daily life, the information from these stars and your personal cells becomes synchronized. This brings you back to your true task in this life, but it also gives you access to the Universal information field. The direct connection with this intelligence will naturally provide you with all the information and life force required for you to fulfill the true life-task.

The earth's rotation around its axis creates a strong electromagnetic field. The wobbling of the earth's axis creates different stellar influences with enormous effects on the conditions of our planet.

Fig. 5.6

Earth Axis Wobbling and Poleshifts

The earth has three movements: it rotates around the sun (one year); it rotates around its own axis (one day); and the axis wobbles. The projection of the earth's axis to the north creates a circular form between Vega and Polaris. There is a strong electromagnetic belt around the earth because of the rotational force. This belt is strongest around the equator and weakest at the poles. The South Pole is directed towards the center of the Milky Way while the North Pole is directed towards the outside.

For this reason the energy that comes through the North Pole is clearer and more subtle than the one which comes in from the South Pole. The northern sky is governed by the energy of the North Star and its 28 constellations and is considered richer in terms of star and galactic energies.

The wobbling movement of the axis of the earth has a strong effect on human civilization and the quality of life on earth. It takes 25,800 years for the earth to make a full 360° movement around its axis. The strongest activation of energy occurs when the axis is directed straight towards Polaris (the North Star at the turn of the millennium).

Around the year 2,102 the North Star will be in perfect line with the earth axis. This will highly increase the influence of spiritual energy on our planet.

The galactic year: Movement of our solar system around the center of the Milky Way. Speed 300 km/sec, 230 million years to make a complete cycle.

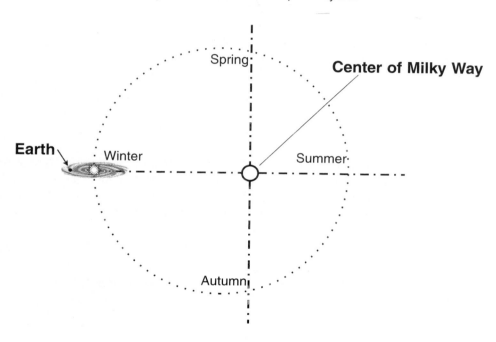

Fig. 5.7 Galactic Year

During the 230 million years (a galactic year) it takes our solar system to orbit the center of the Milky Way, it will be located at different distances from this center, which will create varying gravitational conditions in the solar system and on our planet.

The energy of Polaris is the yang energy from heaven related to the Governing Vessel. The energy of Vega is the yin energy from heaven related to the Conception Vessel.

During a 25,800 year cycle, the period of Polaris was traditionally seen as the light period. There was a flourishing spiritual life on earth and a period of happiness and good luck. The period of Vega (12,900 years later) is seen as the arrival of the dark period with destruction of society and a low spiritual level on our planet.

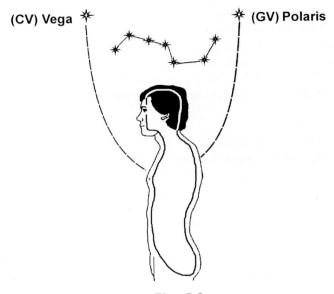

Fig. 5.8

When Polaris is above the earth axis the Crystal Room Governing Vessel receives information and transfers it to the Conception Vessel where it is integrated. When Vega is above our earth axis, the energy is directly absorbed into the lower centers without the spiritual / universal connection. The result is isolation, arrogance and destruction.

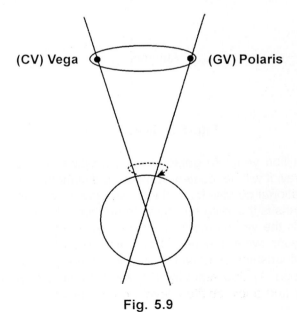

Fig. 5.9

Pole shifts: The rotational force of the earth creates a centrifugal force. When this expanding force reaches a peak, an axis shift occurs. If we roll an egg away from us, at a certain point it starts wobbling and than suddenly flips over, creating another axis and new poles. According to some sources many of these pole shifts have occurred on earth. These shifts happen in a few days, creating giant shifts of the water and land and the death of millions of humans and animals. In different civilizations these shifts and floods have been known and described.

Although scientists do not agree, some believe that the famous sphinx from Giza in Egypt must have been built long before Pharaoh Chefren 2,700 B.C. The sphinx is the biggest one-piece statue on earth. The famous Egyptologist, Schwaller de Lubicz, thinks that the erosion on the head of the sphinx could only have been caused by water. Around 15,000 BC the last ice age must have been at its peak. The big floods caused by the melting ice caps all happened between 10 and 12,000 B.C. As we explained before, these floods were caused by earth axis shifts under influence of the North Star of that time: Vega.

This data suggests that the sphinx might have come from a civilization of more than 12,000 years ago. This would also explain the mystery of Egyptian culture in many areas. Although the pyramids were built with an unknown skill and technology, the Egyptologist Borchardt states that at that time the Egyptian culture was certainly not yet highly advanced. Structures were probably built on the fragments of a lost civilization. Study of sediment in paleo-climatological research has shown that severe flooding must have occurred around 12,000 years ago. Many books from around the world speak of the lost civilization of Atlantis. It is believed to have been swallowed by the sea because of a great deluge about 12,000 years ago. Atlanteans knew of the impending destruction and sent out groups to other continents. Perhaps these emissaries from "lost Atlantis" were responsible for the spiritually advanced cultures that followed. There are other theories relating to the link between these ancient civilizations and extraterrestrial life; most notably between the Egyptian pyramids, spinning disk technology and life on Mars. Taoist masters were not alone in recognizing the 25,800 year earth axis wobble and polar shifts. This process is described by several ancient cultures.

Fig. 5.10

As previously discussed there are many different influences affecting us at the same time. All of these influences have a unique rhythm. It is the concentration of all these rhythms, influences and positions that create a unique Universal condition at every moment of our lives. Another strong influence on human awareness is the Photon Belt. A field that our planet is slowly arriving into now. Satellites discovered the Photon Belt in 1961. Photons are very small light particles of electromagnetic energy, without mass and electrical charge and of an undefinable life span. These photons are in our atmosphere all the time but their number is gradually increasing because our planet is traveling through the Photon Belt for greater periods of time every year. From the year 2013, we will be constantly surrounded and immersed by these photons for a period of about 2000 years. The activity of the North Star and of the Photon Belt represents a unique spiritual possibility to all of us. The North American Indians, the Mayans, Tibetans and the Egyptians were amongst the ancient cultures that were quite aware of the age of light which would begin at the start of the 21st century.

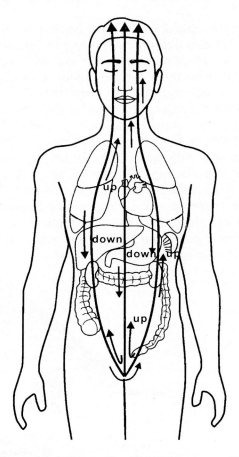

Fig. 5.11 Three Thrusting Channels: Chi Energy can Flow Up or Down.

Universal Tao Practices that connect you with the unique Universal Conditions

The strong Polaris energy, which carries the information of all the stars of the northern sky, will shine straight down into the crown. It has a direct connection with the thrusting channels. These channels run through the central part of the body between the crown and the perineum.

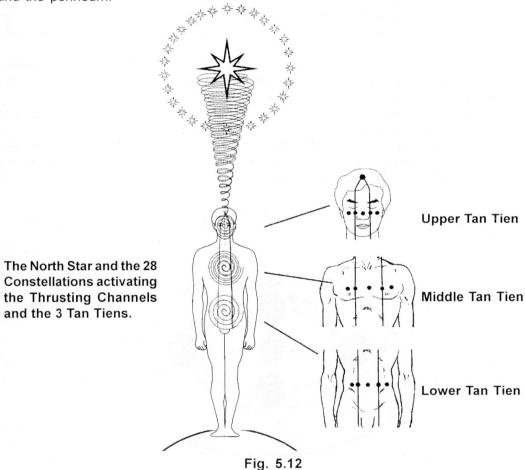

The North Star and the 28 Constellations activating the Thrusting Channels and the 3 Tan Tiens.

Upper Tan Tien

Middle Tan Tien

Lower Tan Tien

Fig. 5.12

There are Three Thrusting Channels: one central, one left and one right. They create left/right balance and a direct vertical connection between all the important organs. The influence of this spiritual activation is already quite apparent in present human behavior and interest. More and more people are attracted to meditation, spirituality and self-development. In the next century, their number and the depth of their spiritual growth will certainly increase.

Another clear sign that humanity is quickly moving towards a new phase in its evolution and into a new direction is the fact that many things in society are changing at a dazzling speed. More than any time before in human history, the pace of life has quickened; many people feel highly pressured and confused, as they desperately try to keep up with the changes in all dimensions of social life and social realities, with encompassing changes occurring in such domains as science and technology, family ties, communications and security. Many people experience this whirlpool of change as a direct challenge to their currently weak condition and as a major reason for loss of energy.

The arrival of the light period in connection with the North Star activation must be seen as a possibility we have to fill in ourselves and not as a gift that will be automatically delivered to our home.

Although the transformation of energy is in principle available to everybody, our overall condition and the direction of our focus will greatly determine the level of integrating the newly arising condition of energy in the universe.

It is important to remember that health and freedom greatly depend on our ability to follow and integrate these universal changes. In the same way as an amoebae opens and closes and the heart expands and contracts, human evolution goes through phases (every 25,800 years) in which it flourishes and enters into decline. These phases are dictated by the earth's axis in the northern sky.

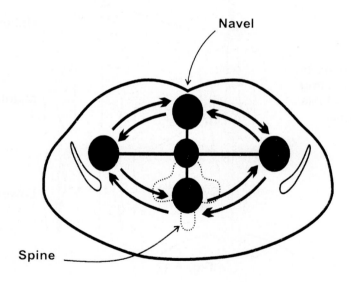

Fig. 5.13
Belt and Thrusting Channels at the Level of the Navel:
These Energy Channels run throughout the Body and are Interconnected by Circular
Horizontal Energy Bridges.

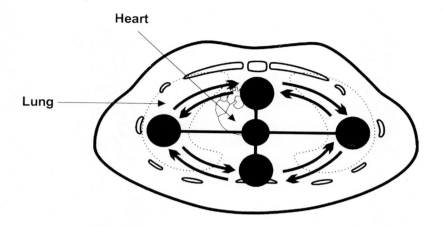

Heart

Lung

Fig. 5.14 Belt and Thrusting Channels at the Level of the Heart

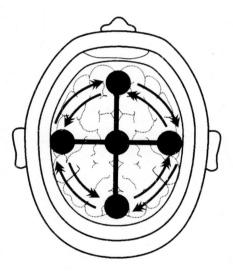

Fig. 5.15 Belt and Thrusting Channels at the Level of the Crown

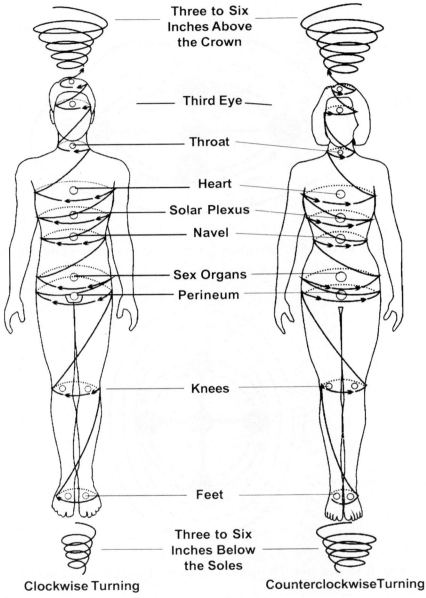

Three to Six
Inches Above
the Crown

Third Eye

Throat

Heart

Solar Plexus

Navel

Sex Organs

Perineum

Knees

Feet

Three to Six
Inches Below
the Soles

Clockwise Turning   CounterclockwiseTurning

Fig. 5.16

Practicing the Universal Tao techniques which will align you with this unique situation in the universe will open several spiritual channels. The first step in this process is the opening of the Microcosmic Orbit (MCO). This is a channel directly connected to all the orbits in the universe reaching to the source. If this channel is open the information from the universe can be easily picked up and integrated. As you can see in fig. 5.18, there are many different points on the MCO which need to be opened and connected.

These points are directly connected with the Tan Tiens (front and back) and with the points where the Tan Tiens are connected with each other and with the environment. As fig. 5.18 shows, the MCO points, the Tan Tiens and the chakras (as they are known in the Hindu tradition) actually have the same location.

When the MCO opens and connects with the Tan Tiens, the Thrusting Channels will also start to open up. This enhances the heaven/earth connection and energizes and detoxifies the body. Then all the five channels (the front and back channels and the three thrusting channels) connect with the Belt Channels. These are horizontal circular channels, which conserve and protect your life force. When these channels are open and connected, your energy level and your healing capacity will greatly increase. The Belt Channels connect the conception vessel/ governing vessel/ the left/ and the right Thrusting Channel

By activating the Tan Tiens and fusing the energy into one 'pearl' in the Tan Tien, the dualistic experience of time in a manifested past and a vibrational future diminishes and finally dissolves into one infinite experience of now.

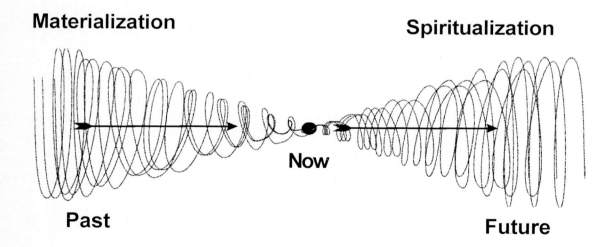

Fig. 5.17 Human Evolution

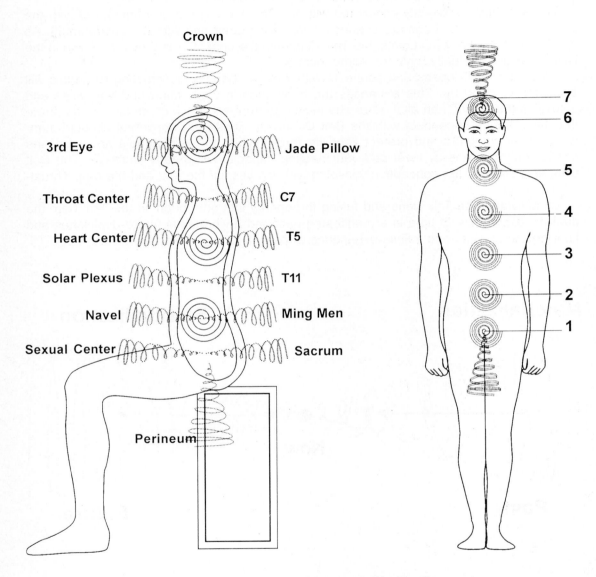

Fig. 5.18 Microcosmic Orbit - Tan Tiens - Chakra Comparison

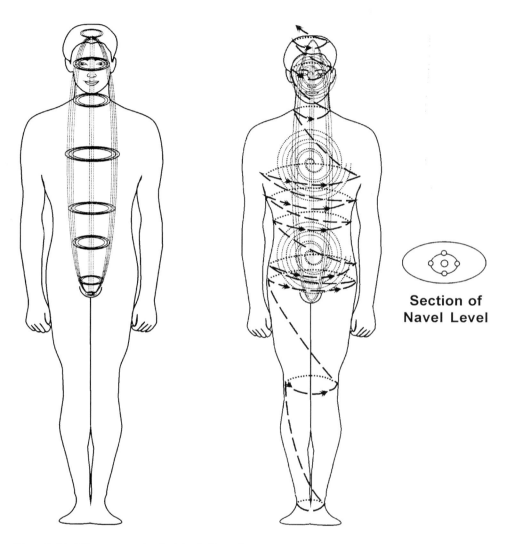

Fig. 5.19 Microcosmic Orbit, 3 Tan Tiens, Thrusting Channels, Belt Channels,
Tan Tien Comparison.

Chapter VI
The Development of Humanity

Simultaneous Development of Humanity and the Universe

Our planet started its materialization process about 4.5 to 5 billion years ago. After the formation of a dense core and a protective atmosphere, the whole planet was covered with water. In this ancient sea, life emerged about 3.2 billion years ago, in its most primitive forms; viruses and bacteria. This, of course, is not when life began in the universe. We, in our true immortal state, are pure life and intelligence in human form. But around that time we began to manifest in physical existence.

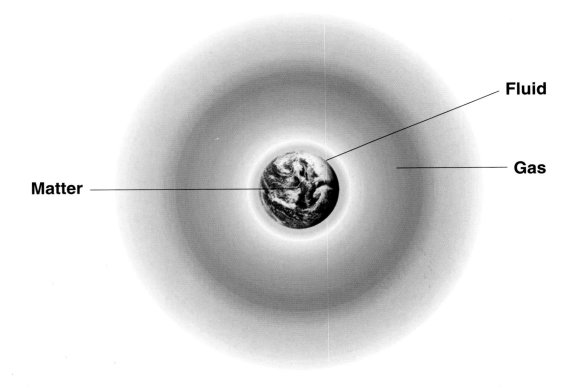

Fig. 6.1

The intelligence that materializes/manifests in the visible world and dematerializes/disappears in other dimensions is one and omnipresent. When the solar system and the Milky Way developed further and became more structured, life on earth developed simultaneously. When the solar system started to form, the Milky Way had already been in existence for billions of years.

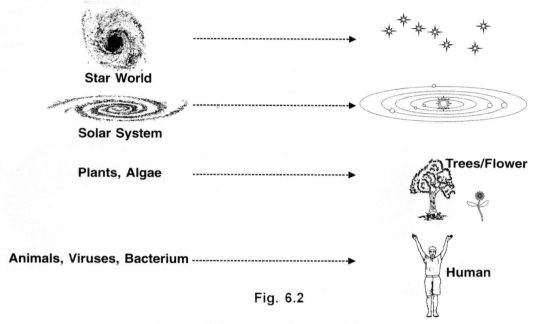

Star World

Solar System

Plants, Algae → **Trees/Flower**

Animals, Viruses, Bacterium → **Human**

Fig. 6.2

The formation of the solar system and humanity is due to a contracting/materializing force or spiral. This spiral crystallizes energetic laws and Chi causing the formation of our solar system and the earth. The unique earthly atmosphere has attracted life with humanity as its highest manifestation. Cosmic dust and particles gather and form elements around the already energetic (present in the world of law and Chi) human structure.

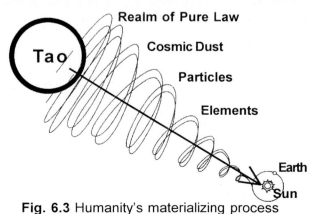

Fig. 6.3 Humanity's materializing process

Humankind in the Solar System

The human form can be seen in the solar system if we look at the deforming electromagnetic field of the earth, caused by the solar wind. This causes a flattening on the sunny side and an enlarging on the dark side of the field. An electromagnetic field is caused by the rotation around the earth's axis. In figure 6.4, the earth would be at the place of the throat center. This center is seen as a center of expression but also of growth and the place where our two bodies (trunk and head) are fused. In an upright position on the earth, the body grows downwards and the head upwards from the throat.

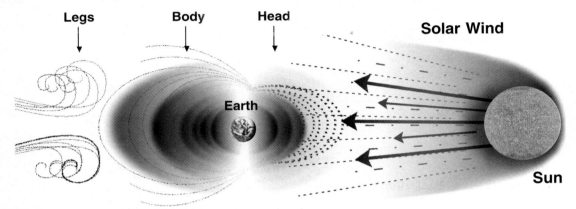

Force from the Outer Planets

Fig. 6.4 Solar Wind - Earth

The earth and heaven forces are in a balance of about 1:7. The earth is creating the rising force or the formation of the head. The heaven is the descending force or the formation of the body. This is according to growth and development. If we look at the energetic functions of the head and the body, the head would be the heaven force center, the lower body would be the earth force center.

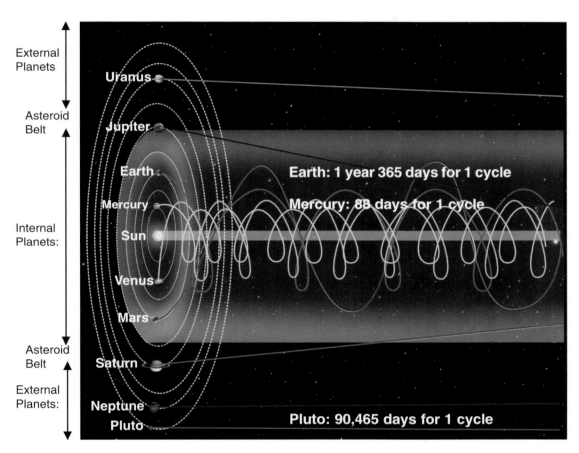

Fig. 6.5 Movement of the Solar System through Space.

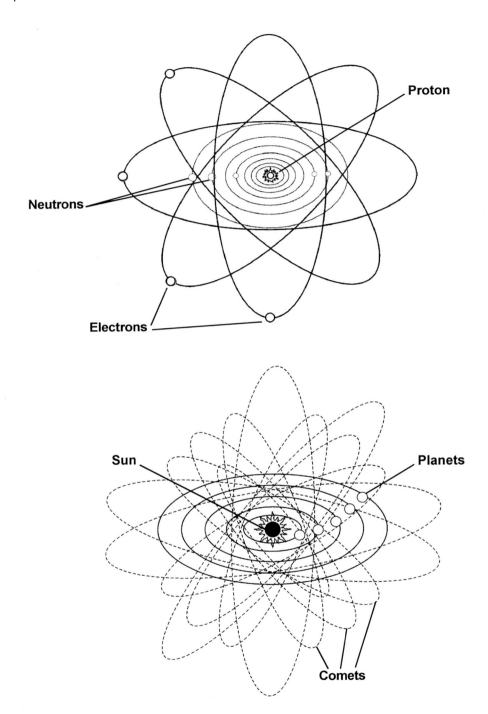

Fig 6.6 Atomic Structure and Solar System Structure

Comparison between Milky Way/Solar System and Human Cells/DNA Structure

If we look at the paths the sun and the planets are making, as they move around the center of the Milky Way, we observe a very interesting spiral structure. Because of the increasing rotation of the planets as we move outward through the solar system, the spiral structure becomes larger from Mercury to Pluto (rotation time for Mercury: 88 days, Pluto: 90,465 days).

The long stretched spiral shows a similarity to a DNA structure. These structures belong to the most fundamental building blocks of the body cells and also contain a complicated transmitter and receiver system that pick up the continuous changes in the solar system, the Milky Way and the vibrational world.

If we compare the form of the spiraling Milky Way and DNA seen from above, the shape becomes even more similar.

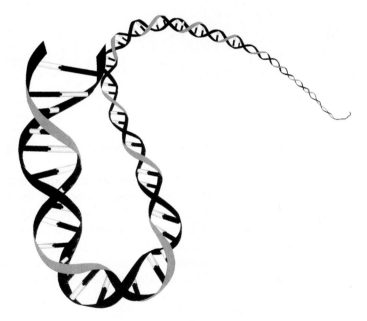

Fig. 6.7 DNA Double Helix

The structure of the solar system is found to be very similar to the structure of an atom (See fig. 6.7). The sun and the planets represent the nucleus of the atom, the sun with a positive charge and the planets a balancing charge. The sun would be the proton and the planets the neutrons. The comets of the solar system are comparable with the electrons of an atom, carrying a negative charge. There's a striking relationship between the I Tjing and the genetic structure, with the number 64 as the central aspect, illustrating the relationship between spiritual laws and genetic structure.

Energetic Embryology

The original unity of man and woman is symbolically seen in the Tai Chi Tsu. The yin and yang in perfect balance together. One stage before this they were still one indistinguishable entity; the Wu Chi state. The energy of man and woman also originates from this oneness. This state is still deeply inherent in all our body cells. So, before the egg and sperm physically fused, man and woman united on a vibrational level. The original oneness literally draws the egg and sperm together.

A recent research project found that in at least 85% of the cases, women were unconsciously acting on a deep drive to fertilize an egg. Something inside of them decides that now is the time. This strong desire then intuitively triggers the attention of the man. This shows the interaction of the karmic charge in the soul and the individual awareness field of human beings.

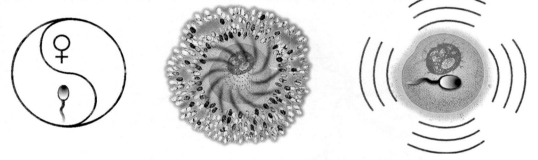

Fig. 6.8 Egg and Sperm, the Big Bang and the Little Bang

At the moment of fertilization, or when the sperm penetrates through the egg's membrane wall, a mini light explosion happens. This series of events contains the complete evolutionary process of universe and humanity. Connected to the information of the egg and sperm and the Universal consciousness, the cell knows how to produce a human being.

This process is very much like the birth process of a star. Energy and then gas build up potential between different stars. The potential rises to a peak where a cloud implodes and falls into different eggs or cocoons. Through the increasing density and pressure a nuclear reaction follows automatically and a new star comes into existence.

The creative ability of the intelligence present in this one cell can only be called miraculous. Everyone could be enlightened from the abilities of the young embryo. Although modern science can demonstrate interesting observations and pictures of how a fully grown human being manifests from this one cell, it cannot understand the theological perspective as to why?

More open-minded scientists agree that the mystery of life cannot be explained by chemistry, genes and chromosomes. Many of them now realize that cells should not be thought of as a rigid unit, but rather as a momentary aspect of spatially ordered (submicroscopic), metabolic movement (same for tissues and organs). All normal cells in the human ovum have the same chromosomes, yet they differ in various ways, so the way genes react must be dictated by external information that enters through the membrane into the cytoplasm and the nucleus.

The vibrational potential between the parents resonates with the soul, which is externally present and interactive long before conception. It enters the embryo around the 49th day after fertilization. The fertilized egg shows (during the first 3 days) a process of splitting, comparable to the earth axis shift that we described before in chapter V (see fig. 5.9). Three or four new axes are created during that time, bringing the number of cells to about 16. This process is also described in the I Ching.

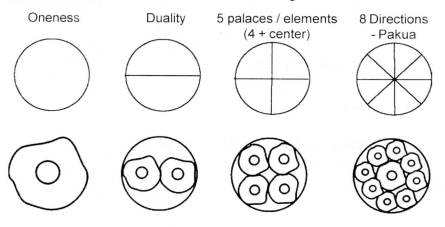

Oneness   Duality   5 palaces / elements   8 Directions
                      (4 + center)   - Pakua

Fig. 6.9 In Embryology this stage is called the Morula.
The one gives rise to the two, the two gives rise to four, the four to the eight.

The fertilized egg stores much of its information in the space and charge between the inside and the outside. The inside is related to the woman's energy and the Conception Vessel. The outside holds the fathers' energy and the Governing Vessel energy. The Governing Vessel functions as a receiving station that picks up all external vibrations. The Conception Vessel internalizes the information and acts as an internal transmission system. In later development the male energy stays more in the vibrational field and gathers around the nervous system and Governing Vessel.

The female energy gathers through the blood production system in the belly, organs, and the Conception Vessel. The Governing Vessel is seen as the source of yang vessels, the Conception Vessel as the source of yin vessels. Until day 16, the embryo consists of 2 layers: the ectoderm and endoderm. Around that time a third layer called the mesoderm will materialize along the central axis of the embryo. The Chong Mo (invisible axis of the cell) has been there all the time, but not in a manifested form. The Chong Mo creates the connection between the Jing (sex potential) and the Shen (spiritual potential).

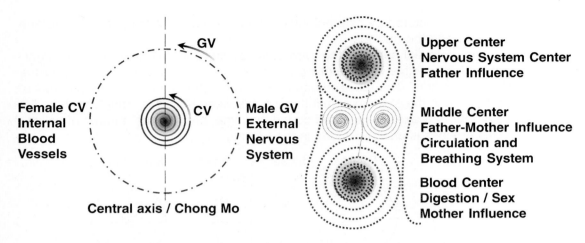

Fig. 6.10 Parental influences on embryonic development.

Energetic Human Model in the Universe

Source	Universal Laws	Chong Mo	CV/GV Extraordinary Channels	12 Meridians Triple Warmer	Acupuncture points / Chakras	All Body Cells

Extraordinary Vessels

Fig. 6.11 Embryo-Source

In Chinese medicine, the triple warmer is directly related to the source. It is directly related to the fascia system as a mechanism to form or shape the fascia, according to the energetic spiral network.

From the 3-layer embryo, the five different elements divide.

The fire element is divided into two parts: primary and secondary fire expressing the high complexity of the human heart/fire quality. So, six meridian couples are formed. This meridian network spreads out in the body with over a thousand vital points, where the electromagnetic force gathers.

> Ectoderm
- Secondary Fire Triple Warmer
           Heart Governor
- Metal   Large Intestine
           Lungs

> Mesoderm
- Earth   Spleen
           Stomach
- Wood   Liver
           Gallbladder

> Endoderm
- Primary Fire   Heart
           Small Intestine
- Water   Kidneys
           Bladder

Waves of Endless Motion

As we have pointed out, humanity developed following one simultaneous materialization process that manifested the entire solar system, the earth and human society. We can say the universe is evolving as a whole. This can happen only with a wavelike motion of life and death or materialization and dematerialization. Just as stars and solar systems are born and come into existence all of it will one day be subject to destruction, decline and dematerialization. The model that is currently used on human development is mainly based on written history, although many facts show that there must have been highly developed civilizations over five thousand years ago. Egyptian, Mayan, Tibetan and Hindu cultures speak of previous civilizations dated long before the times that are generally accepted.

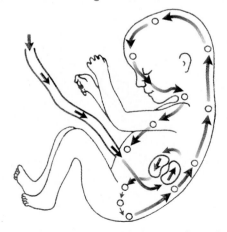

Fig. 6.12 Waves of Endless Creation

The old Newtonian material, rational identification with our external senses, prevents us seeing the authenticity of our true origin. It would be narrow minded to limit ourselves to written material as our only proof. The use of wisdom, life experience and intelligence is the way to penetrate deep behind the limits of the senses. Otherwise we block ourselves and only experience life in our physical boundaries, denying the endless, nature of life. As we see in fig. 6.14, all life comes out of this timeless and formless void, the source. The play, the interaction of polarity creates waves that differentiate in time and space, through the physical universe, the Milky Way, the solar system, the earth, in the body with all its cells, particles and waves. The deeper we go into our physical existence the lower the vibration. Freedom lies in the experience of all these different vibrations while relating to the same timeless and spaceless reality.

Expanding Human Consciousness through the Ages

The work of Rudolf Steiner, the founder of anthroposophy shows many interesting references to planetary energies and human development. This work is more connected to Greek mythology than to Chinese literature. It gives an interesting picture of the link between the universe and human development. Greek mythology places its own qualities on the planets, as do the Taoist or Chinese astrologers.

The planets are the purest symbols of the personality and emotional/social human behaviors. The planetary world is the world of the soul, with the sun as the middle point or the core of the field of consciousness. This chapter is inspired by philosophy of anthroposophy.

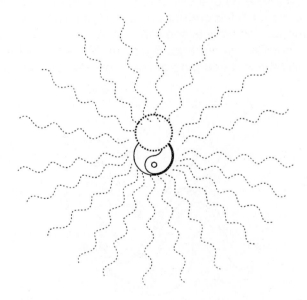

Fig. 6.14 Sun expressing Cosmic Law and Chi

For a long time in the West, astronomy was based on the Ptolemaic view of the solar system (second century Greek astronomer). In this view, the earth was the unmoving center of the universe and all planets circled around it (which is true of course looking from the standpoint of the observer). In anthroposophy, this Ptolemaic point of view is still used as a map to describe the evolution of the soul.

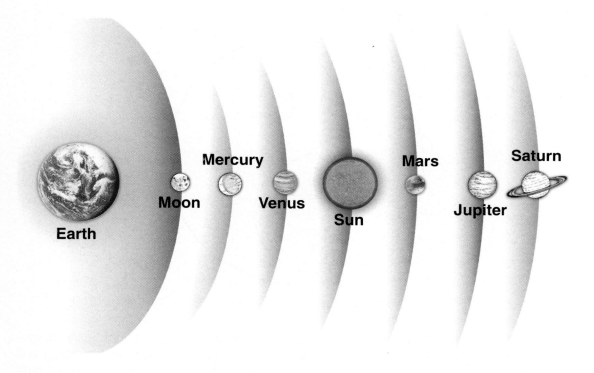

Fig. 6.15 Solar System according to Ptolemy

The earth is the physical place where the human soul connects with the body. Earth, sun and moon form the basic energies for the development of humanity. The deep contents of these energies rise when they meet each other.

The meeting of sun and moon represents the interaction between the consciousness and unconsciousness.

But on another level it can also be seen as consciousness of mind (sun) and consciousness of the body (moon).

Fig. 6.17 Sun and Moon

Mercury represents the ability to connect on a neutral, non-emotional basis. It connects the energy of sun and moon. Among primitive tribes, the group functions as a unit and is more important than the individual. Connection - the quality of Mercury - gives birth to the Venus quality, which has safety and security as its key attributes. They are the unconscious goal of forming a group. People gradually learned to increase their survival rate and enhanced their security through control of the environment (agriculture, hunting).

Mars is the desire to be independent. It stands for the formation of the conscious ego. This is a reaction to the contractive energy of the group. To create balance between this expanding and contractive force another energy was needed. This energy was found in the gods by rituals and prayers (religion). This quality is related to Jupiter. The deeper and higher unity within the group and growing consciousness. The experience of pleasure and pain related to the internal/external struggle in a search for balance and growing consciousness is related to Saturn. It highlights the process of decision making based on your experiences of pleasure and pain.

The discovery of the three trans-saturnal planets created an extra dimension or a higher octave in our solar system's awareness.

Chapter VII
The Soul in the Planetary World

The solar system is an energy structure composed of a central area largely consisting of mass and light and nine awareness belts encircling its center. The planets are the materialized forms of these belts. Each of these belts has unique frequencies and qualities. Since the soul remains strongly connected to the sun, throughout life an evolution through the solar awareness belts takes place.

The Taoist masters clearly distinguish two forms of souls. The sun related cloud soul (hun) and the moon related white soul (p'o). The p'o (one of the stages of the soul) constituent of this dual soul comes into being immediately upon birth, preceding the emergence of the hun which is the yang element of the spiritual nature.

In the following pages we will not use the dualistic principle of the soul, but rather see the soul as one.

The process of Incarnation and Excarnation

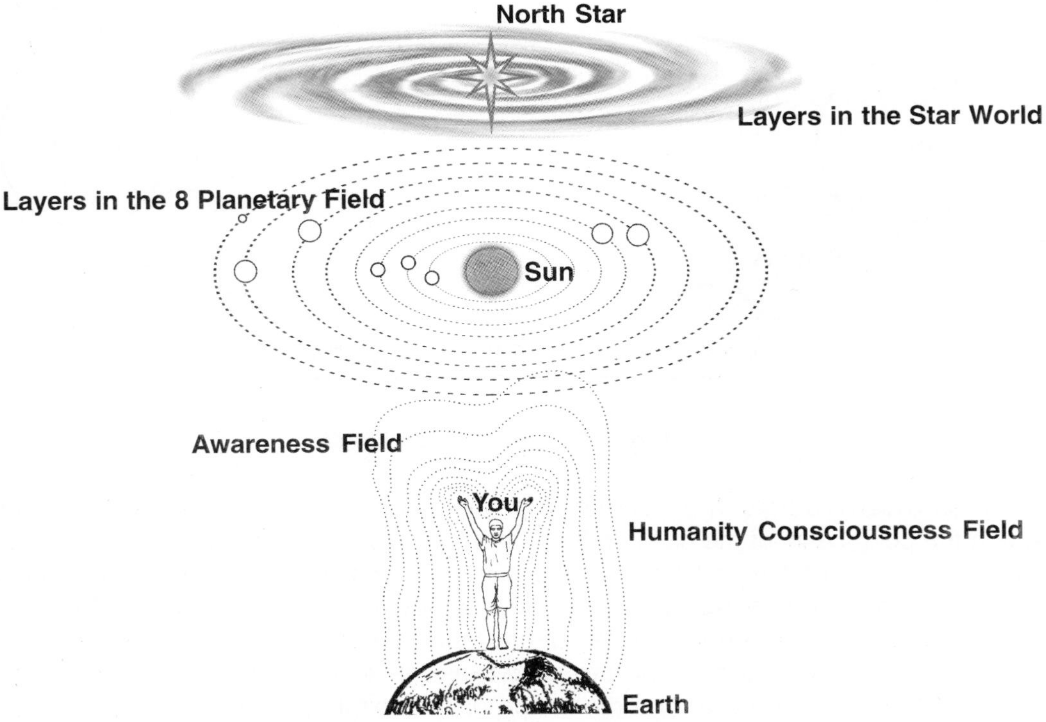

North Star

Layers in the Star World

Layers in the 8 Planetary Field

Sun

Awareness Field

You

Humanity Consciousness Field

Earth

Fig. 7.1 Star World-Planetary World-Human Awareness Field

When the soul starts its incarnation process it moves through the world of stars and is attracted by the unity of our solar system with the sun as its medium. The sun (a star in the solar system) functions as a giant satellite station between the worlds of stars and planets.

According to the karmic information carried by the soul, it will remain a shorter or longer period in the frequencies of some planets. During these stays it receives the necessary information that will create or awaken our specific learning possibilities.

Each soul remains longer in one sphere than another, creating a very distinctive quality in the character of that person. We have greater connections to some of these planets and weaker ones to others. During this incarnation process the soul will move from the unmanifested world through the star world, the external planets, the internal planets and the moon-earth sphere; it will be constantly attracted by the force of the sun and later the earth.

The electro-plasmic force of humanity around the earth functions as an awareness belt that connects the soul with life on earth

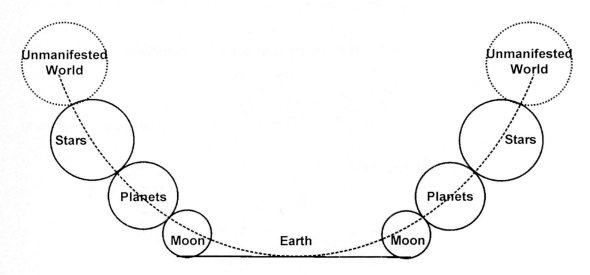

Fig. 7.2 Birth - Life - Death

When a baby is born, the incarnation process is not yet complete, as we can clearly see in the personality of the child. In the first two life cycles (7 year cycle) the full incarnation of the soul still has to be completed. Often around puberty, at the beginning of the third stage, the true personality reveals itself, sometimes even as a shock to the parents. The same happens in the last cycles of life. The person increasingly loses interest and connection with earth and life on the planet, as the soul withdraws towards the higher worlds. Although they are on the other side of the spiral of life, children and old people often dwell with their soul still or already in a higher realm.

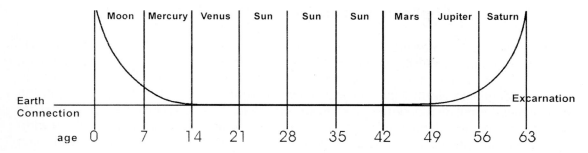

Fig. 7.3 Development of the Soul through the Planetary World Based on Anthroposofical Theory.

In the above picture based on the anthroposophical view of the growth of the soul, the earth is seen as the physical middle point and the sun as the center of soul development. The sun reflects the law of triple unity in the universe. Three planets are placed on each side, the sun is placed in threefold, in the central region.

The stages of incomplete incarnation would be in the stage of the moon and Mercury for the child and of beginning excarnation in the stage of Jupiter and Saturn for elder people.

The discovery of the three trans-saturnal planets has also occurred together with growing human life expectations. This creates a different schedule. In modern society the period of withdrawal from active life and into retirement has clearly become longer than in past centuries. This increased period extends in the trans-saturnal sphere of Uranus, Neptune and Pluto. Because of the low energy and awareness level of many people, this 21 extra years is simply an extension, which results in an increased life span but of a lower quality of life.

Most people have wasted most of their life force before they enter into the trans-saturnal period. This often creates an inability to integrate these planetary influences, with the result that the awareness level drastically diminishes during the last stages of life.

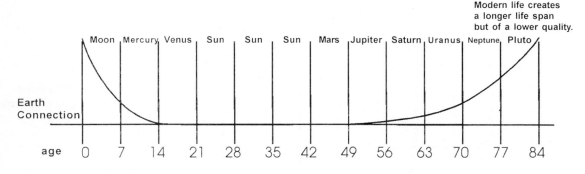

Fig. 7.4

Application in the Universal Tao Practice

In the Universal Tao practice the period of the sun (ages 21 to 42 years) is used to build up a strong connection with the sun and then the North Star consciousness (See fig. 7.5). The North Star is the Taoist spiritual gate. Once the connection with the source is established through the North Star and the Universal light, the effect of the planets on the practitioners' emotional and mental state will be reduced. To establish this sun/North Star connection, the five elemental forces must be balanced and the frequencies of the awareness belts around the sun (related to the planets) must be integrated. During the sun period, the collective consciousness inherent in each cell of our body will be nurtured by the high quality of the sun's frequency. This energy is mostly used to manifest oneself in the world; relationships, work, house, children, etc.

In Taoist practice the awakening light of the sun period is a perfect time to establish the North Star/spiritual connection. Once the connection with the spiritual realm is established we can distinguish two different realities. The planetary influences will still affect us but the rooting to earth and heaven will make it much easier to stay in connection with the spiritual laws, the life in our body and their interaction. This way we stop nurturing the ego and begin to live a life beyond the personality and the related planetary spheres.

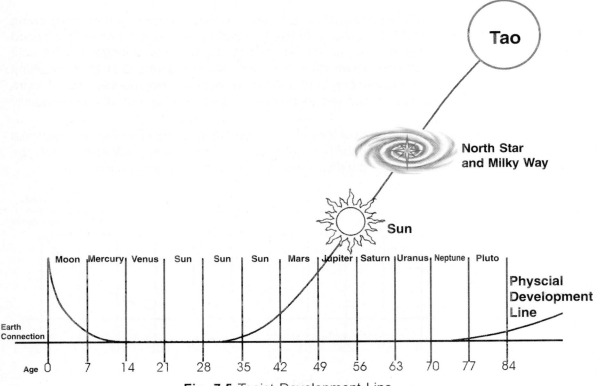

Fig. 7.5 Taoist Development Line

Through the Universal Tao practice the sun period can be used to cultivate the soul and spirit body. The soul is the medium between the physical plane and the spiritual world. The soul naturally follows the evolution through the planetary world but the spirit does not have this limitation. The determining factor is the point of identification and realization. The sun period is also the time when the level of Chi in the physical body is at its peak. The physical and biological development is at its peak at around 28 years of age in men and 24 years of age in women. At that time the body becomes a temple in which the soul and spirit can be cultivated. Taoist practitioners cultivate quantity (life span) combined with quality (spiritual realization).

Through the Universal Tao practices this peak state can be kept and even improved upon during the following decades. Just like many Taoist masters, some isolated tribes found that getting older does not have to mean getting weaker. They became fitter as they grew older, which was confirmed by western doctors. These people were wise and had clear connections to the gods. Is this not a better idea about getting older: "I get wiser, more experienced and intelligent, I integrate this in my body, so I will be fit and strong in my old age". Since most people waste this energy upon superficial satisfaction, it leaks away and when they reach old age, when they have lost most of their energy, they feel weak, scattered and disconnected from their spiritual task. When the sun/North Star connection is open, your whole life will be inspired and guided by the unlimited wisdom of the universe. The connection with the light will enable you to lead an active but peaceful life. You will still experience the growth of the soul through the more emotional planetary world, but the spiritual connection will allow you to observe this process, see reality through the emotions and integrate it within the physical body.

In this way the energy of the experience is integrated to nurture the consciousness. Rudolf Steiner said that the goal in life is to balance the planetary qualities to reach the highest state in the solar system which he called "the sun awareness".

During the excarnation, the soul will move again through the planetary world and will be purified from all earthly, materialistic and emotional experiences.
The fruits of the past life are harvested and condensed to form the seeds for the next life. This process is continued outside the planetary world in the world of stars and the immaterialized realm or the world of vibrations.

In the Universal Tao, the Fusion of the Five Elements practice is used to balance the qualities of the five elements in the body. This practice is also called internal alchemy. After strengthening and purifying the body during the basic practices and fusion practice, the energy and virtues of the five vital organs will be cultivated (kidney, heart, spleen, lungs, liver). These energies will be gathered in specific areas around the navel called the collection points (pakuas). From the collection points, the energy will be drawn to another pakua that is formed around the navel. From this pakua the energy is blended, purified and stored in the center (Lower Tan Tien).

Fig. 7.6 Immortal Meditating

The energy will be condensed until it becomes a radiating pearl. This pearl will be held at the original meeting point, or the point where the information of the first cell or basic spark in your body is kept. Taoists use the metaphor of the pearl or crystal, to refer to the highly concentrated purified energy.

This pearl will be cultivated and slowly transformed into spiritual energy. It will become the house of the soul and spirit body, one's balance, control and Universal connection point.

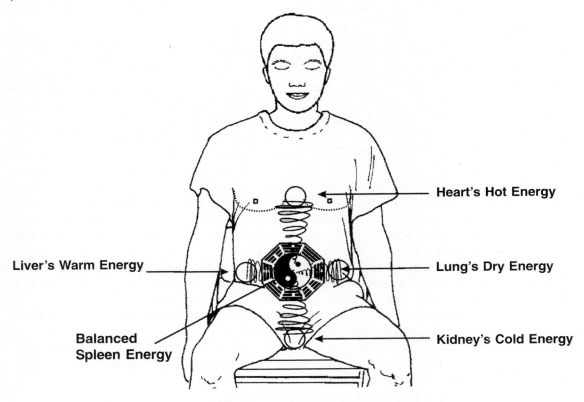

Heart's Hot Energy

Liver's Warm Energy

Lung's Dry Energy

Balanced
Spleen Energy

Kidney's Cold Energy

Fig. 7.7 Pakua Collection Points

The pearl will then serve to open different energy channels in the body and to travel outside the physical body through the world of planets/stars and vibrations. The pearl has the same function as the sun in our solar system: centering, collecting, controlling and connecting to higher realms. When the center is weak (no pearl), there is no central point of consciousness or control. This implies weakness and inability to decide where to go or what to do. When we use the mind to gather the energy at one point, the spark that is still glowing inside of you will create ignition and start to shine again. Just as our solar system formed some 5 billion years ago.

Comparing Solar System and Organ System

Fig. 7.8 Contracting Spiral - Energy gathering in the Center - Spontaneous Inflammation.

When the pearl is shining and stable in the Tan Tien, it will be the source of energy for all the organs. The place where the pearl is kept is the area of the small intestine. In Chinese medicine this is the yang meridian of primary fire, the center of transformation.

When the pearl is stronger and more refined, it can be moved towards the heart center. While the small intestine fire is more a physical fire, the fire of the heart carries a higher vibration. This fire is related to the quality of the sun, the soul and the state of compassion. It is the practitioner's task to create the right internal condition for this by self-cultivation and good deeds to the benefit of all beings. In the Kan and Li or immortal practices, the pearl moves up to the center of the head. It moves up by itself as the fruit of self-transformation. At this point the pearl changes and acquires a very high frequency, related to the world of spirit. During meditation practice it is good to expand one's energy field and connect with all forces of the universe. Subsequently contracting and storing in the Tan Tien will make these energies available in your daily life. During meditation we can use the moon and earth force in the Lower Tan Tien, the sun energy in the Middle Tan Tien and the North Star energy in the Upper Tan Tien.

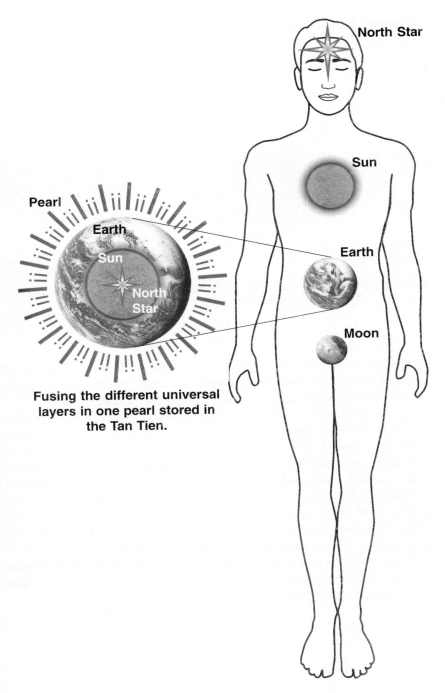

Fusing the different universal layers in one pearl stored in the Tan Tien.

Fig. 7.9 Fusing the Pearl

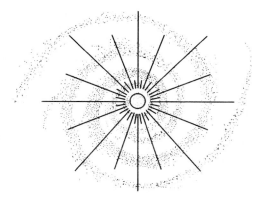

Fig. 7.10 The Pearl in the Tan Tien has a Function Similar to that
of the Sun in our Solar System.

At the end of the meditation the North Star will be brought into the sun in the middle Tan Tien. After that both will be put in the earth or the Lower Tan Tien ("Three in one principle"). This connective and gathering process symbolizes unification, or the spiritual world becoming the core of your life.

Use of Planetary Energies in East and West

In China the planets have been used in connection with the five elements and the Five Heavenly Palaces in their relationship with the 28 lunar mansions for thousands of years. The planets were called the "naked eye five" or the "five stars" or sometimes the "five pacers". The precise movements of the planets as seen from the earth was not a focus point for the ancient Taoist, although the trajectories were approximately known by about the fifth century. The translation of the Chinese name of the planets gives us an idea of the nature of their energy.

Translation	Chinese English Spelling	Western Name	Element
Chronographic Star	Ch'en Hsing	Mercury	Water
Grand White	T'ai Po	Venus	Metal
Sparkling Diluter	Ying Huo	Mars	Fire
Year Star	Sui Hsing	Jupiter	Wood
Quelling Star	Chen Hsing	Saturn	Earth

Outside China there is a long history of the astrological use of planets, recorded since the third millennium B.C. in the Babylonian civilization. The Babylonians also connected the planets with different gods and goddesses, a link found in many cultures.

Planet	Babylonian	Hindu	Egyptian	Greek	Roman
Sun	Shamash	Surya	Ra	Helios	Apollo
Moon	Sin	Chandra	Chamse	Artemis	Diana
Mercury	Nabu	Hanuman	Toth	Hermis	Mercurius
Venus	Ishtar	Lalita	Hathoor	Aphrodite	Venus
Mars	Nergal	Mangala	Horus	Ares	Mars
Jupiter	Marduk	Indra	Amoun	Zeus	Jupiter
Saturn	Ninurta	Brahma	Sebek	Kronos	Saturn

Western astrological signs are different, but comparable with Taoist astrology - the base of our stellar and planetary initiation. It uses signs for the planets that have slightly different connections with the world of soul and spirit, where the sun is the image of concentrated spirit.

The circle is a sign of wholeness and the dot represents the center of the solar system.

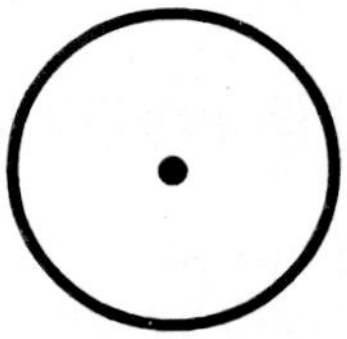

Fig. 7.11

The vertical division of the circle, or the half circle is the symbol for the moon and also for the soul (divided consciousness).

Fig. 7.12

When we integrate matter or the cross in the circle of spirit we get the sign for the earth: matter in spirit.

Fig. 7.13

Fig. 7.14 Venus is the Sign of Spirit over Matter.

Fig. 7.15 Mars shows the Cross of Matter over spirit.

Fig. 7.16 Mercury as the Planet of Connection Mediates between the different Forces or is the Spirit as a Bridge between Soul and Body.

Fig. 7.17 Jupiter shows the Soul Elevated over the Cross of Matter.

Fig. 7.18 Saturn is the Cross of Matter above the Crescent of the Soul.

In Greek mythology and related anthroposophical studies, soul types are described based on the expression of the planets. The observations of the expression of these heavenly bodies was the vehicle to get in contact with the higher psychic world.

In the Taoist practices the planets are seen from the Tao and its manifestation in the five elements and so the internal energy of the planets have a relation with the colors of the five elements and the seasonal cycle. Because of this different point of view (their interpretation of male/female planets), the connection they make with the body organs and systems and also the personality connected to a particular planet, is different between Chinese and Western astrology.

For instance in the West the planet Venus is a female planet connected with the Greek goddess of love and beauty, Aphrodite. While Jupiter is known as a male planet with a dominating, controlling energy and the god Zeus.

In the East, wood is the quality for spring. Spring gives birth to new life (so it is female). Since wood is the planet of Jupiter it is considered to be a female planet. Metal is the quality for autumn. In autumn life withdraws and contracts (male). Venus is in the East, so it is seen as a male planet. The planets Mercury and Venus seem to be used in opposite ways in the two systems.

So, it is important to use the planets according to one system only and not to mix them together.

Modality	Lungs		Kidneys		Liver		Heart		Spleen	
Emotion	Sadness, Grief	Righteousness, Courage	Fear, Stress, Fright	Gentleness	Anger	Kindness	Impatience, Cruelty, Hate	Love, Honor, Respect	Worry	Fairness, Openness
Shape	Collapsed, Flattened Ball	Tall, Straight	Awkward, Tiny, Compressed	Round, Full, Expansive	Spear-like, Sharp	Round, Smooth	Moving, Spiny	Straight, Open	Irregular	Open, Wide, Big
Color	Grey	Bright White	Dark Grey, Cloudy	Bright Sky Blue	Red, Cloudy	Soft Green	Orange, Muddy	Bright Red	Cloudy	Mellow Yellow
Smell	Musty	Pure, Fresh	Foul, Urine	Fresh	Pungent	Sweet, Fragrant	Sharp Burnt	Aromatic Incense	Sour	Clean, Dry
Temperature	Cold	Comfortable, Warm	Cold, Chilly	Cool, Comfortable	Hot, Explosive	Warm, Pleasant	Unsteady	Warm, Full	Humid	Warm, Mid-range
Sound	Low, No Force	Strong Firm, Resonant	Hight-pitched Shrill	Whisper, Pleasant to the Ear	Flashing, Loud	Melodious	Noisy, Irregular	Deep, Stable, Steady, Solid	Shaky	Clear, Soft, in Tune
Feeling	No Energy, Exhausted	Uplifted	Tight, Closed in	Relaxed, High, Centered	Pain, Tough, Rough	Nurtured	Irregular	Stable, Protected	Uncertain	Balanced, Even
Texture	Crumpled	Firm but Comfortable	Slippery	Velvety	Rough	Soft	Cactus-like	Comfortable, Secure	Sticky	Smooth, Firm
Size	Deflated, Low	Expanding Upward	Small	Limitless	Expanding, Exploding	Expanding, Gently	Small, Pointed	Expanding	Out of Proportion	Big, Deep
Taste	Salty	Satisfying	Salty	Mild, Honey	Bitter	Sweet	Acidic	Satisfying	Sour	Smooth, Clean
Direction	Downward	Upward	Scattered	Circular	Attacking	Enfolding	Scattered	Open, Steady	Constricted	Horizontal

Fig. 7.19
Typical qualities of the five vital organs

Chapter VIII
Cranium: a Projection of the Five Elements, the Five Star Palaces and the Five Planetary Forces

Development of Craniosacral Rhythm

Taoist theory on the structure of the universe and the invisible world can be partly recognized on a more physical and chemical level in more recent discoveries in science and bodywork. An interesting link was discovered between the five elements - the five planets, the cranium and the five vital organs. These more recent discoveries make the Taoist esoteric knowledge pragmatic in meditations and treatments. Taoist masters always mentioned that the power of the Governing Vessel is controlled by the power in its two poles: the **sacrum** and the **cranium**.

Since the Governing Vessel is a reflection of the Universal orbits, coming all the way from the Tao, a free flow of energy between the two poles is essential to provide the body with the right information to function in accordance to the Universal law. The treatment of the physical manifestation of this system is developed in a specialized art of bodywork, deriving from osteopathy, called craniosacral therapy. Touching the crown to connect another person to the light is well known in several cultures and thousands of years old.

The governing vessel has been used as a spiritual channel for more than 5,000 years, but the art of working with craniosacral rhythm is about 100 years old and focuses on other energy levels of the human skull. The discovery of this bodily intelligence would appear to be directly connected with Universal and human evolution. It is a further development of awareness and sensitivity of the bioplasmic (personal aura) and electroplasmic field (shared with all other humans). Long ago humans were only aware of their rhythm of breathing. The primitive human being recognized the breath as a sign of life. They were strongly physically dependent and oriented. The breath provided them with vital energy (Cosmic light) and oxygen to nourish the exchange process between their and outer world and the transformation process in the belly.

The heart center was undeveloped and the cardiovascular system situated more deeply inside of the body. They were not aware of their heartbeat. The development of the heart center gave birth to a more conscious soul connection. As the breathing developed and grew into the heart center, the sociability of the lung energy came forward.

System	Level	Connection
* Meridian rhythm (cycle)	- Spiritual	- Unmanifested world
* Cranial rhythm	- Higher mental/spiritual	- Star connection
* Heart rhythm	- Lower mental/social/emotional	- Sun connection
* Breathing rhythm	- Physical	- Earth/Moon connection

In the heart center, the connection with other beings, the emotions and virtues arise. When the heart center developed into a higher state, compassion evolved as a bridge to the higher mental and spiritual level. Chi and awareness in the nervous system or spiritual center is known in every spiritual tradition but the rhythm of the craniosacral system is a relatively new discovery.

The Craniosacral System

The craniosacral rhythm develops through the subtle cranial shifts that occur during the unfolding of the embryonic nervous system and is a translation of the information in the Governing Vessel. The brain and its ventricles produce a liquid called cerebrospinal fluid. This fluid is rhythmically pumped into the sub-arachnoidal space around the spinal cord between the surrounding fascia layers (the meninges). The Governing Vessel is located at the back of the spinal cord - in the same space between the arachnoid and pia mater, all the way from the perineum to the upper lip (and internally back down to the perineum). In this way the Governing Vessel is constantly charging the cerebrospinal fluid and the spine.

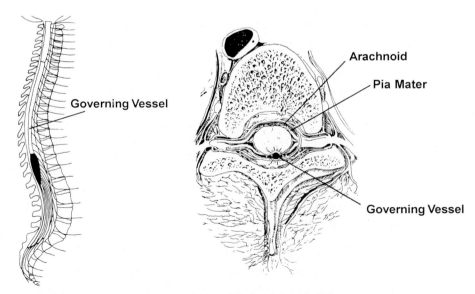

Fig. 8.1 The Meningsal System contains the Energy of the Governing Vessel.

The cerebrospinal fluid is produced in the ventricles of the brain and is completely renewed every 5 to 6 hours. There is about 135 cm^3 of this fluid present in the body and the ventricles secrete more than half a litre daily. It must circulate continuously; take this information as encouragement to do **spinal cord breathing** frequently during the day! (refer to Cosmic Healing I). Besides the spiritual information in the Governing Vessel the cerebrospinal fluid contains the deep memory of biological evolution from the oldest planetary oceans. A period of more than three billions years of evolution from bacteria and viruses to human beings is stored there. The high and low "water marks" in the system have a rate of about 8 to 12 times per minute. During the phases the membrane system in the head contracts and expands causing the movement of cerebrospinal fluid in the spine. The cranial movements, created through these waves, are 0.04 to 1.5 millimeters, but with some training they can be felt throughout the whole body. It is important to remember that the craniosacral rhythm is fully independent of the breathing process.

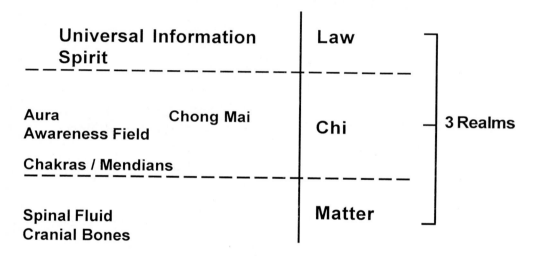

Fig. 8.2 Three Realms in the Universe and in the Human Body

In a meditative state confusion may occur between these two rhythms. Touching the skull very lightly and stopping the breathing for about 10 seconds in the outbreath can help you out of this confusion.

Even though the energy in the cranial system is more spiritually oriented, four different dimensions can be recognized (spiritual, mental, emotional, physical).

Any kind of impact on one of these four layers changes the quality and energy in the other three: treatment, meditation, thoughts, physical stress or strong emotions.

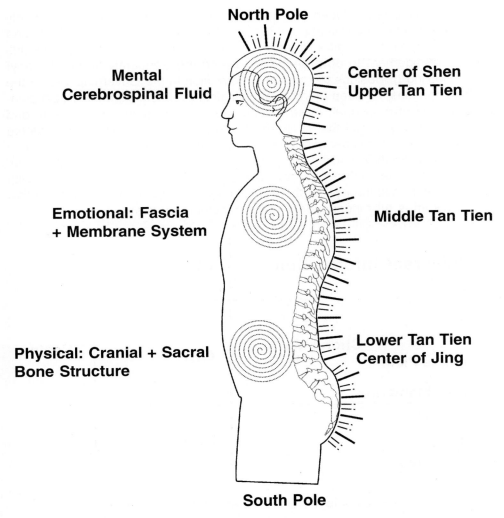

North Pole

**Mental
Cerebrospinal Fluid**

**Center of Shen
Upper Tan Tien**

**Emotional: Fascia
+ Membrane System**

Middle Tan Tien

**Physical: Cranial + Sacral
Bone Structure**

**Lower Tan Tien
Center of Jing**

South Pole

Fig. 8.3 Spiritual Governing vessel and its aware expression (Craniosacral System)

The whole cranial system is a big antenna and transmitter of information to all the different energy levels in the body. To work with it in our treatments or just for our own meditations, it is necessary to practice, to feel and study the different layers of the system.

The physical layer (cranial bones) and the spiritual layer (Governing Vessel) are the most easy and most practical ones to register in your body. This mental / spinal fluid and emotional fascia needs more study and practice. The craniosacral system has a north pole, the cranium and a south pole, the sacrum. Under normal conditions they work together in perfect rhythm. The cranium is the pneumatic/mechanical driving force; the sacrum follows the cranium impulses. In cases of stress or blockages there can be small timing differences between the two.

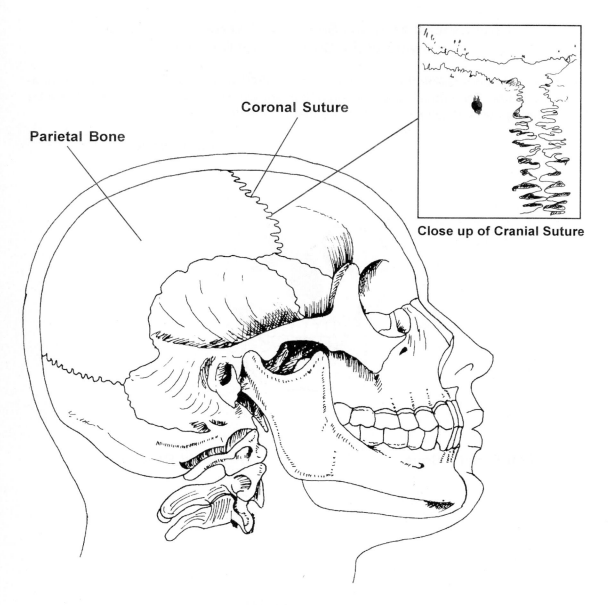

Close up of Cranial Suture

Fig.8.4 Cranial Bone

The suture lines in the cranial system form zigzag pointed protrusions that have a function in receiving stellar vibrations. From these structures subtle energy information channels spread out through the whole body.

Craniosacral Anatomy Sensitivity Exercises to become Aware of the Craniosacral Rhythm

To be able to understand the craniosacral system we have to look at some simple anatomical charts. The cranial bowl contains 10 major external bones, five of which will be used during our meditations: you can see them in the drawings below.

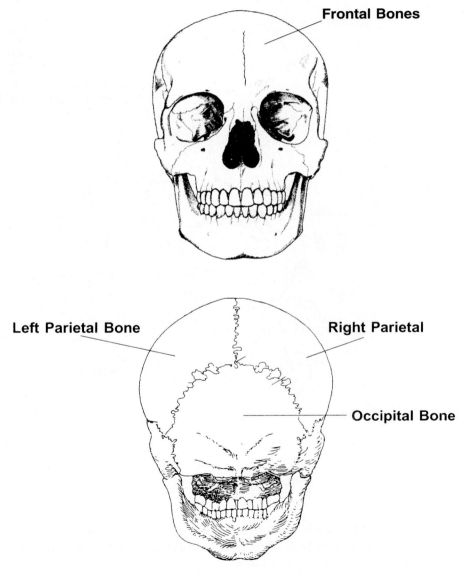

Fig.8.5 Skull Front View and Skull Rear View

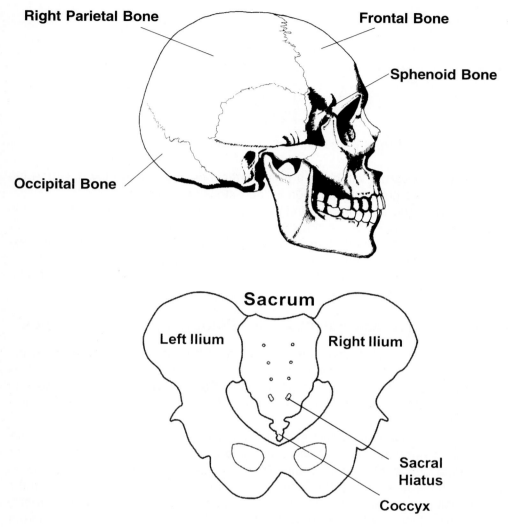

Fig. 8.6

As described before, the craniosacral system has a high and low tide according to the movement of the cranial bones and membranes in the cranium. Each individual bone has a very specific movement plus a bending factor of the bone itself. This means that the bones can actually bend like a piece of hard rubber. We can also see a general movement of the cranium (seen as one piece). In the flexion stage the cranium becomes wider and shorter. In the extension stage the skull becomes smaller and longer. You can compare it with a balloon you hold on both sides. If you softly press and release every 6 to 7 seconds, you get an effect similar to the cranium during flexion/extension.

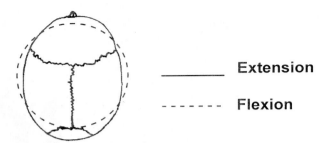

Fig. 8.7 Flexion and Extension Stage

Simultaneously, the sacrum will be in a more vertical position (if you lay down) in the flexion stage and a more horizontal position in the extension stage.

In the flexion stage, the arms/hands and legs/feet have a slight outward rotation. On the extension stage they make an inward rotation.

Spend some time feeling this rhythm in your head, arms, hips, sacrum, legs and expand the movements into the aural field.

You will feel a deep relaxation and at the same time a great improvement in your sensitivity and body awareness.

Five Elements - Five Star Palaces - Five Planets-Five Cranial Bones

The five planets are the physical representation of the different awareness layers in the solar system and at the same time a materialized form of the law of the five elements. This five elements law is an important foundation in ancient and modern Chinese society. In medicine, astrology, politics as well as in a variety of other fields this principle of five directions is used.

There are Taoist meditation practices where the planets are linked with the cranial bones. But in some methods connections are made among the stars and the sutures between the crainal bones. One comparable Taoist meditation of unknown origin places the planet Saturn in the heart, Mars above the head, Mercury under the feet, Venus in the right palm and Jupiter in the left palm. The cranial system is our own compact mini-representation of the five planets or the more central part of the solar system and on a larger scale the five star palaces.

It is in direct connection with this planetary/galactic/five element world and reacts directly on all information coming through this channel. From the cranial bowl, the energy moves down into the organs and different body systems.

Awareness of the cranial system and its connections to the planetary/galactic and five elemental forces helps us to:
* Create a direct contact with the universe. It is an enormous energy source.
* Get insight in our karmic charge, how the soul is basically influenced by some and less by other panets/stars.
* Develop the ability to understand our present lives, our reactions, our physical, emotional, mental condition.
* Acquire an ability to stabilize these imbalances.

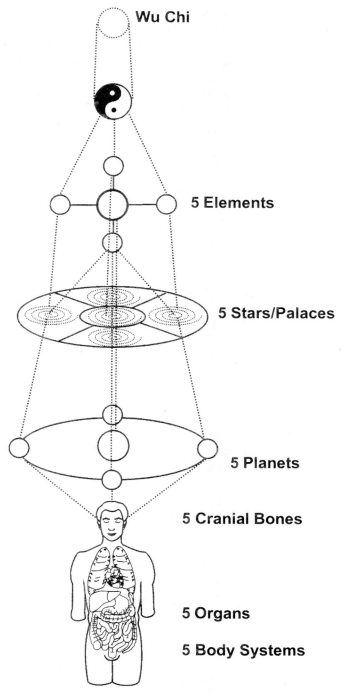

Wu Chi

5 Elements

5 Stars/Palaces

5 Planets

5 Cranial Bones

5 Organs

5 Body Systems

Fig. 8.8 Five Elements, Palaces, Planets, Cranial Bones

Once a clear connection with the planets is established, the galaxy energies from the five palaces can be integrated. See chapter 11, meditation 4. On a high level, a direct contact with the law of five elements in the vibrational world can be achieved.

The bone structure is our most dense body system. The crystalline and mineral structure of the bones has (besides its supportive function) a primary function in attracting high frequencies. Also, the hormonal activities in the glands in the head have an important role. Both the hormones and mineral structures are very condensed substances that have the ability to attract extremely high vibrations: spiritual energies and star frequencies.

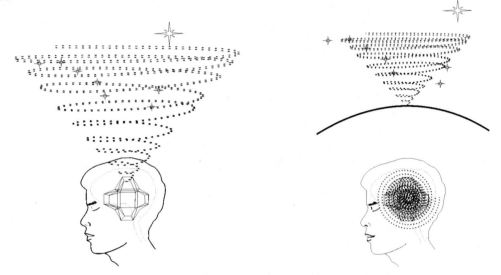

Fig. 8.9 When the Crystal Room is Open, there is a Universal Connection; when the Crystal Room is stuck there is no Universal Connection.
Too much Mental Activity: Stress, Low Energy, Negative Emotion.

The glands serve as transmitters and transformers of the subtle (high) energy frequencies, which can then enter into the organs and the layers of the body with a lower vibration.

These vertical connecting channels can only be experienced in the silence of the empty spaces between the turbulent horizontal activity caused by the emotions and thoughts. The planetary and stellar connection generally depends on two different factors: prenatal and postnatal.

Prenatal
The karmic information, based on the tasks and messages the soul has received during the incarnation process (according to the sum of past life information).

Postnatal

The physical, emotional and mental condition determines the ability to receive information from the universe. If we get very busy, and mentally overactive, stress gathers in our body and the feeling of separation will increase in and outside of ourselves. In this way the left brain becomes very active and a state of separation from the environment and an inability to connect with ourselves arises. This condition makes it impossible to take in information from the universe.

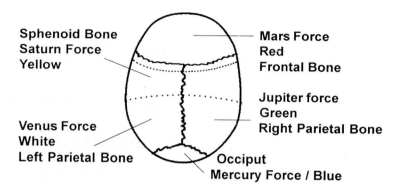

Sphenoid Bone
Saturn Force
Yellow

Mars Force
Red
Frontal Bone

Jupiter force
Green
Right Parietal Bone

Venus Force
White
Left Parietal Bone

Occiput
Mercury Force / Blue

Fig. 8.10 Top View of the Cranium

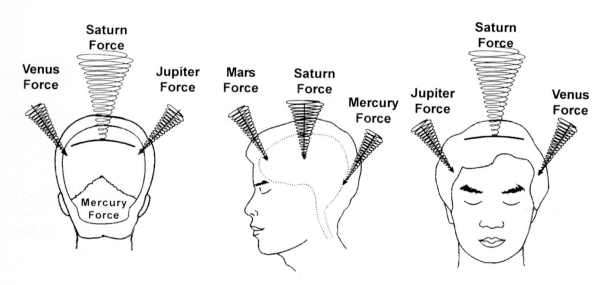

Fig. 8.11 Back View, Left Side, Front Side of the Cranium and the Planet Forces

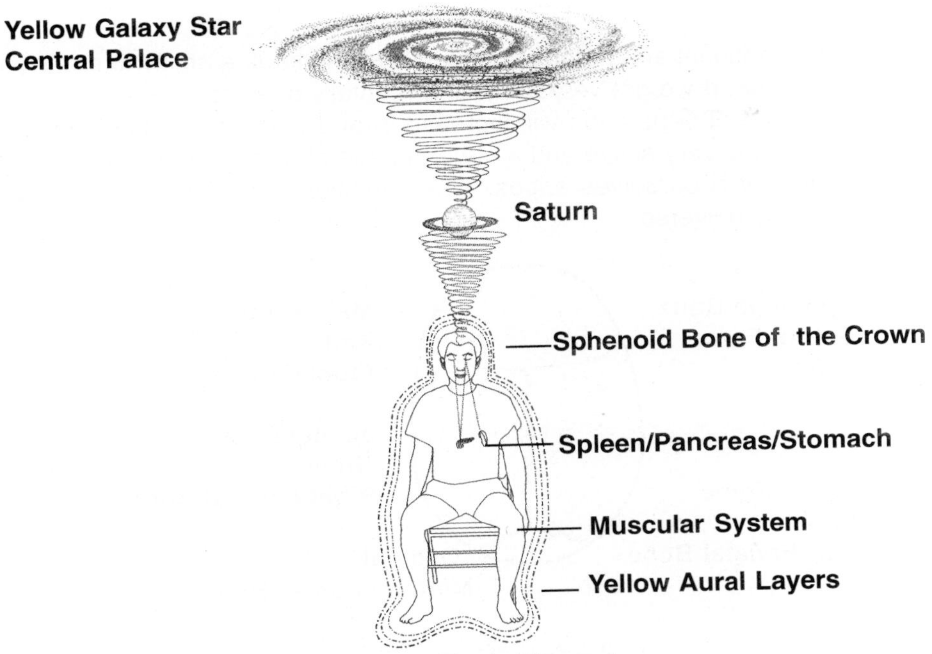

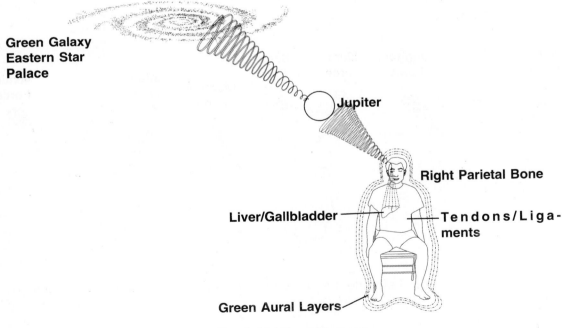

**Yellow Galaxy Star
Central Palace**

Saturn

Sphenoid Bone of the Crown

Spleen/Pancreas/Stomach

Muscular System

Yellow Aural Layers

Fig. 8.12 Earth Element

**Green Galaxy
Eastern Star
Palace**

Jupiter

Right Parietal Bone

Liver/Gallbladder

**Tendons/Liga-
ments**

Green Aural Layers

Fig. 8.13 Wood Element

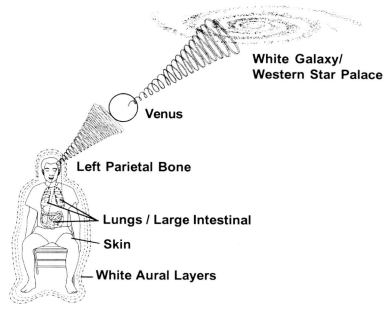

White Galaxy/ Western Star Palace

Venus

Left Parietal Bone

Lungs / Large Intestinal

Skin

White Aural Layers

Fig. 8.14 Metal Element

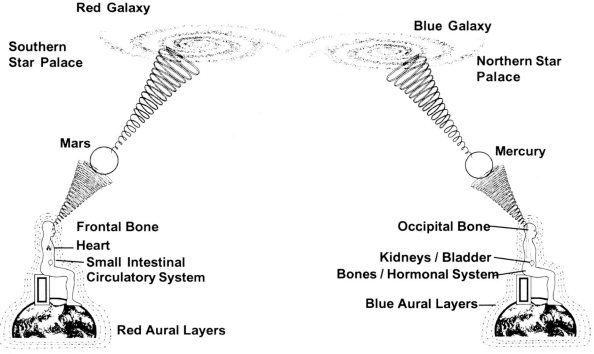

Red Galaxy

Southern Star Palace

Blue Galaxy

Northern Star Palace

Mars

Mercury

Frontal Bone

Heart

Small Intestinal Circulatory System

Occipital Bone

Kidneys / Bladder

Bones / Hormonal System

Blue Aural Layers

Red Aural Layers

Fig. 8.15 Fire Element

Fig. 8.16 Water Element

Fig. 8.17 Inner Balance

Balancing the Planetary Energy with Nature's Energy and the Earth Force Creating a more Harmonious Energy Quality

To prevent overheating it is necessary to mix the planetary or heavenly energy with the five nature forces and the cooling energy of the planet earth itself. The combination of planetary and five earthly elements gives a more balanced and stable energy. We can breathe in these energies through the third eye or the skin to the related organ or directly through the navel area in the center.

Five earthly connections for the planetary energies are:

Jupiter	- Liver	- Tree/Wood Energy	-	Green
Mars	- Heart	- Fire/Flame Energy	-	Red
Saturn	- Spleen	- Earth/Soil Energy	-	Yellow
Venus	- Lungs	- Lake/Metal Energy	-	White
Mercury	- Kidneys	- Water/River Energy	-	Blue

The energies of the wind, sky, thunder, lightning mountains and flowers are also very useful. All natural energies are a direct source of cosmic energy for us.

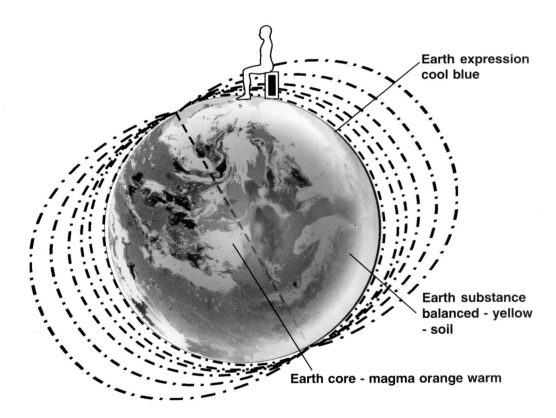

Earth expression
cool blue

Earth substance
balanced - yellow
- soil

Earth core - magma orange warm

Fig. 8.18 Three Aspects of the Earth Force

Three Aspects of the Earth Force

The planet earth has three different energies. Many discussions about the energetic quality and color of the earth and other planets is based on the fact that different people tune in on different planetary layers or use another method of looking at things. Always give yourself enough space to perceive energies in your own way, but know at the same time that if you perceive the energy and color differently from someone else you are probably tuning in to a different energetic layer. If we tune in to the earth, we connect to the earth/soil quality which is yellow. If we tune in to the energy radiated by the earth created by the centrifugal force, we receive blue, cool energy.

If we go deeper into the earth with our mind and bring this energy into our body we can perceive orange/red, related to the more central part of the earth (fire, magma).

The inner earth has a very different quality. Not only is the temperature very different, but also the movement and speed of the central part varies with that of the outside layer.

The inner earth relates more to the deep female qualities while the expession of the earth is the male quality. Exactly the same discussions occur about male/female energy qualities as with planets and again it is just a matter of where you are tuning in to.

According to the Taoist masters, women are more yin, in their overall energetic constitution. In the same way that the earth's (the female source) center has a different energy. Women are warmer inside than men. This warmth is also found in the quality of the eggs in the ovaries. Taoists knew long ago that the eggs and the earth/moon energy are directly related. Understanding this relationship, they knew that the fertilized ovum had a similar turning motion similar to the planet earth. Western science has discovered this turning motion only this century.

Men on the other hand have a more warm energy on the outside, but deep inside their basic quality in accordance with the sperm is cool.

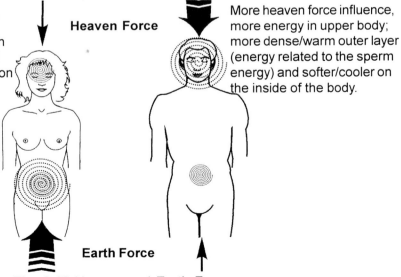

More earth force influence, more energy in the lower body; more density/warmth in the Tan Tien (stability of the egg) and softer/cooler on the outside of the body.

Heaven Force

More heaven force influence, more energy in upper body; more dense/warm outer layer (energy related to the sperm energy) and softer/cooler on the inside of the body.

Earth Force

Fig. 8.19 Heaven and Earth Forces

Relationship Between the Five Planets and the Star World

As in the planetary world, the star world is divided into five parts called the five palaces (four directions and one central part)

To concentrate the energy from the galaxies, all energy can be visualized in one central star in the middle of the galaxy.

The five palaces in relationship with the 28 lunar mansions are fundamental in Chinese astrology. The 28 constellations are divided into four groups of seven around the central palace of the North Star, the Big Dipper and related stars. There is a total of one hundred and eighty two stars collected around the central palace. In the past the four groups of constellations were seen as four giant constellations related to the following animals.

Green Dragon	- East	(32 Stars)
Blue or Black Turtle	- North	(35 Stars)
White Tiger	- West	(51 Stars)
Vermilion Bird	- South	(64 Stars)

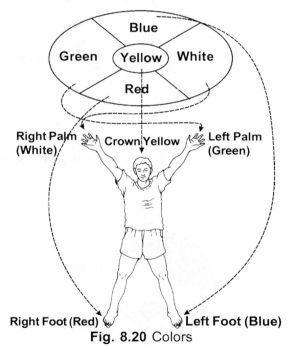

Fig. 8.20 Colors

These mythical animals were called the guardians of the four directional palaces.

In the Taoist immortality practice, or Kan and Li, the palaces are connected with the hands and feet.

Through the connection of the extremities and the crown with the five palaces we can integrate the galactic energy more easily.

Long ago the planets were seen as special stars related to the five elements :

Fire Star - Mars
Earth Star - Saturn
Metal Star - Venus
Water Star - Mercury
Wood Star - Jupiter

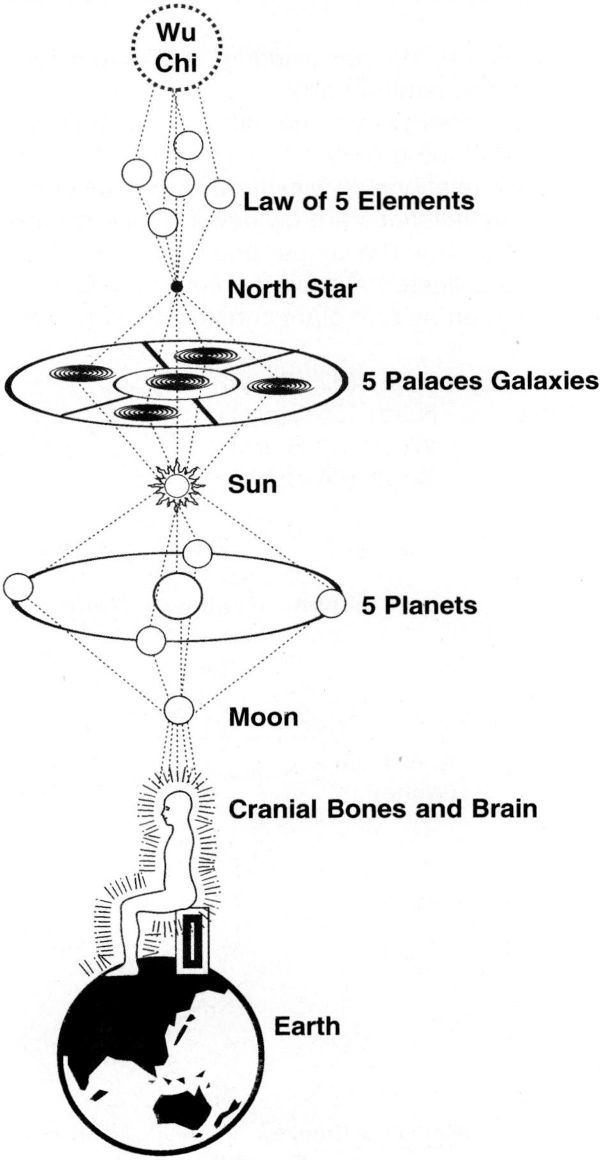

Fig. 8.21 Universal Forces

The North Star is the balancing point above the galaxies and the sun is the balancing point above the planets. The sun and the North Star are gates to a higher dimension and frequency in the universe. In order to pass through these gates a balance and integration of the underlying energies is required.

Earth and also the moon will be used to keep the grounding and to integrate the high frequency energy in the physical body.

The galaxy meditation of the five palaces brings the energies of all stars and galaxies placed in that direction of the sky together in one galaxy.

Balancing the Cranial System

Many therapists work with techniques on the craniosacral system these days. In the last 20 years craniosacral therapy has evolved to a great art of bodywork to create balance, release blockages and energize the body. Most of these therapists work with the bones, the membranes, the fascia and the cerebrospinal fluid. Planetary and stellar energies can create an extra dimension to this art because it helps to get closer to the origin of the system and how it relates to Universal principles. In many cases the craniosacral system is treated as a separate unit of the body or, by some therapists, as the only important system in the body. Miracle therapies have been brought forward many times throughout the ages but after a while it always becomes clear that they are just another part of the puzzle. The Universal laws organize all the parts of the puzzle. Stellar and planetary initiations can be a valuable method to create an extra dimension in the consciousness and deeper understanding of healers and bodyworkers.

The meditations described in this book demand only a basic theoretical and practical knowledge. Essential, however, is sensitivity and energy cultivation. Of course, people with a deeper understanding of the craniosacral system can integrate the meditation and awareness practices into their regular treatment method. More detailed descriptions of how to use the meditations during treatment will be published in a book on the therapeutic applications.

Since the origin of this method is located in the world of the soul and spirit, balancing the planet and star energies will result in deep, long lasting changes in the life of the practitioner and the patient. When the energies get balanced, Universal information naturally reaches you in a more harmonious way. Many of the blockages on a physical, emotional and mental level will get connected and receive the information that was missing before. As a result of the balancing they will gradually dissolve.

It is necessary to realize that the bodyworker/healer of the future will have an important teaching task. The qualities required to practice as a therapist in this new age are a fusion of awareness with knowledge and sensitivity with skill.

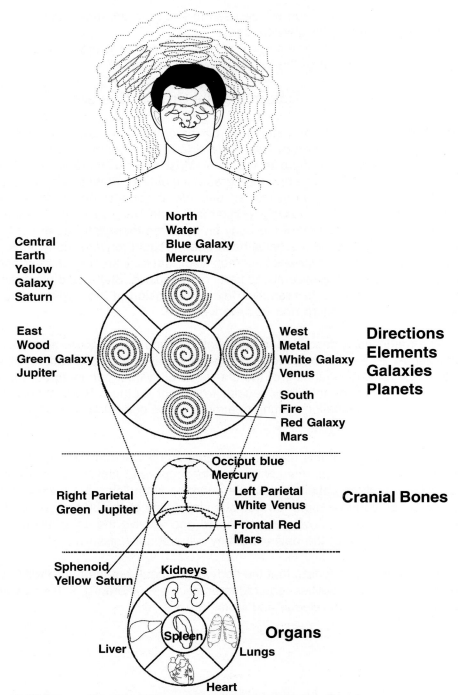

North
Water
Blue Galaxy
Mercury

Central
Earth
Yellow
Galaxy
Saturn

East
Wood
Green Galaxy
Jupiter

West
Metal
White Galaxy
Venus

South
Fire
Red Galaxy
Mars

**Directions
Elements
Galaxies
Planets**

Occiput blue
Mercury

Right Parietal
Green Jupiter

Left Parietal
White Venus

Frontal Red
Mars

Cranial Bones

Sphenoid
Yellow Saturn

Kidneys

Spleen

Liver

Lungs

Heart

Organs

Fig. 8.22 Integrating the Different Frequencies into the Cranium.

Chapter IX
How to use Planetary Forces in your Life

In cranial osteopathy the sphenoid bone is considered to be the central, mechanical, driving bone. It connects the temple bones and forms the central axis of the cranium where all major cranial bones are attached. In the planetary world of our solar system, according to the five elements, the earth element and saturn are the central aspects. The central yellow galaxy with the yellow star in its core is the earth element of the star world. The four other planetary/galaxy connections of the cranium are functioning as two complementary couples paired up around the central point. The five planets are ruled by the sun.

Sun - Moon

The sun/moon balance is an important preparatory practice, (see also meditation 1 in chapter 11). The sun and moon energies form a major influence in the development of human consciousness derived from the more primitive life-forms (mammals and reptiles).

	Biological evolution
Neocortex: self-consciousness, human	200 million years ago
Limbic system: feelings, emotions, mammal state	300 million years ago
Brain stem: most basic life features, the reptile state	500 million years ago

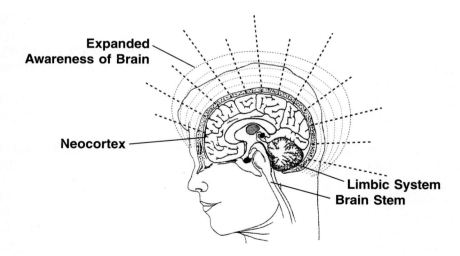

Fig. 9.1 Limbic System - Brain Stem - Neocortex

The development of the neocortex as well as the etheric brain is the end product of a 500 million year process. About 100 million years ago, the multiple layer structure of the neocortex was formed. This process is still in evolution. Only at the highest level of awareness can the neocortex expand energetically beyond the physical boundaries of the skull. This expanded aural brain shows connections to the godly level, clairvoyance, vision and enlightenment. This is similar to the golden crowns or halos that are seen in paintings of Christian saints.

The hot essence of accumulated yang energy generates fire and gives birth to the sun. The cold essence of accumulated yin makes water and gives birth to the moon. Sun's cloud soul and moon's white soul are the yin and yang manifestations of the energy around our planet.

As heaven is one, the yang is realized in three: heaven, the sun and the constellations. The associated animal with sun energy is the three legged crow. This sun crow stands for the lively consciousness. Names that were used for the sun are "Radiant Numen" (Yao Ling), "Vermilion Luminosity" (Chu Ming).

As in most cultures the Taoists saw the sun as the supreme life-giving force on earth. The crow in the sun belongs to the west (metal energy), it is of the yin class and in this way clarifies and balances the light of the sun.

The moon is the grand yin aspect and complementary to the sun. The moon animal is the toad; its nature is cold and watery. The toad on the moon belongs to the east (wood energy); it is of the yang class, which strengthens and illuminates the moon.

The moon plays a vital role in planetary existence and its value is frequently underestimated. This point is based on the social status of women in the east but also the imbalanced view of male/female energy around the world. The moon is the 'potential' around the world - the receptive form of spirit. Its true brightness is latent and dependent on the light of the sun. But its cool yin energy is constant and independent. Men have lost the ability to see light and feel energy in the dark, due to a lack of inner peace and silence.

The moon is the magic mirror, reflecting consciousness in the sunrays and bringing them to the core of the body, to our sexual potential. The water energy is closely related to the sexual energy and all body fluids. The phase of the moon strongly influences all fluids in the body and from there, human behavior. The moon's journey around the earth represents the yin principle in the cosmos and in our world.

The sun has a connection with the third eye and the pituitary gland. It is the star connected with consciousness and future vision. It functions as a source of consciousness and compassion and a gate to the higher universe.

The moon finds its most important entrance point in the sacrum (the sacred part) and represents the unconscious relation to the past, sexuality and basic instinctive reactions.

The place where their essence is stored is located more centrally in the body.

The sun/moon energies contribute in keeping a balance between the lower and middle Tan Tien (belly/heart). Imbalances can also relate to the influences of the other five planets. When the five other planets are not in balance it will be hard to receive the deep frequencies of the sun and the sexual energy will get distorted. A strong connection to the sun will have a balancing function throughout the whole body.

Once the sun energy is collected in the heart and moon energy in the sexual center, these two energies can be moved towards the Tan Tien. The most vital blood channels in the body, the aorta and the vena cava, can be used for this: The artery system, which the aorta belongs to, distributes the blood outward. It works with clear, red, oxygenated blood and is more yang/future oriented, so it has more sun qualities.

The vein structure like the vena cave withdraws the blood from the outside. More bluish or dark blood is transported here, which will first go through the kidneys to be purified. So it is a more yin/past oriented system and has moon-like qualities.

Harmonizing the aorta/vena cava and the rest of the cardiovascular system will magnify the sun/moon meditations.

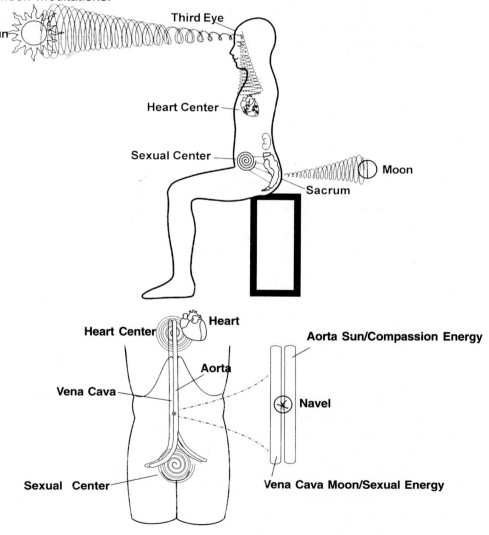

A strong moon connection can give access to deeper unconscious behavior and gives us the ability to shine a light in the dark or transform unconsciousness into consciousness. The sexual essence governed by the moon energy will stimulate all energies in the body, both positive and negative. A strong stimulus of the moon energy without an open sun connection can cause emotional problems and distorted sexual behavior.

In the Taoist way of energy cultivation the sun controls the hours between midnight and noon (yang energy). The moon controls the energy between noon and midnight (yin energy).

Sometimes it is said: All hours of sleep before midnight count double, because of the strong yin energy which charges us at that time.

Taoist masters also saw the sun and moon as the eyes of heaven, corresponding to the human eyes. The left rational or intellectual brain relates to the sun, while the right more intuitive part of the brain relates to the moon.

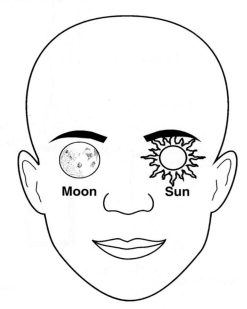

We can use the sun/moon energies to create balance between the two hemispheres. If used during meditation, always integrate the sun/moon energies in the heart center, third eye and the sexual center/sacrum first. This is to prevent overheating the heart. Practice and integrate meditation 1 in chapter 11 before you try this meditation.

It is important to utilize the moon/sun frequencies to get a balance between water and fire energy in the body and then to increase the amount of energy of both.

The moon's color is yellow, its essence is red and its rays are silver white. The Taoist practices for the moon are done according to the eight articulations of the moon power which occur during the two solstices, the two equinoxes and the first day of the four seasons.

In the second century manual "Can Dong Chi" the interaction of sun/moon is used in relation to the Daiwa, the twelve directions and the five elements. These pictures contain the deep secrets of the Taoist immortality practice.

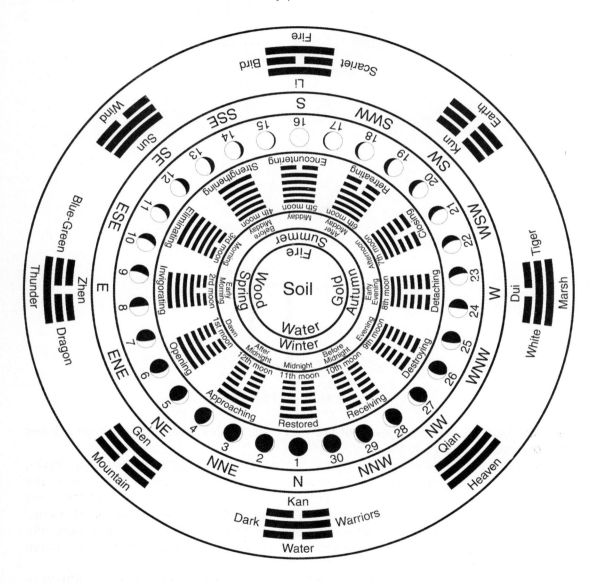

Fig. 9.4 The Method of the Elixir

Mars - Mercury

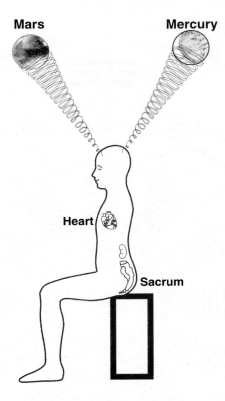

Fig. 9.5 Mars and Mercury

Mars and Mercury are the planets of fire and water respectively. They are on a lower vibration level compared to the sun.

The sun is the father of fire and Mars is the planet of fire. Mars relates to the tongue, speech and the physical heart. The heart is placed to the left of center in the chest; the sun is connected to the heart center, behind the sternum and is related to the heart governor. We can say that the sun has a controlling/regulating effect on the heart energy.

Medical research on yogis has proved that their physical heart operates more efficiently after many years of meditation and that the tip of the tongue often makes a curve in the palate in the direction of the center of the crystal room.

Mars energy is more male and future oriented. If the Mars energy is too strong in comparison to the other energies, one may get aggressive and too talkative. This is often caused by weakness of the kidneys. Most heart problems are caused by depletion of the kidneys and the sexual energy. If Mars is too weak, the heart function/fire is withdrawn and the person feels weak.

Since the kidneys are the seat of the sexual essence and store the ancestral energy, they have a governing function on the sexual center. If the kidneys are depleted, sexual energy will also be weak. Fire is inactive in isolation and needs the presence of the other elements to stay balanced. Keep the fire in your stove and you won't burn your house down. (see chapter II).

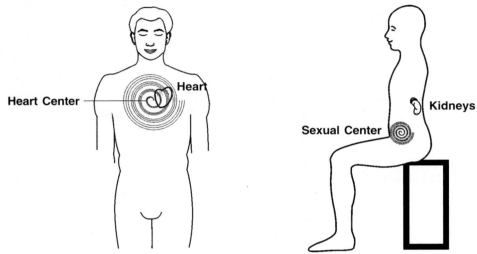

Fig. 9.6

The play between water and fire is found in the controlling cycle of the five elements. Mars and the sun can be seen as fire qualities - Mercury and the moon as water qualities; this demonstrates the double nature in the fire element (primary and secondary fires) and the double formation of the water element (urogenital system).

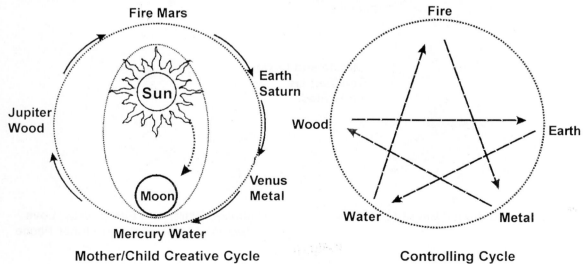

Fig. 9.6

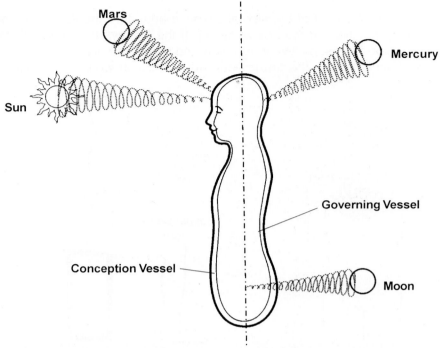

Fig. 9.8 Conception Vessel Sun-Mars and Governing Vessel Moon-Mercury.

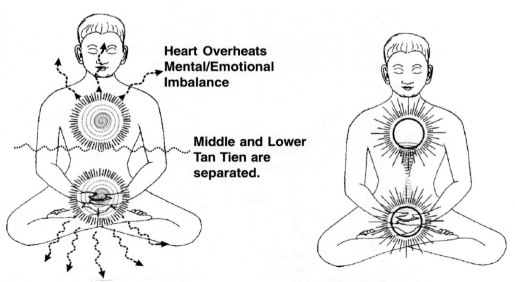

Heart Overheats Mental/Emotional Imbalance

Middle and Lower Tan Tien are separated.

Kidney and Sexual Energy Leak out

Balanced Water and Fire Energy, Love and Sex lead to Strength and Inner Peace

Fig. 9.9

The sun and moon can be placed internally. In the five element creative cycle water will give birth to wood, wood to fire, fire to earth, earth to metal. It is a cycle of expansion and contraction in five stages (see Fusion 1 book). In the Taoist spiritual practice this interaction is compared with cooking. Water controls fire. If the sexual energy potential dries up, the fire has no more control. At the same time there is a controlling cycle which balances the five elements. Water controls fire. So kidney/sex energy has a cooling balancing effect on heart and heart governor. On the other hand, if the fire is too weak, the body often gets very cold and the spine and hip area can become very stiff.

The water-fire balance is related to the Jing/Shen interaction and is a fundamental step in the Taoist immortal practice, Kan and Li.

The sun/moon meditation and to a lesser degree Mars/Mercury meditation can help people who have problems balancing their life according to the future and past. Today many people are stuck in past experiences. These experiences have an emotional charge and are connected with pain which may be constantly denied or at the most intellectually controlled. For these people, the sun connection will bring relief, more vision of the future and another view of their past. Some are only striving for future experiences, running away from themselves constantly. The moon/mercury meditations will bring them closer to where they come from and to the forces and influences which have shaped their emotional body.

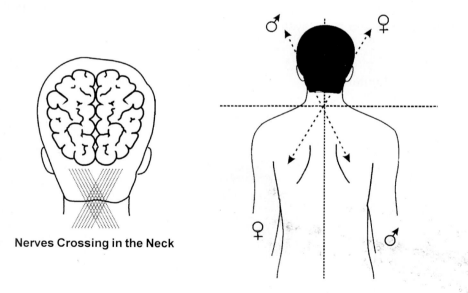

Nerves Crossing in the Neck

Fig. 9.10 Body on a Mental/Emotional Level

Venus - Jupiter

The left/right brain activity has been a popular topic for many decades. As stated before, the focus point in heaven and in the body determines how you will perceive this reality.

There is a strong influence of the five element forces with wood on the right, metal on the left and earth in the middle as the balance point. This is a direct influence from the realm of spiritual law straight down to the physical body (see Fig. 9.11). The Tan Tien energy shows the same structure, according to the energy collection points, just like the initial connection of the spirit with the deep body energy or the Shen with the Jing. This process happens without directly interfering with the lower mental/emotional field. The central stabilizing earth aspect is also found in the energy of the spleen and pancreas.

If we look from the perspective of stars and planets, the core of the activity will be on the emotional and mental level and related to the activity of the brain.

The white stars and Venus are activating the left, more rational and social part of the brain, more male energy. The green stars and Jupiter are activating the right, more emotional part of the brain, more female quality.

From this point of view the nerves are crossing in the neck. So the left brain is associated with the function of the nervous system, regulating the right side of the body with the liver as the center point. The right brain regulates the left side of the body, with the spleen and the pancreas as the center point. (see Fig. 9.10) These energies will enter more directly into the organs and body system.

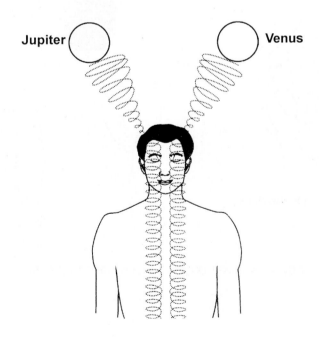

Fig. 9.11 Jupiter and Venus

The right brain is related to individual/body emotional awareness, downward energy related to the spleen. The left brain deals mostly with social, external, controlling, rational activities; more rising energy related to the liver and gall bladder. The elemental influence is weaker in this new point.

We have to remember that the cortex and the human brain consciousness developed from the limbic system, which is evolved from the mammal state. In these primitive states the mental, intellectual and social abilities are very limited. The limbic system has a basic center in both hemispheres of the brain. These centers called the amigdala, deal with deep emotional experiences (affection, safety and other primal needs). A human being is directly related with the neocortex and the ability to connect with other people and the universe. But we must not forget to be in touch with our feelings and our body. Just as the Taoist masters say: "Help and heal yourself and then help others".

If the right brain is overactive and the left brain energy is blocked, the person will tend to feel isolated, overemotional and stuck in the past (no spirit connection).

If the left brain is overactive and the right brain energy is blocked, the person has a hard time getting in touch with the emotions and body awareness. They tend to rationalize things and they have a hard time feeling involved with others or even with themselves.

Left/right brain balance is crucial for a state of well-being. The planetary and star initiations can be a tremendous help in keeping or creating this balance.

In western astrology and Greek mythology these two planets are exactly in opposition (Venus/female-Jupiter/male) to the Taoist view.

Saturn Energy

The universal earth element is the center point in the planetary and star system. It balances the energies of Mars-Mercury and Jupiter-Venus. It is also related with the central thrusting channel. It connects the crown with the perineum. The universal earth quality of Saturn meets the earthly earth quality in the solar plexus and the Tan Tien. The Saturn and earth quality is of major importance to balance the energy in the solar plexus between liver/gallbladder and on the other side spleen/stomach. Bodily stress is created by an imbalance between the internal and external world, primarily stored in the solar plexus. These days most people have great trouble with their digestive system. Men tend to get a blocked and overheated liver/gall bladder, caused by irritation and anger. Women often suffer from spleen weakness; caused by worry/doubt, from which fear/kidney imbalances originate. Saturn energy has a strong balancing effect that is often experienced physically in the skull during meditations, in the form of movements, pain or pressure.

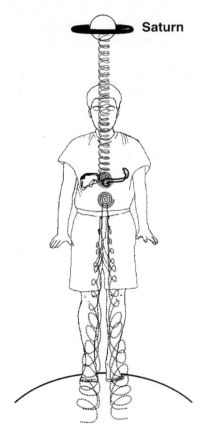

Saturn

Fig. 9.12 Let the Saturn Force go down through the Perineum.

How to find your Strongest and Weakest Planet of Influence

The easiest way to do this is to observe how you connect with the qualities, colors and pictures that are used with each planet (reactions in your body, ability to feel the energy). If you take some time with each of them you will soon find which quality/element feels natural and easy. On the other hand you will also feel what is missing. If you study the typical qualities of this element you will recognize much in your daily life (also, use the meditations in chapter 11). Regular evaluation will soon make it clear that one of them is always there and another may be deficient. It is interesting to meet people who have an abundance of the qualities that you are missing. To some extent they are your masters, but often you will not like them because you feel that they confront you too much. Observe and feel where and how they get this energy. Remember that the first goal is the sun state. The sun state or the state of compassion will grow out of the virtues of all the other organs/planets.

Breaking through the Circle of Attractions and Addictions

Balancing the planetary/galactic/elemental forces brings us to the underlying cause of many problems in life, such as emotional patterns, addictions, irresponsible behavior and low self-esteem. At an emotional level they can only be temporarily released; at a mental level they are often ignored or rigidly controlled. When we get to the higher meaning and origin of these problems and balance the information and energy imbalances that are causing them, they lose their reason for existing and gradually dissolve.

The Three Trans-Saturnal Planets

The trans-saturnal planets are not commonly used in the eastern astrological systems because they were undiscovered until the last century. They can be seen as the higher octaves or frequencies of the internal planets reflecting the co-evolution of human consciousness with universal changes.

Water	- Mercury	- Uranus	- Thyroid Gland
Metal	- Venus	- Neptune	- Thymus Gland
Fire	- Mars	- Pluto	- Adrenal Gland

It is not necessary to work with these planets in your meditations, but they can be used to provide an extra dimension. Sometimes they come up spontaneously during meditation. Because of their influence on the social field, they often occur in group meditations.

In the Universal Tao eight planets are used in the pakua as seen in fig. 9.13.

More study and meditation will bring clearer information on these three planets and their cranial connection. According to our and other practitioners' experiences during group meditations, the following entrance points can be used for the trans-saturnal planets.

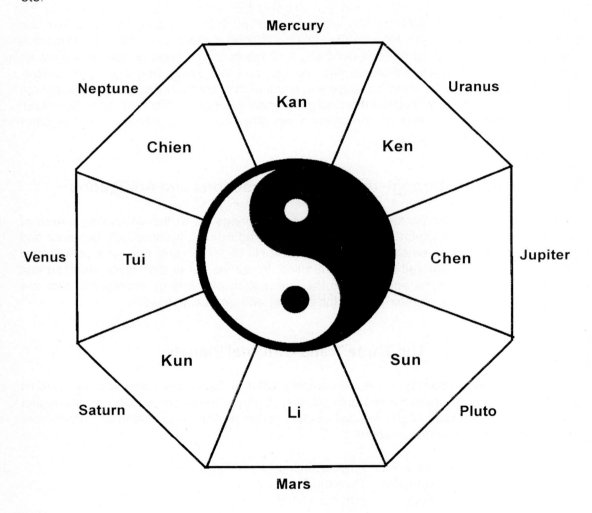

Fig. 9.13 Pakua

The trans-saturnal planets are the field between the basic planets (organs) and the stars (glands). They work on the lower frequency and the more physical, hormonal function of the glands.

Pluto enters above the Mars area.
Neptune around the hair spiral area above the Mercury area.
Uranus at an angle of about 45° (just a few cm above the ears).

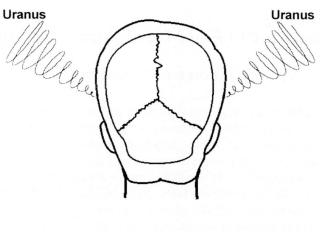

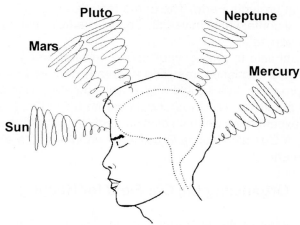

Fig. 9.14 Planet Energies

Chapter X
Universal Healing Connection

Create a Chi Field for Cosmic Healing

Visualization into Actualization!

Think of a Chi Field as being a containment area for all the Chi you might want for your Chi practice. The area can be as large or as small as you want. It could cover a city, a farm, your neighborhood or home, your room, a group of people, or just yourself. You can create Chi Fields within Chi Fields — as many as you like.

Use your power of visualization to project a dome-shaped protective covering around yourself, a group of people, or whatever suits your situation. Think of the dome as being like a semipermeable membrane that will allow Chi in and that will not allow it to leak out. It will also prevent unwanted forces or emanations from coming into your space, somewhat like the ozone layer that protects Earth. The dome may be as large or small as you want it to be. This Chi Field will contain the Universal, Cosmic Particle and environmental Chi that you draw into it when you set it up.

You can create a Chi field to protect your house. In rural areas, Chi Fields have been used to protect and fortify farmlands, resulting in greatly enriched produce and increased yields of agricultural products. We should also cover ourselves with a Chi Field when we do our Chi cultivation practices. Teachers should create a Chi Field to work in, in order to impart more powerful experiences when guiding students in meditative processes for awareness and experience. A Cosmic Healing Practitioner should create a Chi Field for a powerful healing environment.

Organizing the Chi Field for Healing

1. Connect with the forces of the six directions and create a Chi Field. Creating a Chi Field is very important. It is like you are painting a beautiful picture inside yourself in the Chi Field. Sense thunder and lightning coming down. Create a domed Chi Field to cover the room you are doing a healing session in. Sense that the room has become electrified, that thunder and lightning has come in. Draw in the power of the lakes, forests, oceans, Sun, Stars, and high mountains. When you are ready, inhale; draw the energy from the Galaxy and Universe.
2. Be aware of your Tan Tien and pour the energy over the crown. Feel the energy come to your crown and let the energy flow. Feel numbness and tingling. Focus on the soles of the feet.

3. Gradually feel that the room has become charged with Universal Chi. Close your eyes and feel the personal stars of the participants. Start to link them together from the left corner of the room.
4. Spiral out clockwise to link them together with your own personal star, you can project an individual vertical connection from the energy body to each participant. Link all the stars, including your own star, to an energy body.
5. Project an Energy Body above you in the dome. The size and shape of the Energy Body is not important; just have the idea and the sense that it is there for you to use. This tool provides you with an immediate resource to draw from when you distribute energy to the participants. When you are guiding and teaching a meditative process, keep your awareness of your Tan Tien and the Universe and guide the students via the Energy Body for enhanced power and effectiveness. For yourself; first empty the mind down and fill the Tan Tien with 'Smiling Sunshine' Chi. Be aware of your heart; empty love, joy and happiness into the Tan Tien. Extend your Tan Tien up to the Universe, multiply, draw down to the energy body and distribute it to those present.

Opening the Three Tan Tiens to the Six Directions

Introduction

Opening the Three Tan Tiens is a Chi Kung meditation that strengthens our connection to the Universe, opening us up to the primordial force of the Cosmos and the energy within Nature. We are dynamically connected to the infinite. "As above, so below" is an echo of wisdom heard from sages and mystics throughout the ages. When we can connect to and absorb the energy that surrounds us, we are able to tap into the many splendors of the Universe.

We exist because of the unique combination of the forces that are around and within us. The two main forces are electricity and magnetism. 'Bio-electro magnetism' is the Western term for life force and what the Tao refers to as Chi. For the last 5000 years, the Taoists have utilized this bio-electro-magnetic energy to enhance their way of life and establish a relationship with the Universe. Bio signifies life, electro refers to the universal energies (Yang) of the stars and planets and the magnetic force refers to the Earth force (Yin) or gravitational force present on all planets and stars. As we align ourselves with these forces, we become a conduit through which we can absorb and digest these energies through the body, mind and spirit establishing a direct connection with the Universe. The Taoists recognized this connection and created the Chi Kung form of 'Opening the Three Tan Tiens to the Six Directions' to enhance our relationship to and our understanding of this connection.

Humans normally access bio-electro-magnetic energy through their food and air. Plants take the universal energies of the sun and the magnetic energies of the Earth and digest and transform them, thereby making these energies available to all living beings. Taoists believe that the food sources with the purest form of energy are the green leafy vegetables. These have taken sunlight directly into their cells. Rather than waiting until the energy in the Universe is processed through plants, the Taoist goes directly to the source of this primordial energy. Through Chi Kung and meditation, the Taoists direct the energy of the Universe precisely. Opening the Three Tan Tiens is a meditational Chi Kung exercise that focuses on how to directly tap into the source of energy all around us.

Activating the Three Fires

The Three Fires refers to the fire energy contained within the lower abdomen, the Door of Life (the adrenal fire) and the heart center. Opening these centers fills the body with energy and life force.

1. Stand with the feet together. Feel the connection to the Earth through the soles of the feet. Project your mind and extend your Chi into the Earth. Continue extending your mind power and Chi until you feel the connection to the infinite space beyond the Earth.
2. Hold the palms down, parallel to the ground, lifting up the fingers. Connect to the Earth energy through the center of the palms .
3. Move the arms and palms out slightly to the front of the body (palms still facing down). As the arms move, expand your mind and feel the connection to the Earth and the infinite space below you.
4. Gently, pull the hands and arms back toward the body. As the arms move, feel the Chi flow through your body and condensing into the lower Tan Tien. Continue to push and pull 6-9 times, expanding your mind and gathering Chi from the infinite space into the lower Tan Tien.
5. Lift your arms and face the palms toward the lower Tan Tien. Feel as if you are holding a huge Chi ball on the lower Tan Tien. Feel the connection between the fire in the lower Tan Tien and the fire energy in the Universe. Feel the warmth spread through the entire body.
6. Expand your awareness to the infinite space behind you. Move your hands to the back and hold a huge Chi fire ball on the Door of Life (Ming Men).
7. Feel the Chi ball pulsing and breathing, drawing energy into the body from the infinite space behind you.
8. Lift the hands, palms facing up, to the sides of the body under the arm pits. Feel the Chi from the fingers extend into your chest, igniting the fire in the heart center.
9. Allow the heart center to open, pulsing and breathing with Chi.
10. Feel all three fires activated and resonating together; the lower Tan Tien, the Door of Life and the Heart Center.

Healing with the Chi Field and Energy Body

1. Ask the students to start to empty the mind down.
2. Connect with the energy body. Move your hands down. Touch your navel; touch your navel. Concentrate on the Tan Tien. Ask your students to follow you. Your fingers touch the navel; focus on the Door of Life. Feel a numbness, a tingling sensation of energy flow. When you feel it, transfer it up to the crown. Expand to the Universe and multiply the feeling. Guide the Universal energy down to the Energy Body. Always spiral the energy in the Tan Tien. Transfer, guide the energy, the feeling, down from the Universe to the Energy Body.
3. Take time to work with the Tan Tien. Transfer your Chi (feeling) to the other people. When your Tan Tien is very full, you actually feel the energy charge up the whole brain. So, your brain has a lot of Chi to extend up to the Universe.
4. At this level, there is no particular color for the energy body — it depends on what you are doing. Just transfer the feeling up, the feeling of the Chi. The Chi feeling gives you a pattern. And that pattern can multiply in the Universe. When it multiplies, it can be abundant when it comes back down.

You cannot teach somebody something that you do not first have yourself . When you are teaching, you are controlling the energy. You are guiding the students' energy. If you are happy, they feel happy. You feel joy and they feel joy. When you have the feeling of the bone marrow, you transfer the feeling of the bone marrow up. Therefore, the students can only be as good as you can are at that moment. You may feel pain in your body at times; just pick out the good feeling and transfer that up. Otherwise, the student might feel pain and it is not his or her pain.

You have to multiply what you are feeling first before transferring your energy to the students. When you have that feeling (very nice, very good, happy, laughing bones, funny bones — tingling, numbness, etc.), transfer it up to the mind and out to the universe. From there, you spiral a few times — just spiral the energy and multiply— and then bring the increased Chi down to the energy body and it will spread out to the participants by itself.

(see the illustration on page 207)

World Link Meditation

Explanation

The Three Minds are the Upper, Middle & Lower or the Three Tan Tiens. The Upper Mind is good for planning and figuring out numbers, but any negative emotions that are present will stir up the brain with excess thinking and worrying. It spends and drains out too much energy. We should train this brain while resting to just observe. The key is to lower your Upper Mind and use it in the Lower Mind to do your thinking; "seek the released mind".

At first, I did not understand this. When my Master taught me to lower and sink my mind down to the lower Tan Tien, I started to understand. I understood this further, when I found that Western technology had discovered that the nerve endings in the stomach and intestines, especially related to emotional responses, are the same as those in the Upper Mind. So by just smiling to the lower Tan Tien you can activate the Lower Mind. By using the awareness, consciousness, and observing minds together in the abdomen you can do all your thinking.

The Upper Mind works practically all the time, stirring up the emotions and using up to 80% of your body energy. Western science has discovered that the lower mind can do a lot of things that the Upper Mind does without using the senses. The difference is it does it with pure awareness without questioning, as the Upper Mind does. If you can use the lower brain more, the Upper Mind can rest and listen (observe) from the abdomen. The Upper Mind, or as the Taoists refer to it, the monkey mind, when activated will suppress consciousness or awareness. Once the Upper Mind rests you can be conscious and aware of things you were never conscious or aware of before. You then can rest, be more aware and save energy using the lower (second) brain. So your upper brain can rest and build up strength for any daily tasks.

The Three Minds

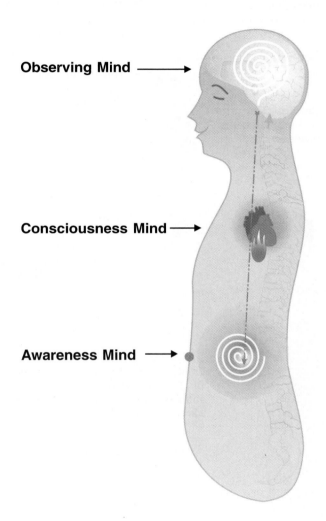

Observing Mind ————▶

Consciousness Mind ————▶

Awareness Mind ——▶

Fig. 10.1 Empty your Mind Down to the Tan Tien.
Let the Awareness and Consciousness Combine Together.

Preparation

Stand or sit alone or with others in a group meditation. Relax and empty your mind down to the Tan Tien by smiling down to your lower abdomen. Bring your awareness to your abdomen and fill your abdominal brain with Chi.

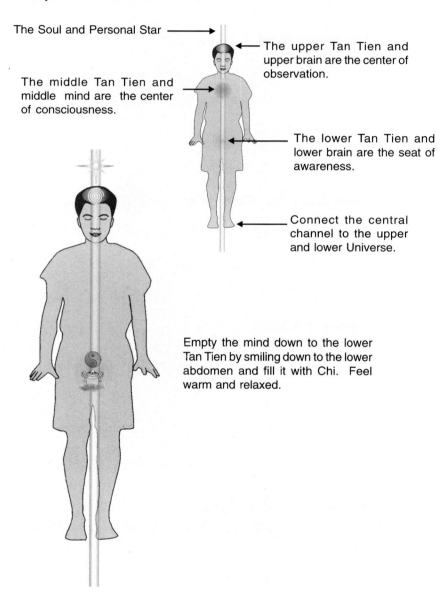

The Soul and Personal Star

The upper Tan Tien and upper brain are the center of observation.

The middle Tan Tien and middle mind are the center of consciousness.

The lower Tan Tien and lower brain are the seat of awareness.

Connect the central channel to the upper and lower Universe.

Empty the mind down to the lower Tan Tien by smiling down to the lower abdomen and fill it with Chi. Feel warm and relaxed.

Fig. 10.2

Activate the Consciousness of the Three Fires
Tan Tien, Kidney and Heart Fires

1. **Tan Tien Fire (Abdomen):** Feel the energy behind the navel become warm as you direct a golden sunshine smile down from your face. Imagine that the energy in your abdomen is like a fireball behind the navel and below, a stove burning with fire. The stove is situated below the navel and close to the sacrum and lumbar vertebrae. Create the fireball above the stove behind the navel. The Taoists describe it as a burning stove that energizes the other fires in the body.

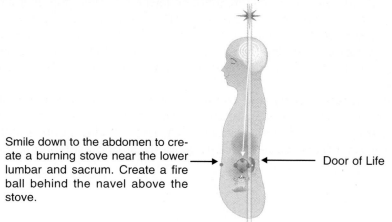

Smile down to the abdomen to create a burning stove near the lower lumbar and sacrum. Create a fire ball behind the navel above the stove.

Door of Life

Fig. 10.3

2. **Fire under the Sea (Kidney):** Be aware of the Yang energy of the Adrenals on top of the Kidneys. Move that Yang energy down into the center of each kidney at the Door of Life (Yang within the Yin), thus lighting the Fire under the Sea. Expand the activated kidneys' energy to the Door of Life point on the spine opposite the navel just below the kidneys.

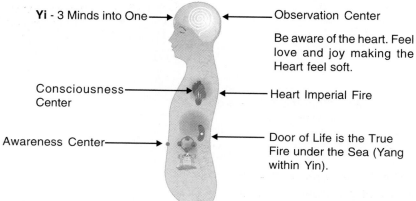

Yi - 3 Minds into One

Observation Center

Be aware of the heart. Feel love and joy making the Heart feel soft.

Consciousness Center

Heart Imperial Fire

Awareness Center

Door of Life is the True Fire under the Sea (Yang within Yin).

Fig. 10.4

3. **Imperial Fire (Heart):** Activate the consciousness by smiling down to the Heart making it feel soft. Be aware of the 'Fire in the Heart'. Feel the fire of love, joy, happiness and compassion creating softness in the Heart (Yin within the Yang). This will activate the consciousness of the Heart. Make a triangle, connecting the heart down to the kidneys and then down to the fireball behind the navel (Tan Tien). Connect the fireball to the kidneys and back to the Heart. This triangulation doubles or triples the Chi Fire Power.

Fuse the three minds into one mind *(Yi - pronounced "ee")*: When the abdomen is filled with Chi and feels nice and warm, it will rise and fill the upper brain with Chi. Lower the upper mind and the middle mind to the lower Tan Tien, combining the three minds into one mind, *Yi*. The three mind powers will move to the mid-eyebrow. You can use this *Yi* to make correct decisions and to take the correct action or non-action.

Expand to the 6 Directions: Combine the power of the three minds with the power of the one mind, *Yi*. Bring the *Yi* power into the third eye and expand it to the Six Directions of the Universe.

Link Personal Stars, Energy Body and Universe: With the *Yi* power connect to your *Personal Star* six inches above your head. Expand your awareness and consciousness to your personal star and out to the whole Universe. If in a group, spiral out and link with their Personal Stars. Create an Energy Body, linking everyone together with the Universe.

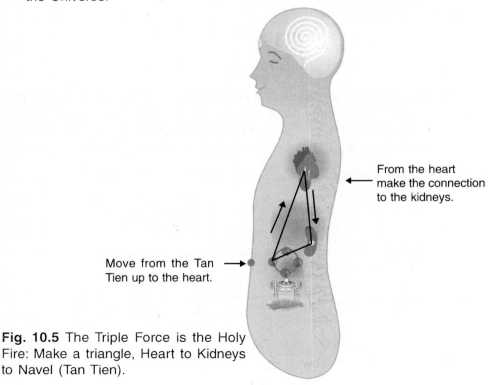

From the heart make the connection to the kidneys.

Move from the Tan Tien up to the heart.

Fig. 10.5 The Triple Force is the Holy Fire: Make a triangle, Heart to Kidneys to Navel (Tan Tien).

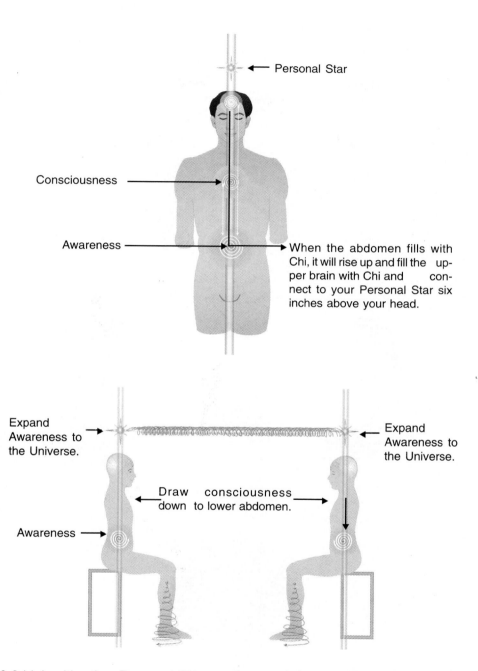

Personal Star

Consciousness

Awareness

When the abdomen fills with Chi, it will rise up and fill the upper brain with Chi and connect to your Personal Star six inches above your head.

Expand Awareness to the Universe.

Expand Awareness to the Universe.

Draw consciousness down to lower abdomen.

Awareness

Fig. 10.6 Link with other Personal Stars and expand the awareness from the abdomen.

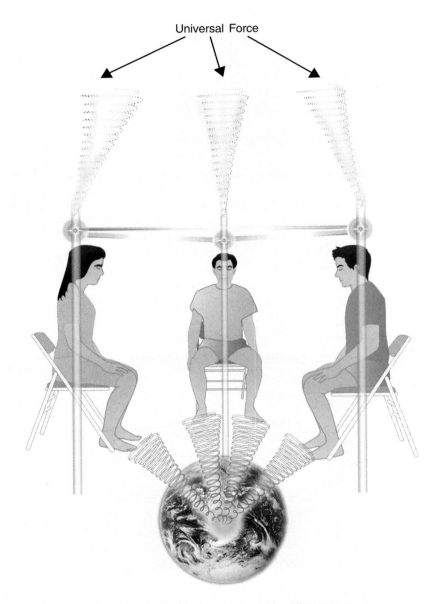

Fig. 10.7 Link with other Personal Stars.

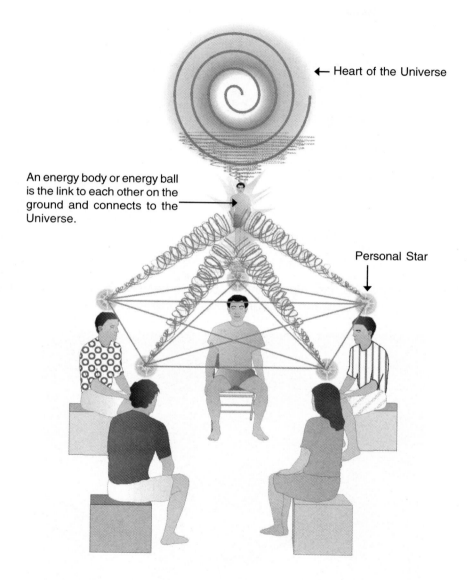

Heart of the Universe

An energy body or energy ball is the link to each other on the ground and connects to the Universe.

Personal Star

Fig. 10.8 A Group can Link their Personal Stars Together.

Link to friends, instructors, or others in the Universal Tao, or to others who are doing similar work.

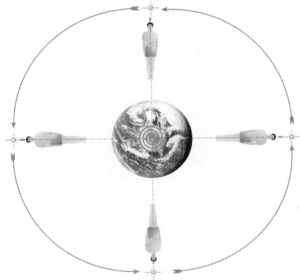

Fig. 10.9 Like a Satellite, the World Link Meditators become a Communication Link between the Earth and the Universe.

Fig. 10.10 Linking to the Heart of the Universe (God) is a way of 'being in' Unconditional Love.

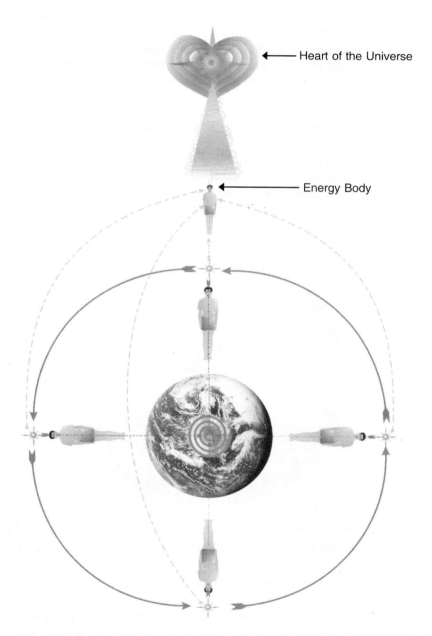

Fig. 10.11 The *Energy Command Communication Center* for each person and group can connect to their 'own' Heart of the Universe.

Protective Sacred Circle of Fire

The **Sacred Circle of Fire** has the power to protect us from all evil, whether it be sickness, misfortune, or negative thinking from those around us. It allows us to connect with the power of the Universe. It helps us remove doubts of our own worthiness, so that we may reclaim the best that life has to offer; our birthright. Additionally, the **Protective Ring** connects us with the elemental essences of Forces in the Universe which both strengthen and protect us.

Sacred Fire Circle and Golden Chi Field

This method is an inner visualization using the power of the three minds (the observation, consciousness, and awareness) fused into one mind, the **Yi**. Its purpose is to get in touch with the **Guardian Essence (Guardian Angel)** or the forces of the **Six Protective Guardian Animals** of the **Six Directions**.

Fig. 10.12 The *Sacred Fire Circle* and *Golden Chi Field* have the Power to Protect us from Evil and Negative Thinking from around us.

Visualization into Actualization

When we use awareness and consciousness, we turn our visualization into actualization; using our trust and belief, we can manifest and let it happen in consciousness and awareness, with good intentions.

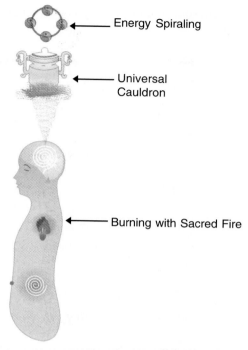

Fig. 10.13 Project a Cauldron of Fire Burning in the Cosmos.

1. Use visualization and imagine a big cauldron burning with fire in the cosmos. Feel the awareness and let it happen.

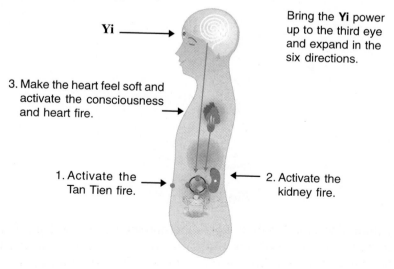

Fig. 10.14

2. Be aware of yourself holding a long wand. Reach out to the cauldron and ignite the wand with fire.

Fig. 10.15

3. Use the Yi power to draw on the ground with the burning wand a Circle of Fire, 7 feet (2 meters) in diameter.

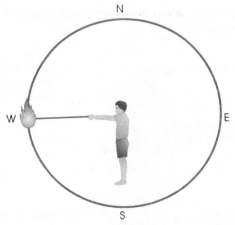

Fig.10.16

4. Stand in the center. Face the North. Imagine the burning wand and light up the Northern section outside the circle with fire. Pass the wand in an arc towards the South edge of the circle and ignite the Southern section with fire. Then swing it to the Eastern edge and ignite that section with fire.

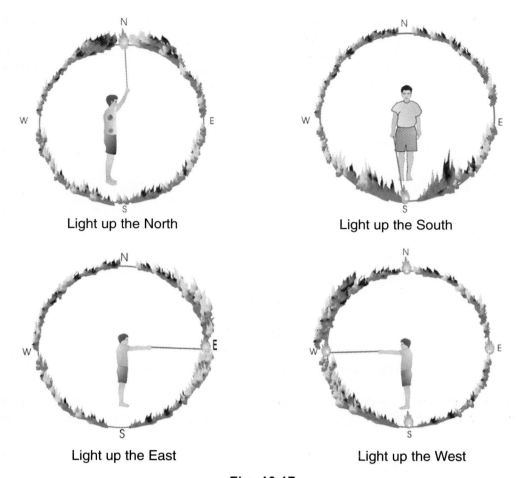

Light up the North

Light up the South

Light up the East

Light up the West

Fig. 10.17

5. Position the wand directly overhead. Turn left to face West and ignite it with fire.
6. Expand the fire to the whole circle, protecting you from all evil, whether it be in the form off sickness, misfortune, or negative thinking from those around you. Place the wand at the edge of the circle.

   Squat down facing North. In each direction place a Protective Animal (Guardian Essence or Angel): In front (North) place a Blue Tortoise, in back (South) a Red Pheasant, Right (East) a Green Dragon, Left (West) a White Tiger, Above (Center) a Yellow Phoenix, and Below (Earth) a Black Tortoise.
8. Create a protective Golden Dome Chi Field over you. Let go of all concerns and empty yourself. Ask each animal for protection. These Protective Animals of the 6 Directions are the same protective animals that are associated with the vital organs. Therefore, for energetic protection, ask the Blue Tortoise for Gentleness; Red Pheasant for Joy; Green Dragon for Kindness; White Tiger for Courage; Yellow Phoenix for

Fairness; and Black Tortoise for Stillness (Beneath). Connect with Universal Love, saying "I am worthy of Divine Love and Protection".

9. Remain in this position for several minutes. Be aware of the Sacred Fire burning all around the circle and the Golden Dome Chi Field surrounding you. This forms a permanent magnetic Sacred Circle that is literally indestructible.

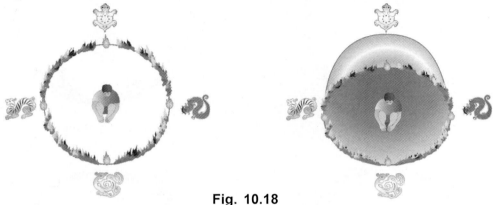

Fig. 10.18

Practice

Affirmations Peace within your own Heart

Calm the mind, emptying down to the abdomen and expand the awareness out to the Universe, repeating the following affirmations from the center of your awareness and consciousness.

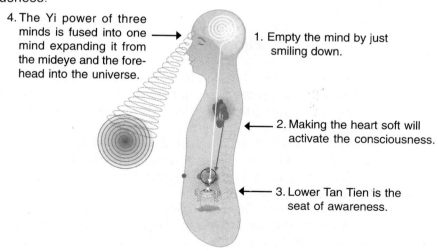

4. The Yi power of three minds is fused into one mind expanding it from the mideye and the forehead into the universe.

1. Empty the mind by just smiling down.

2. Making the heart soft will activate the consciousness.

3. Lower Tan Tien is the seat of awareness.

Fig. 10.19

Empty the mind by smiling to the lower Tan Tien and direct the conscious mind of the heart down to the awareness of the lower Tan Tien, combining the three minds to fuse into the one mind (Yi). The Yi mind is the most powerful mind to connect with the universe.

I am at peace, feeling love & compassion in Myself (Touch Heart).
I am calm, warm, and still in my Center (Touch Lower Abdomen).
I am at peace with my Family and people close to me (Picture Them).
I am at peace with my Neighbors (Picture Them).
I am at peace with my Friends and Co-workers (Picture Them).
I am at peace with my Community (Picture Them).
I am at peace with myself and all sentient beings (Feel them).

Healing Yourself and Others

Personal Connection
1) Empty the Mind by starting a **smile** in your face. Let the Smiling Energy flow down to the neck and in to the Heart area (the seat of consciousness). Make the heart feel soft and full of love, joy and happiness activating the consciopus mind.
2) Continue smiling and relaxing down to the abdomen (the center of awareness). Smile, emptying the mind and senses (eyes, ears, nose and mouth) down until the navel area feels warm, activating the awareness.
3) Feel the observing mind of the head and the conscious mind of the heart going down to combine with the awareness mind of the Lower Tan Tien. Combine and fuse these three minds into one mind: "Yi" at the mideye. Expand the awareness out from the abdomen beyond your physical limits to the cosmos and universe, connecting with the Universal Energy (God).

Take the Yi and spiral it upwards through the crown into the vast pool of energy in the universe. Continue spiraling in the universe and let it multiply. Then, spiral it down to your Personal Star and into your whole body.

Forest Green Energy

Picture an ancient forest with bright green leaves up in the universe. Picture a beautiful emerald green light coming from heaven and spiral it down to you. Spiral the green light down through your community, Tao Garden, your house and then into your crown. Let it clean your whole body, binding and absorbing any negativity, burdens, worries and sick energy and draining it all out of your body. Let it flow down deep into the ground. Dig a hole and bury the sick, negative energy in the ground. Let your heart be happy (3-6 times), for serious illness (36-81 times).

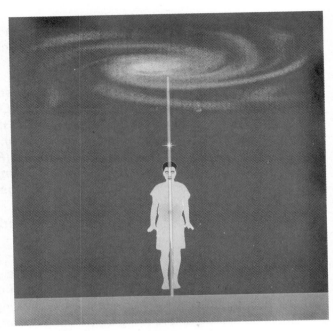

Forest Green Energy Keep the Tan Tien warm and expand the Yi mind to the universe, picturing a beautiful emerald green light in the universe.

Fig. 10.20

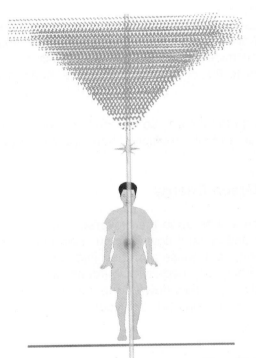

Spiral it down through your community, your home and then into your crown.

Fig. 10.21

Let the energy cleanse all that it comes in contact with.
Then spiral it down into the ground.

Fig. 10.22

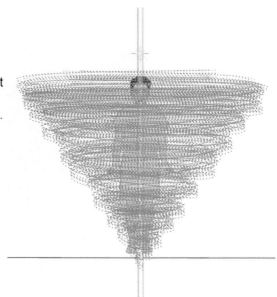

Dig a hole and bury the sick, negative energy deep into the ground, never to return. It will be transformed by the Earth into positive energy.

Fig. 10.23

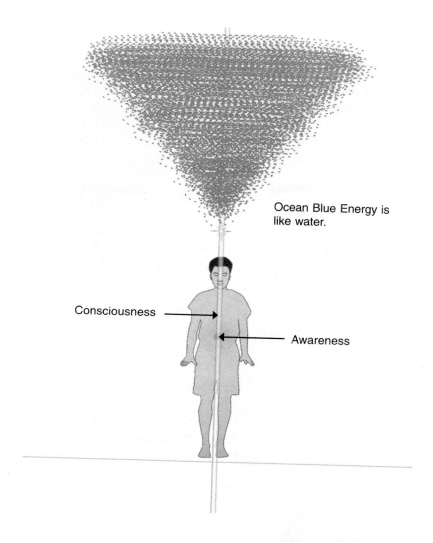

Fig. 10.24 Keep the Tan Tien Warm.
Stay Connected to the Awareness and Consciousness of the Yi
as you Flush the Blue Light through your Body.

Electric/Universal Violet Energy

Picture violet light, the most abundant energy in the universe. Picture it coming from the North Star and the Big Dipper. Gather the energy in the cup of the Big Dipper. Hold the handle and pour the violet down over the Crown. Spiral the energy down and fill all the cells of your body, together with the Energy Body (6 times).

Fig. 10.25 The North Star is a major source of violet light.
The Big Dipper is a major source of red and infra-red light.

Healing and Strengthening the Whole Body

1. Fill the brain with violet light, saying "Let all sickness go away and let the brain be at its best."
2. Follow this method for your organs. Using the same affirmation for every organ. You can also group the organs;
   Eyes, ears, nose, mouth, tongue, teeth.
   Thyroid, parathyroid, thymus, pancreas, prostate, uterus.
   Lungs, heart, stomach, small intestines, large intestines.
   Liver, spleen, kidneys, ovaries, testicles.
Doing this with your mind, stay conscious of the Lower Tan Tien. Expand your awareness to the universe and the universe will fill you with healing energy.

Activate the Immune System and Defense System

1. Touch the sacrum and feel your fingers grow 'long' with Chi and penetrate into the sacrum and bone marrow, activating the bone marrow. Put your mind into the Tan Tien and the universe. Hold until the universe fills the sacrum and Chi rises up the spine to the forehead. Feel the pulsating in the temple bones. This increases the production of healthy white blood cells for the immune system. Keep the Tan Tien warm and feel the Chi flow up the spinal cord, then let it spiral up into the universe. The universe will fill you with healing energy.

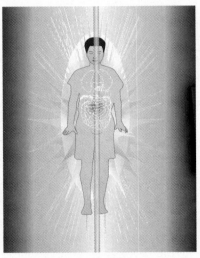

Fig. 10.26 Feel your whole body radiate, clean and shining with light.

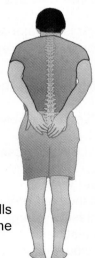

Fig. 10.27 Hold until the universe fills the sacrum and Chi rises up the spine to the forehead.

Activate the Immune System. Empty the mind down. Keep the Tan Tien warm. Touch above the pubic bone and feel your fingers grow 'long' with Chi. Let them penetrate into the sacrum and bone marrow to activate the immune system's production of red and white blood cells. Leave your fingers there and lower your mind into the 'Tan Tien and the Universe'. Feel the funny, happy, laughing and tingling electrifying sensations in the bones.

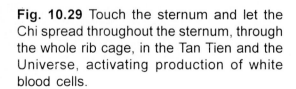

Fig. 10.28 Touch and feel the pubic bone. Leave your fingers there. Lower your mind into the Tan Tien and the Universe.

Fig. 10.29 Touch the sternum and let the Chi spread throughout the sternum, through the whole rib cage, in the Tan Tien and the Universe, activating production of white blood cells.

Touch the femur bone's middle point (upper legs) and feel your fingers grow 'long', penetrating the bone marrow of your legs. This should give a tingling sensation through the whole leg. It also increases the production of red blood cells.

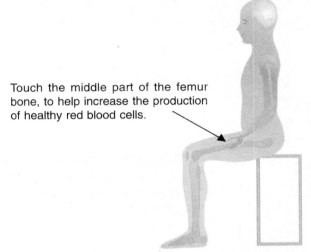

Touch the middle part of the femur bone, to help increase the production of healthy red blood cells.

Fig. 10.30 Touch the Middle Point of Femur Bones.

1. Touch the middle point of the humerus (upper arm) and feel your fingers grow 'long' penetrating the bone marrow of the arm, activating production of healthy red blood cells.
2. Touch the sternum, feeling your fingers grow 'long' and project the Chi into the chest cavity activating the thymus gland. Feel the connection to the thyroid and parathyroid glands. This activates the immune system and increases the production of the T-cells (the anti-virus 'commando' cells of the body).

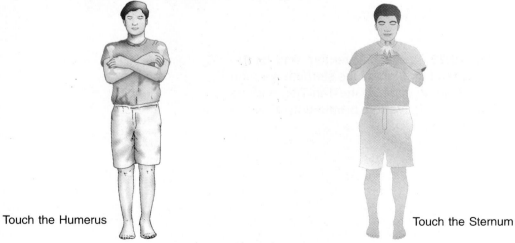

Touch the Humerus

Touch the Sternum

Fig. 10.31

Manifestations

Virtue Mind Power: our Subconscious Guilt

In order to increase the Virtue Mind Power, you need to get rid of subconscious guilt. Our subconscious guilt-complexes are major obstacles to our health and progress. They are the major causes of illness and frustrations. It is as if we have an inner program that says we do not deserve to have health, wealth and happiness. This guilt makes us feel like powerless victims.

Other guilt-complexes assume that we are sinners requiring punishment in the form of ill health or misfortune. We can never bring ourselves to ask the Universe for anything that we do not feel worthy to receive. God made the human in his own image. Humankind is naturally entitled to everything that the Earth and the Universe can provide for our happiness and well being. As children of God we deserve the best. We can command the Cosmos, providing that we make our command in the right way and with good intent.

Being Unwanted

Being unwanted is one of the worst situations for many people. This is true for all those who feel alone, especially children and old people, who might feel left all alone to die. Subconsciously, they will send out messages to the Cosmos to make themselves sick. The more attention that is given to sickness and ill health, the more energy is received from the Cosmos to make that happen. We get exactly what is projected by the subconscious mind.

Negative Self-Talk and Negative Thinking

Every thought whether positive or negative, is a command to the Universe. If our lives are not how we would like them to be, it is because we have unwittingly given negative commands to the Cosmos, we will receive negative results. Humans have a deep need for love and attention. Sometimes we become needy and try to get sympathy and attention through being sick, or by becoming a victim. If in our subconscious mind we believe that our motives are unrighteous or impure, then the Cosmos will keep us poor, sick, or both.

Your command to the Cosmos always brings results. We get exactly what we command, whether good or bad. Therefore, we must be careful of what we think, feel and say, if we want our lives to change for the better. We can remove all the unworthy, guilty, sinful thoughts and ideas, replacing them with the realization that we are the Children of God (the Cosmos). We can accept the best the Universe and Earth have to offer. Be glad to see other people have gained wealth honestly and that they are healthy and happy. If we develop jealous or negative feelings towards them, then we immediately return to the state of being self-righteously poor.

We need not accept the results of our negative thinking. We can initiate a positive course of action. To fully use this power you must replace negative thought patterns with a new command of the cosmic force. You must take action when you receive the energy and information. The way to get extra energy is by breathing the red light into the heart 3 to 6 times letting it radiate into the whole body into the heart. You will feel a lot of energy helping you to take the actions necessary to complete your tasks.

Direct Command

To make a positive statement is to make a direct command. A command given in the present tense – in the now – is the most powerful command that we can give to the Cosmos. A command to the Cosmos should be phrased clearly, as an individual statement and, always said aloud.

For example, if we make the command to ourselves, "I am well, I am healthy, I am happy, I am wealthy," it doesn't matter how sick or poor we are. The fact is, we have already begun to take on that quality because of the command that we have given. The change will begin very rapidly. The Cosmic force will begin work on our inner functions immediately, according to what qualities we have claimed. Success in using Cosmic power depends upon our working with and our exercise of the command, in the right way, to take action and responsibility. Practicing Positive Mind Power, fusing the three minds into one, the Inner Smile, or Chi Kung will help.

Once you have set the cosmic force in motion with a direct command, you must take action. You must be willing to take responsibility for yourself. The Universe can not accomplish everything on its own. The key is to use the Cosmic force to aid your actions. There is no limit to what the individual can accomplish when combining the Cosmic force with individual intent.

Manifestations: 'Yi' Mind Power

Start by smiling and empty the mind to fuse the three minds as one (Yi), in the lower abdomen. Move the Chi up to open the frontal lobe of the brain at the Third Eye. Create a triangle from the third eye to the temple bones filling it with Chi. Expand the awareness to the Universe.

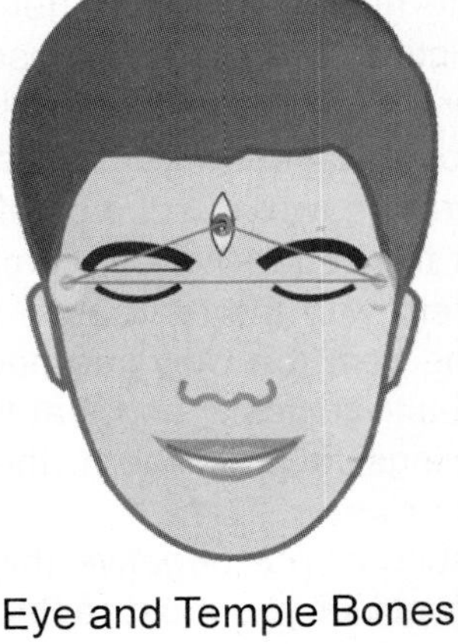

Fig. 10.32 Third Eye and Temple Bones are in a Triangle.

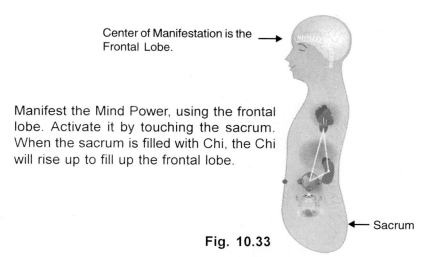

Center of Manifestation is the → Frontal Lobe.

Manifest the Mind Power, using the frontal lobe. Activate it by touching the sacrum. When the sacrum is filled with Chi, the Chi will rise up to fill up the frontal lobe.

← Sacrum

Fig. 10.33

We manifest our affirmations in the physical, emotional, mental and spiritual body by starting to manifest from the center of awareness, by placing the attention in the abdomen. Next bring the thought that you want to manifest up to the heart connection, then to the upper mind, the frontal lobe and the mid-eyebrow. Broadcast it out to the entire Universe. This affirmation is multiplied many times by the abundant Universal energy. It will return to you to be manifested, but you must wait with your awareness anchored in the second brain - the lower abdomen.

Physical Image

Picture yourself at an age you would like to be, and hold that image very clearly. Hold it in the center of your second brain (lower abdomen) and move it up to the center of your consciousness, in the heart area. Continue to hold this image very clearly and move it up to the forehead and then send it out to the Universe in all six directions, saying, "I am well and perfectly healthy."

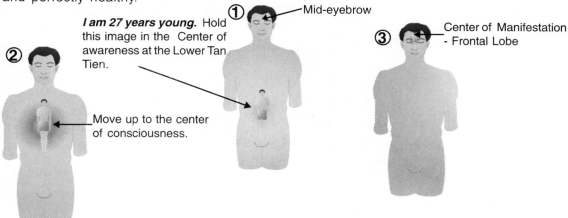

① Mid-eyebrow

I am 27 years young. Hold this image in the Center of awareness at the Lower Tan Tien.

② Move up to the center of consciousness.

③ Center of Manifestation - Frontal Lobe

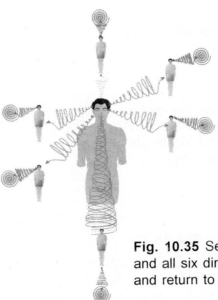

Fig. 10.35 Send the image out into the Universe and all six directions. The affirmation will multiply and return to you to be manifested.

Emotional Image

Picture your emotional body: See a body-shaped image close around your physical body, composed of all kinds of moving colors, saying: "I let go of old emotional experiences, seeing them for what they are and fill myself with radiant joy, love and compassion." Bring the image up the heart center and then to the frontal lobe. Send it out to the Universe and the Universe will multiply it many times and it will be sent back to you. Just wait for it to return with your awareness in the lower brain.

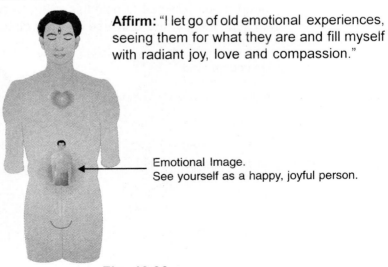

Affirm: "I let go of old emotional experiences, seeing them for what they are and fill myself with radiant joy, love and compassion."

Emotional Image.
See yourself as a happy, joyful person.

Fig. 10.36

Mental Image

Picture your mental body, saying: "I make an agreement with myself to enjoy the best of life and to live the full wealth of my potential in harmony with Nature and the Universe." Follow the same sequence of moving the image up to the heart, the frontal lobe and out to the Universe. Wait for the return with your awareness in the lower brain.

Affirm: "I make an agreement with myself to enjoy the best of life and to live the full wealth of my potential."

Fig. 10.37

Spiritual Image

Picture your spiritual body and higher self, saying: "I am at one with my God (Source) within and manifest its Glory." Follow the same procedure as before.

Problem Solving
Answers and Solutions

A. Take the questions and problems that you have into your center of **Awareness** (Abdominal Brain) then to your **Consciousness** (Heart Brain) and send them out into the Universe through the third eye in your **Observation** center (Mind Brain) broadcasting out to the entire Universe.

B. Wait for the best answers and solutions to return to you clearly and distinctly. Allow them to ripen into full understanding.

C. At any point in the future, if you have any questions or you need to take action or have a problem that needs to be solved, all you need to do is to inhale deeply and allow your awareness in the abdomen to expand far beyond your physical limits.

D. Exhale your problem into the Universe, open yourself, wait for a moment and let go of the problem. You will become conscious of the solutions to your questions or problems you presented. The more you practice this, the quicker and easier the results will come. You must take action when you receive the energy and information. The way to get extra energy is by breathing red light into the heart 3 to 6 times, letting it radiate into the whole body through the heart. You will feel a lot of energy enabling you to take action and complete the task.

E. You can use the same technique to project the goals and the time frame during which you wish to accomplish them. Sometimes it helps to ask for more wisdom from the Universe or Cosmos in order to understand our Life's purpose.

Finish the meditation by resting for a few moments and collecting the energy in your Lower Tan Tien.

Chapter XI
Planetary and Stellar Meditations to increase Awareness and Sensitivity

Feeling the direct connection with the planetary energies is a unique experience which carries multiple benefits for yourself and for the healing practices you carry out. Here follow some of the benefits we noted among practitioners of these meditations:

☯ An increase in emotional stability and in understanding the origin of emotional patterns.
☯ Ability to connect with information and energy from the universe.
☯ Strong healing processes in the organs and the whole body.
☯ A major increase in healing power.
☯ A greater balance between the weak and strong points of character.
☯ A rise in the ability to be deeply in touch with the different organs/systems in the body
☯ both of the practitioner and that of the person being treated.

We advise you to practice the opening of the three Tan Tiens to the six directions first. (see Chapter II). Once the organs and energy centers are connected to the galaxies, the planetary forces can be integrated easily. The planetary meditations are divided into seven parts (five are described in this book); following each one represents a growing level of awareness/sensitivity.

Before you start with the first one, take some time to create a good contact and to integrate these energies into your body. Then proceed with the next one. A good sequence for building up the meditation practices from this book is the following:

Step 1: Iron Shirt Chi Kung, Inner Smile, Six Healing Sounds, Microcosmic Orbit. For those of you who have studied Cosmic Chi Kung (One Finger Art, see the book Cosmic Healing I) this practice is also a perfect preparation.

Step 2: Opening the Three Tan Tiens to the Six Directions.

Step 3: Planetary and Stellar initiations 1 to 5.

To get a direct connection with the frequency of the planetary belts and galaxies, use the information and pictures in Chapter III; Taoist Astrology and the Structure of the Universe. As is the case with all new practices and meditations, it takes some time to build up the connection, but with practice it soon will become easier and once you really get it, you can connect to the energy at any moment during the day when you decide to tune into it.

As with anything in life, you will only get good at it if you master the basic principles and practice daily. If you want to go too quickly in the beginning, you may have to return to the basics at a later stage.

It is important to realize that in these meditations you are interacting with enormous forces. It is not the effort, but the awareness and resonance that determine the results.

The openness to achieve the connection with these energies will give you just enough of what you need and what you are able to manage. This can cause strong emotional, mental and physical shifts in energy, but it is always available in amounts that you can handle. If you try to manipulate the universe you may well suddenly receive a lot more energy, just as you have asked. But you will discover soon that the ego led you in this direction. You will not be able to handle it and will 'burn' yourself. Thus your energy level will decline instead of rise, with disappointment being the result.

A good way to get in contact with the awareness belts in the solar system (planetary frequencies) is to study some basic astronomy and use the pictures of planets/stars in this book as a starting point. Once you have a better understanding of how the solar system really appears, the pictures can be used to tune in to the planetary frequencies. Simply look at the pictures then close your eyes, look out through the cranium and expand your awareness. It is important to respect the correct sequence of building up this meditation practice. Start with what you can clearly register sensorially. Start with the sun (warmth/ seeing it), then move to the earth (seeing, feeling gravity and energy), then shift to the moon (seeing, feeling). You need to contact with these three forces first before you will be able to connect to the other planets. Remember that you do not have to see these planets in order to feel them. What we are getting in contact with is the energy/awareness belts of the planets. The planets in their materialized form are only the center of this belt.

Practice with great respect. Do not try to pull these forces with your willpower. This will not work! Try to attract them.

You can use the eastern or western astrological signs for the planets during the meditations by projecting them into the picture of the planets. But it's better to start with only the color and quality of the element.

Meditation 1
The Earth - Sun - Moon Triangle

1. Warming up exercises (Inner Smile, Chi Kung, Tai Chi, Tao Yin and others)
2. Opening the Three Tan Tiens to the Six Directions, integrate the Inner Smile and the MCO.
3. Connect to Mother Earth. Breath deeply into the earth with every exhalation. Thank the earth for her love and nourishment. Breathe in the cool blue energy through the soles, the palms and the perineum. Store this energy in your center. This will be your safety belt and rooting during your planetary and galactic journey.
4. Bring your attention to the sacrum.
5. Picture a bright full moon behind you, shining on your sacrum. The color of the moon can be seen/felt as silver/white.

The moonlight will be mixed inside the sexual center with the blue sexual energy. Breathe it into the sacrum drawing the moonlight inside and further into the sexual center. At the same time draw the sexual energy inward. Men pull up the sexual organ, perineum and anus and gently squeeze the muscles around the prostate gland. Women softly close and contract the vagina, perineum and anus and gently squeeze the muscles around the ovaries and the uterus. On the exhalation (men and women) release the muscles about 90% but keep the Chi inside.

The squeezing should be very gentle and the other muscles in the body remain very relaxed. Gather the energy at the sexual center. Take about 5 to 10 minutes until you feel the moonlight directly entering into the sexual center.

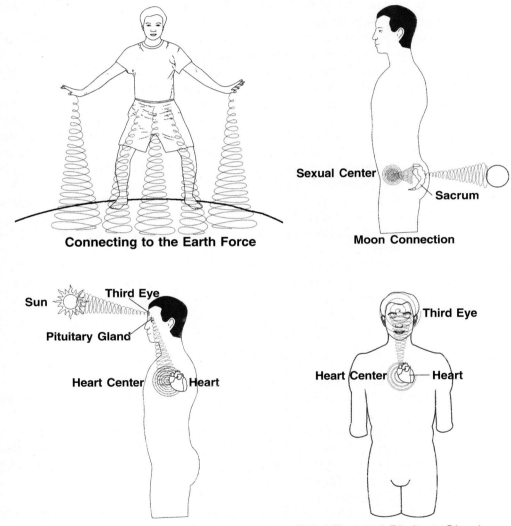

Connecting to the Earth Force

Sexual Center

Sacrum

Moon Connection

Sun

Third Eye

Pituitary Gland

Heart Center   **Heart**

Third Eye

Heart Center   **Heart**

Fig. 11.2 Connecting the Sun with the Third Eye and Pituitary Gland.

6. Bring your attention to the third eye/mid-eyebrow point.
7. Picture a bright gold/yellow sun in front of you. Feel the light particles, the cosmic Chi tingling on your face. Absorb this light in the third eye and the pituitary gland.
8. Breathe in the light and guide it from the third eye and the pituitary gland down into the heart.
9. Make the heart sound to clean it and balance the heart energy. Feel love, peace, patience and respect, while you feel the sun directly shining in your heart. Shift your focus towards the heart center, right in the middle between the nipples, behind the sternum.

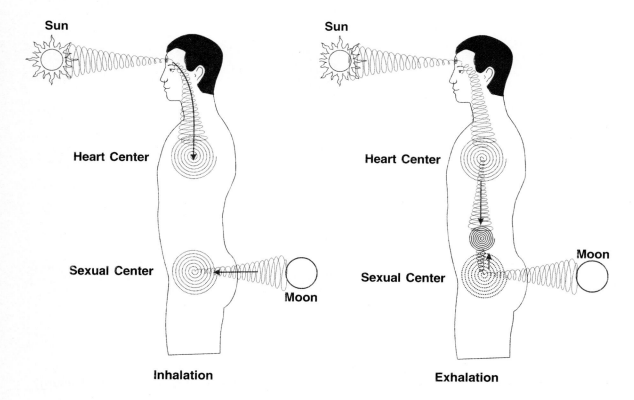

Fig. 11.3

10. Blend the golden/yellow sunlight with the bright red color of love and compassion in the heart center.
11. Gather more sunlight in the heart center. At a certain point the heart center will open up further and connect with the universal love. A deep yet unsentimental love can be experienced. This has been described as the 'blooming of compassion'.
12. On the inbreath draw the silver/white moonlight into the sacrum/sexual center (blue) and at the same time the golden/yellow sunlight into the third eye/heart center (red). On the outbreath condense these two energies in the central point behind the navel. Push the blue/silver/white energy up and the red/golden/yellow energy down. Keep drawing these energies in until you feel a clear connection (10-15 minutes).

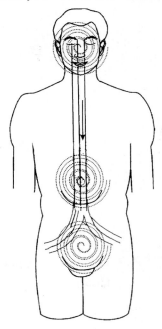

Fig. 11.4

13. Bring the kidney and sexual energy up through the vena cava and the heart energy down through the aorta.
14. Mix both energies in the Tan Tien. If you have difficulties to connect with the aorta/vena cava, just relax and let the two energies come together in the Tan Tien.
15. When the love and sexual energy are combined in the center, a soft orgasmic feeling will start vibrating in the lower Tan Tien and from there on through the whole body.
16. Combined with the sun and the moon force this energy can be multiplied. Start slowly; do not take in too much sun and moonlight or you will begin to overheat. Give your body the time to adjust to the new energy level. If you feel that you are getting too hot, or have any adverse reactions (unpleasant sensations), practice the Six Healing Sounds to cool down and regain equilibrium.

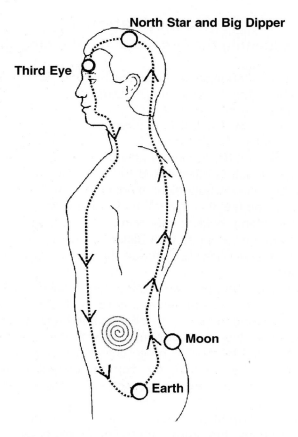

Fig. 11.5 Microcosmic Orbit (MCO)

17. Move the energy from the center down into the perineum and up the MCO.
18. Put the emphasis on the following points and connections:

   Perineum - Earth
   Sacrum - Moon
   Crown - North Star/Big Dipper
   Third Eye - Sun

19. Stop at each of these points and feel the external connection.
20. Circle the energy around 9 to 18 times in the MCO. Gather the energy in the center and rest. Observe your body and energy in the yin stage. Just notice where the energy is moving in your body. Remain in this state for 5 to 15 minutes.
21. End this meditation with Chi Self Massage.

Meditation 2
Strengthening the Organs and Balancing the Emotions

1. Warm up exercises (Inner Smile, Cosmic Chi Kung, Tai Chi, Tao Yin and others).
2. Opening the Three Tan Tiens to the Six Directions.
3. Integrate the Inner Smile and the MCO.
4. Make a firm condensed Chi ball in the center.
5. Connect to the Mother Earth force.
6. Bring your attention to the cranium and softly touch the cranial bones with a minimum of pressure. This touch is often called the butterfly touch, as it is compared with the pressure you feel when a butterfly is landing on your hand; connect to the craniosacral rhythm. Once you feel this rhythm, try to remain with it. Try it without hand contact. Touch without touching, holding your hand 1 to 2 centimeters from the skull.
7. Expand this cranial awareness to a distance of 5 to 50 centimeters away from the physical body. This will greatly increase the sensitivity in your skull and the craniosacral structure.
8. Make the connection between the organs, the cranium and the related planet.
9. Put one hand on the spleen-pancreas area, fill them with the bright yellow light of openness, fairness and trust. Put the second hand (in the form of a beak) softly on the crown point to make the internal connection with the sphenoid bone (See fig. 11.6).
10. Hold the position and let the Chi move between the hands or between the sphenoid and the pancreas/spleen. Once you feel the connection, put the hands together in front of the Tan Tien. Then expand your cranial structure and look up with your eyes through your crown.
11. Visualize a bright yellow planet above you, the planet Saturn. Let the light of the planet Saturn shine down into the crown and the sphenoid bone and than directly down into the spleen and the pancreas. Feel the direct connection and feel how the spleen and pancreas are activated through this direct contact.
12. Feeling this connection may take some time, but once it has been established, the planets become like powerful batteries, charging your organs.
    Use this same procedure for the planets and organs, following the five element cycle:
    Spleen - lungs - kidneys - liver   - heart
    Earth   - metal - water   - wood - fire
13. Use an open hand for the other bones in the cranial system and not a beak hand as on the sphenoid bone.
14. Use your giving hand (usually the predominant one) on the cranium and your receiving one on the organs.
15. Picture all five planets above the crown and let the light shine into the five cranial entrances and further down into the organs. Bring all these energies together in the center.
16. Move the energy in the MCO, making 9 -18 cycles.
17. Gather the energy back into the center, observe the yin stage.
18. End with Chi Self Massage

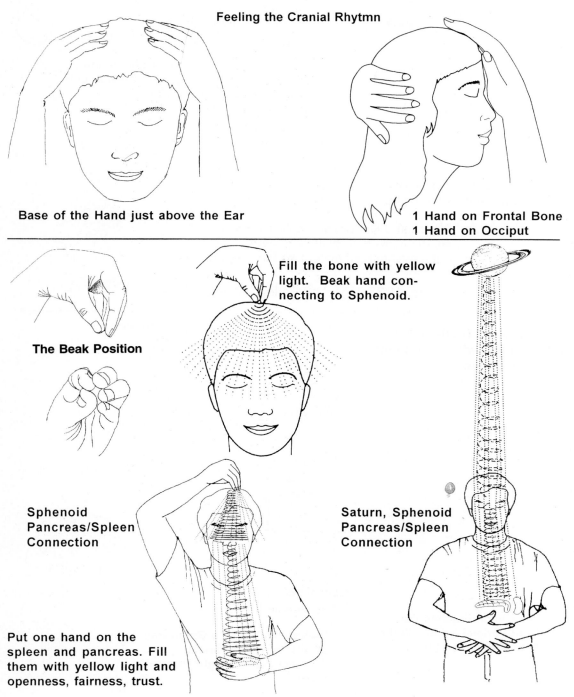

Feeling the Cranial Rhytmn

Base of the Hand just above the Ear

1 Hand on Frontal Bone
1 Hand on Occiput

Fill the bone with yellow light. Beak hand connecting to Sphenoid.

The Beak Position

Sphenoid
Pancreas/Spleen
Connection

Saturn, Sphenoid
Pancreas/Spleen
Connection

Put one hand on the spleen and pancreas. Fill them with yellow light and openness, fairness, trust.

Fig. 11.6 Spleen/Pancreas, Sphenoid bone and Saturn

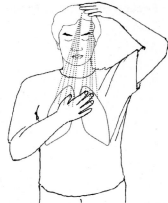

Picture Venus as a White Ball above the Left Parietal and connect Venus Left Parietal.

One hand touches Left Parietal. Fill the bone with White Light.

Other hand just below the Collar Bone. Fill the lungs with White Light and righteousness. Connect Left Parietal and Lung.

Fig. 11.7 Lungs, Left Parietal Bone and Venus

Put one hand on the Liver. Fill the Liver with Green Light and friendliness.

Jupiter

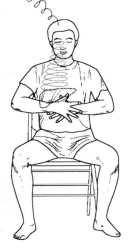

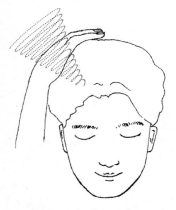

Other hand touches the Right Parietal Bone. Fill the bone with Green Light.

Connect Liver and Right Parietal Bone.

Picture Jupiter as a Green Ball above the Right Parietal. Connect Jupiter Right Parietal Liver.

Fig. 11.8 Liver, Right Parietal Bone and Jupiter

Put one hand on the Heart. Fill the Heart with Red Light, love, peace and respect.

Mars

Picture Mars as a red ball above the frontal bone. Connect Mars, frontal bone and heart.

Other hand touches the Frontal Bone. Fill Frontal Bone with Red light.

Connect Heart and Frontal Bone.

Fig. 11.9 Heart, Frontal Bone and Mars

Put both hands on the Kidneys. Fill the Kidneys with Blue Light and gentleness.

Mercury

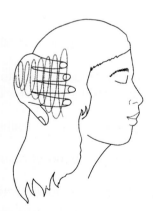

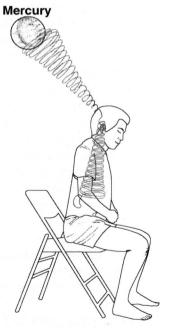

One hand touches Occipital Bone. Fill Occipital Bone with Blue Light.

Other hand toughing Ming Men (Door of Life at Lumbar 2 and 3) Kidney Point. Connect Occipital and Kidneys.

Picture Mercury as Blue Ball above the Occipital. Connect Mercury, Occipital.

Fig. 11.9 Kidney, Occipital and Mecury

Note: During the meditation you may meet different negative or undesirable emotions. Keep smiling down into the organs to enhance the virtue energy. If negative emotions keep bothering you, exhale them deeply into the earth and make the related healing sound. Fill the space with positive or virtue energy.

Meditation 3
Strengthening the Body Systems
Increasing the Energy Field

After you have practiced the second meditation for a while it will become easier to feel the connection with the planetary forces. This third meditation uses the technique of the second meditation but adds two factors:

The five earthly elemental forces.
Expansion of the planet/organ energy into the body structures.

This practice will strengthen the different organs and body systems. It will also create balance in your energy structures. Sickness and negative energy will be discharged. Your energy field will greatly improve.

1. Warm up exercises
2. Open the Three Tan Tiens to the Six Directions.
3. Make a firm, condensed Chi ball in the center.
4. Connect to the Mother Earth force.
5. Go through the same five planets/organ cycle, as in meditation 2, but now add the earthly nature force related to that organ. Spend some time to build up a connection with the different nature forces.
6. Mix the earthly and planetary energy in the organ.
7. Let the energy/color/virtue expand in the muscular system until the whole body is filled with it and the energy radiates out into the aural field.
8. Earth element: spleen - sphenoid bone - Saturn - earth/soil energy - muscular system. Earth energy can also be used in the lymphatic system. Use the same strategy for the four other elements.
9. Metal element: lungs - left - parietal bone - Venus - lake energy, metal - breathing system (lungs, skin).
10. Water element: kidneys - occipital bone - Mercury - water energy - bone structure/hormonal system.
11. Wood element: liver - right - parietal bone - Jupiter - tree energy - tendon/ligament system.
12. Fire Element: Heart - Frontal Bone - Mars - Fire Energy - Arterial/veinous System.

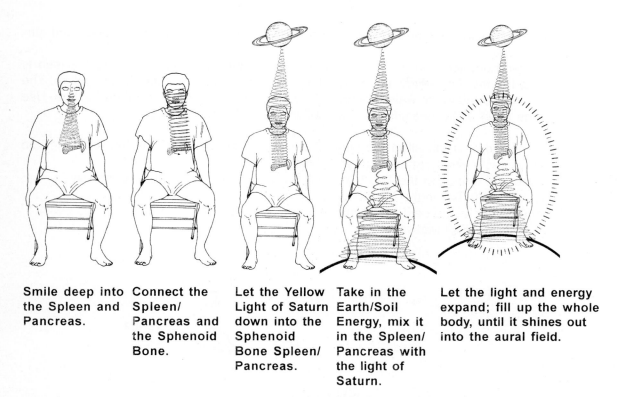

| Smile deep into the Spleen and Pancreas. | Connect the Spleen/Pancreas and the Sphenoid Bone. | Let the Yellow Light of Saturn down into the Sphenoid Bone Spleen/Pancreas. | Take in the Earth/Soil Energy, mix it in the Spleen/Pancreas with the light of Saturn. | Let the light and energy expand; fill up the whole body, until it shines out into the aural field. |

Fig. 11.10 Earth Element: Spleen, Sphenoid Bone, Saturn, Earth/Soil, Muscular System

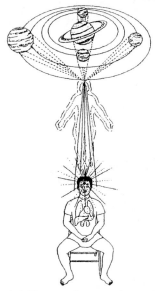

Fig. 11.11 The Planets' Forces beam down to the Crystal Room.

At the end you will feel a strong multicolored energy filling your whole body and surrounding you.

You can complete the meditation by adding the sun and moon energy. The sun is connected to the fire energy, the pericardium, third eye and lymph/immunite system. The moon is connected to the water energy, the sexual organs, sacrum, hormonal system. Use the same order as in meditation 1. This will increase the energy field.

13. At the end envision all of the planets above and around you. Just relax and let the energy move freely throughout your body.
14. Gather the energy in the Tan Tein until you feel a Chi ball. Condense it firmly.
15. Circle the Chi ball in the Microcosmic Orbit.
16. Then gather in the center and observe the yin stage.
17. End with Chi Self Massage.

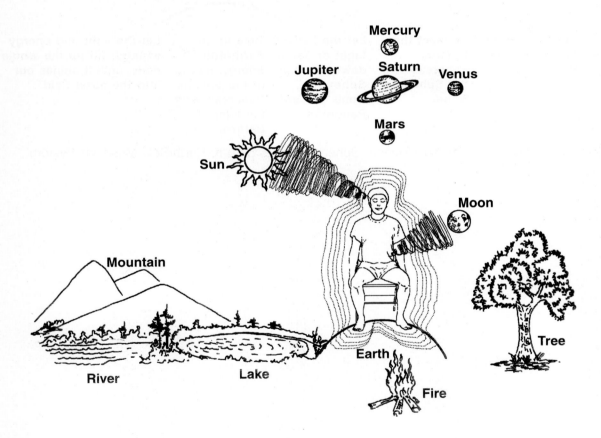

Fig. 11.12 Natural Forces

Meditation 4
Connecting to the Galactic Forces

To connect with the galaxies is a very strong meditation form. It brings enormous amounts of energy in your body. To work with them first use the preparation exercises from chapter II.

The galactic energies can be used in two different ways:
1 Connect with Six Galaxies in the Six Directions.
2 Connect with the North Star and the Five Palaces.

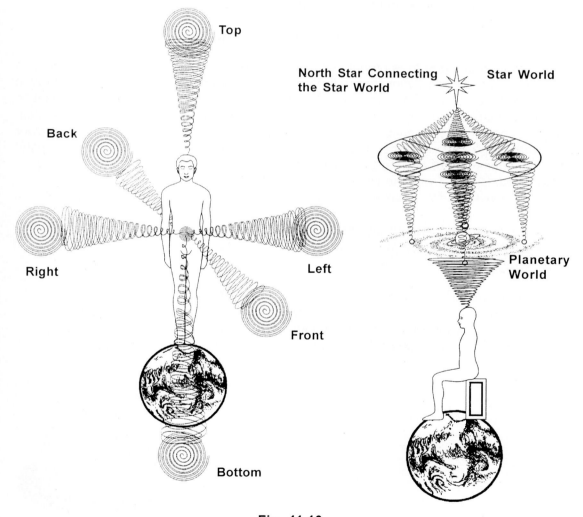

Fig. 11.13
Galaxy Connection in the Six Directions and Galaxy Connection with the Five Palaces

The Six Direction Method

Golden yellow is the color used most frequently but any other colors can be incorporated as they manifest.

The entrance points are the crown, the third eye, the navel, the Door of Life (point in the lower back) and the feet. This meditation will balance the energy throughout the body since the connection points are in the head, body and legs. The bottom galaxy is reached through the earth, which means that good grounding is easy. This takes away the risk of overheating. Always remember that galactic energy is enormously powerful; maintain a respectful attitude as you work with these energies. The best way to build up is to work first with the six directions and then with the five palaces.

The Five Palace Method

In this method, the energy is brought into the body through the cranium so there needs to be a good rooting and connection with the earth to balance this hot Universal energy in the head. Meditation 1, 'Balancing (Earth) Sun and Moon' or the preparation exercises in chapter II, can be used first. It is advisable to begin with planetary connections and meditations. Their frequency and the subsequent amount of heat that is produced is lower than that of the galaxies. Once the planetary energies are balanced in the head, expand the awareness further beyond the Milky Way into the galactic world. Connect with the North Star and build up the connection with the five galaxies placed around the North Star.

Use the same colors and qualities as used in the five elements and bring the energy all the way down to the five organs.

Note: Once you have mastered this meditation you can increase the energy level, specifically by connecting the seven stars of the Big Dipper with the bones of the skull. (Details, see chapter V, page119)

Fig. 11.14 Immortal

Pictures of galaxies that can be used during or as a preparation for meditation.

Central Palace -Yellow Galaxy

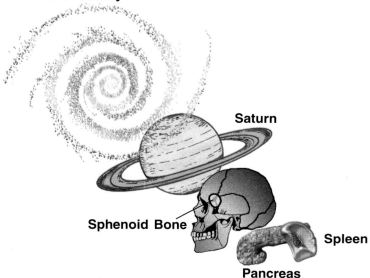

Fig. 11.15

West Palace - White Galaxy

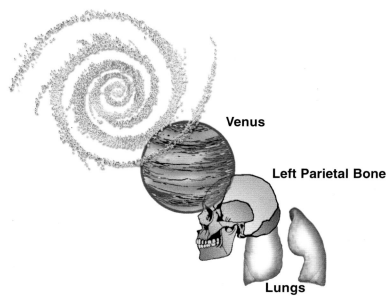

Fig. 11.16

East Palace - Green Galaxy

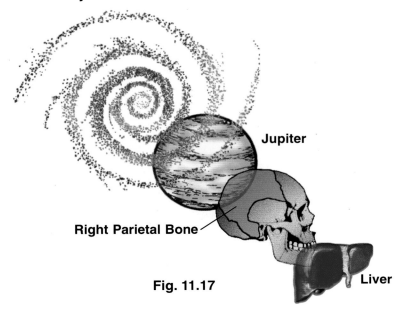

Fig. 11.17

North Palace - Blue Galaxy

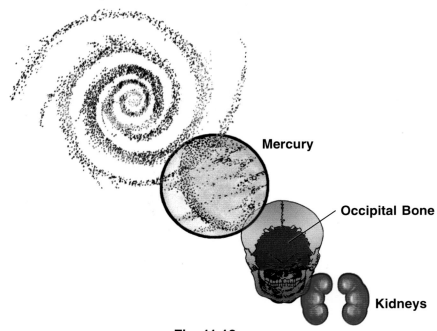

Fig. 11.18

Southern Palace - Red Galaxy

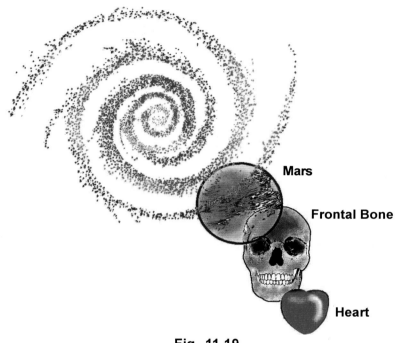

Mars

Frontal Bone

Heart

Fig. 11.19

Meditation 5
Balancing the Planetary and Stellar Influences
and increasing Emotional and Mental Stability

Regular practice of the first four meditations will give you a clear picture which of the five elements is your strong or weak point. It might show up in different ways - emotions, pain, and tension during the meditation. You might notice the weak element through an inability to feel its color, organ or planetary influence.

What you probably have accomplished by now is:

1. The ability to feel the connection with the related planetary and/or stellar frequency.
2. The ability to feel the connection between the cranial bone and the organ.
3. The ability to expand the energy into the related body system.

One of the five planets (sun/moon) - Star Palaces - cranium - organ - body systems will probably be very easy to feel, while another may seem to be absent. This difference originates in all kinds of physical, emotional, mental imbalances which are locked up in between the unconscious minds. It is also possible that you may feel the planetary connection and not the stars of the same direction or the other way around. Try to get the picture as clear as possible, it will give you a lot of information about your personality and also about your soul.

Once you have discovered how this imbalance is anchored in your system, you can use this during meditation as a tool to improve the weakness in your personality and in your physical body.

In this meditation we use the five galaxies and not the six directions method.

The principle of full and empty functions in the body is one of the most fundamental in oriental medicine. The cause of the problem lies basically in a lack of energy and information in one part of the energy system which is internally balanced by overactivity in other parts. Many people are hooked in a fanatical way on a certain more developed part of their personality and abilities. If they wish to balance themselves they must face their fear-based fanaticism which creates the empty or missing opposite.

The imbalance might already be found in the karmic information and can be related to the life task or it might come through in the way this person leads their life. Use the same principle as in the third meditation but work only with the strongest and weakest connection. As an example, let us say that you connect with the liver easily - right parietal bone - Jupiter- green galaxy and have difficulty with the lungs - left parietal bone- Venus- white galaxy. This might also show up in liver overactivity and lung weakness. You might notice a tendency to irritation, anger and on the other side depression, sadness, discouragement; good overviews on situations but tendency to over control.

The principle of this meditation is that you use the excess energy from the overactive organ to create a connection and nurture the deficient organ. If we put more vitality into the weak organ - the information of how to open this closed door often arises spontaneously.

1. Start with the same preparation as in meditation 3.
2. When you have reached the part with the planetary connection, first make the connection with the strongest organ - cranium - planet/star connection, in this case the liver - right parietal bone - Jupiter - green galaxy and fill the body and aura with the related color (green).
3. Then change the color in the body and aural field with the one of the weakest function, in this case the lung/white. Draw this color inside of the lungs. Put both hands on the lungs, until you feel the energy tingling inside the organs.
4. Put one hand on the left parietal and feel the lung - left parietal connection.
5. Once you feel this connection, put your hands together in front of the navel and turn your eyes left and upward looking in and through the left. parietal outside in the direction of Venus and the white galaxy.

6. Visualize a clear white ball above you. At a certain point the energy of Venus will shine down directly into the body; keep your attention and expand your awareness through Venus towards the white galaxy.

Do this transition of color from the strongest to the weakest function several times until the energy feels more balanced.

If the transition does not work, let the green light expand and project through the left parietal/Venus/white galaxy until you feel the white light clearly. Let the light shine on your skull and fill up the whole body and aura with this color.

Feel both liver/Jupiter/green galaxy and lung/Venus/white galaxy and balance them further into the body and the aural field.

7. To increase the effect, expand the energy in the respiratory system. Breathe through the skin of your whole body.
8. Gather the energy in the Tan Tein, making a condensed Chi ball.
9. Circulate it through the MCO.
10. Then gather it again in the center and rest in the yin stage.
11. End with Chi Self Massage.

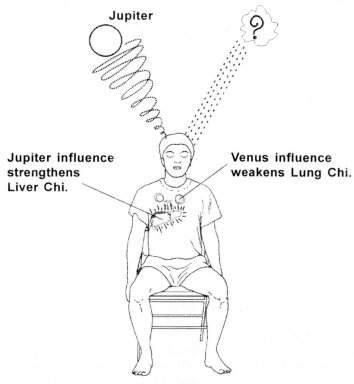

Jupiter

Jupiter influence strengthens Liver Chi.

Venus influence weakens Lung Chi.

Fig. 11.20

Fill the whole body and the aural field with the green light.

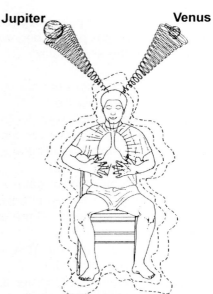

Maintain the energy field and bring it into the lungs. Change the color to white, let it radiate into the whole body and the aural field.

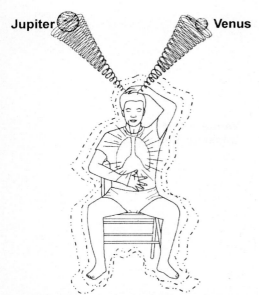

Balance the energies of Jupiter and Venus in the organs and aural field (green/white energy).

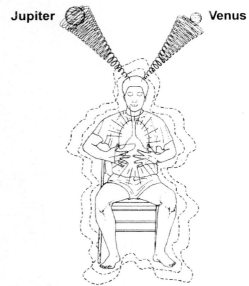

Look out through the left parietal and picture the planet Venus. At a certain point the light will come down from Venus (white galaxy) and start nurturing the energy field and the lungs.

Fig. 11.21

Meditation 6
Balancing the Yin/Yang Extremes in the Star World

The immensity of the star world is difficult for the undeveloped human mind to grasp, yet is a part of the materialized world and in this way part of the world of polarity and yin and yang.

Although many scientists believe that black holes are built around a point of singularity (infinite density) it is clear that infinite density cannot exist. Infinity cannot be found within our limited thinking of the material world. Black holes are indeed points of extreme density but only to the point that extreme yin turns into its opposite. Extreme darkness starts to produce light again. So, although not yet measurable, light particles are still escaping from black holes.

Also the quasars, the brightest objects in the sky are not infinite light but extreme light, until the point turns to its opposite. Dark holes and quasars are the yin/yang extremes of the star world. In this meditation we will use these two poles to project our awareness beyond the world of phenomena.

It is important that you have taken sufficient time to master the first five meditations; only then can this advanced meditation be of great help in your spiritual development. If you are not prepared, it can be harmful. **We advise that you contact an experienced Cosmic Healing Teacher to introduce you into this level. If you suffer regular headaches, heart problems or mental/emotional problems don't do this sixth meditation. Use mediation 1 and mediation 7.**

These are the principles of this meditation:
1. Start with good centering/grounding.
2. Expand your awareness in the star world.
3. Connect high above you with the North Star and Big Dipper.
4. Let the light fill your upper Tan Tien.
5. Connect with two points, placed around the North Star.
6. One extreme light point, quasar (extreme yang).
7. One extreme dark point, dark hole (extreme yin).
8. Let these two points circle around the North Star.
9. Let the process speed up and continue automatically while your attention goes in and through the North Star.
10. At a certain point the process can speed up so much that you start to feel a lifting and the edge between yin and yang start to fade away.
11. Let this process continue naturally, until yin and yang are melting together and the pure yang or ultimate yang energy arises.

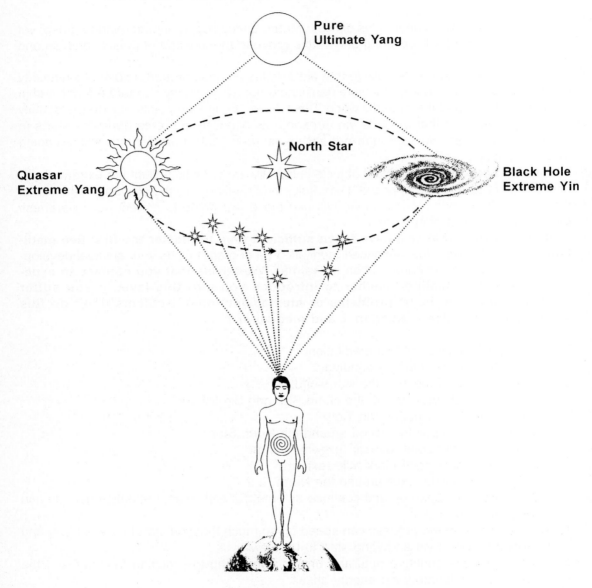

Fig. 11.22

Meditation 7
Yin Stage
Awareness Practice

In this meditation the intention is to let the planetary/galactic forces enter spontaneously. It is important not to use willpower or intention to attract any particular planet, just be open to the planetary/galactic forces, which is an unspecified intention. If you have read the previous parts of this book it will be clear that planetary/galactic forces are influencing us every second of our lives. The only choice we have is to be aware of it or not - the influence is there anyway. For each individual the dominant planetary/galactic influence changes many times in a day. When we sit still and empty the mind we can observe this subtle process of planetary/galaxy energies and shifts in our cranium, our organs and energy field.

During a yin (passive) stage meditation, you can pick up energy from different layers (or combinations) of the universe.
1. Nature energies: Trees, lakes, mountains, thunder, wind, lightning, etc.
2. Planets.
3. Individual stars.
4. Galaxies, quasars, pulsars, black holes.
5. A connection with elemental qualities in common, for instance: Green galaxy-star-Jupiter-tree energy.

When you learn to observe this process you will be able to feel the direct influence of these planets/stars in that particular moment. It will give you the freedom to understand the specific Universal influence and how it determines your physical/energetic condition and your emotions/thinking process free from any astrological prediction. It also will clarify tensions or growing processes in relationships or with friends. If you and your partner or your friend are both practicing these meditations you can meditate together and see how the energy is naturally working on the two of you. It will definitely give you much insight and information.

This yin stage awareness meditation works very well in groups. Many different processes will be occurring at the same time. The planetary/star energies will:

Work on each individual.
Work on processes among several individuals.
Work on the whole group energy as a unit.

Experience shows us that even in big group meditations 50% to 80% of the people experience the same planets/galaxy entering their energetic fields.

The way to build up this meditation (alone or with more people) consists of:
1. Warming up exercises.
2. Opening the Three Tan Tiens to the Six Directions, integrate the Inner Smile and MCO.
3. Make a firm, condensed Chi ball in the center.
4. Connect to the Mother Earth force.
5. Bring your attention to the cranium, feel the rhythm, expand the cranial rhythm into the aural field.
6. Connect to the energy field of the people you are meditating with.
7. Just relax and see what happens; if you want, you can softly say to the others what you feel happening in your body or cranium.

Individual and Triangle Awareness Meditation with Saturn Influence

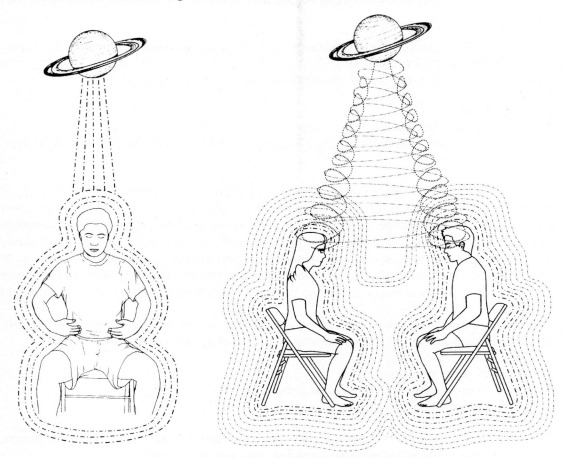

Yin Stage Awareness Meditation - Saturn Influence

Fig. 11.23

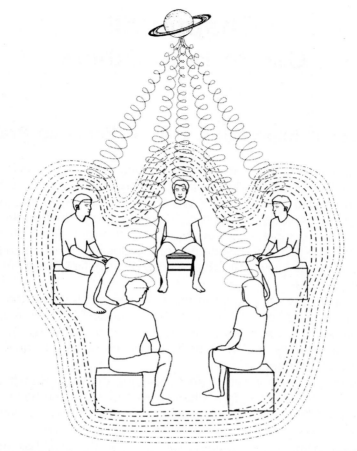

Group Meditation: Yin Stage Meditation - Saturn Influence

Fig. 11.24

8. At the end draw the energy back into your own individual field.
9. Gather into the Tan Tein and make a condensed Chi ball.
10. Circulate throughout the MCO.
11. Then gather it again in the center and rest in the yin stage.
12. End with Chi Self Massage.

First, practice individually or, if you practice in a group, stay with your individual experience. After a while you will be able to distinguish your personal energy field and the shared or group energy field.

If you have difficulty feeling these energies, meditate with someone who has a better connection with the planets, but stay with your own experience.

Be patient, relax. You can be sure that your information/energy source will not run away.

Chapter XII
Use to Help Others

Treatment Expression of your Personal Practice

The therapeutic potential of the previously described practices is unlimited. It can be applied as an individual or self-healing method with great success, but it is also very easy to integrate it into healing and bodywork practices you are using already. This chapter explains some basic techniques on applying Cosmic Healing during a treatment (on one or more students). The complete theoretical and practical procedure on how to help and heal others will be published in the next book of the Cosmic Healing series.

The combination of the Universal Tao practices with Chi Nei Tsang (Internal Organ Chi Massage) is very powerful.

Both methods have the same goal in the treatment: to balance the energies in the body and to activate the life force. Chi Nei Tsang uses the Tan Tien as the main area of diagnosis and treatment. Imbalances in energy and tension in the Tan Tien will be treated with a firm physical pressure and with the three forces of the universe (earth, cosmic, universal) as the nurturing source.

In Cosmic Healing the emphasis is on connecting the body with the five elemental forces of nature, the planets and stars, often without touching the body.

We could say that Chi Nei Tsang works mainly from the Tan Tien towards the universe while Cosmic Healing works from the universe towards the Tan Tien.

The combination of these two systems will give you the ability to integrate internal/external energy in the Tan Tien.

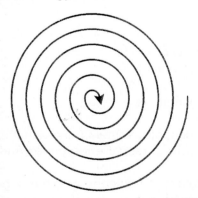 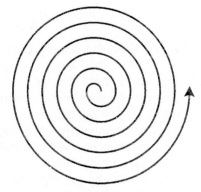

Cosmic Healing: Starting form the universal laws and integrating it into the physical body.

Chi Nei Tsang: Starting from the Tan Tien and connecting with the Universal laws. From matter into subtle energy.

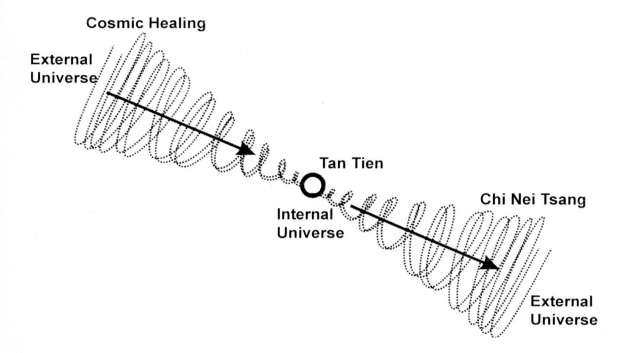

Fig. 12.1

These days many healers are working consciously with the Universal connection from Subtle energy into matter. Different systems are now in use. Some of them work with initiations to connect the student with the same universal source as the teacher or master.

This is the story of a student who was desperately looking for a teacher who could show him how to reach the state of enlightenment. He visited or followed many teachers , but he did not make much progress. None of them gave him satisfying answers to his main questions and most of them were still in search of enlightenment themselves.

One day he traveled to a master who was known to be fully enlightened. When he asked the master if he could show him how to attain enlightenment, the master said, "Sure," and smiled at him. After a long silence the student said, "Well, why don't you tell me?" The master said, "Why confuse you more by telling you something that you surely cannot understand anyway".

This story shows us how useless it is to give initiations to people who are not ready to integrate and understand.

It only creates confusion and illusion. Many students are trying to buy their 'ticket' to heaven by paying thousands of dollars for initiations with a master or guru.

Let us stay clear and grounded. There are no shortcuts on the spiritual path.

Although spectacular healings occur through this practice it must be clear that the goal of the treatment is mainly one of guidance and teaching.

The purpose of planetary and galactic healing is to reconnect students with the energy of nature, planets, stars and the higher universal frequencies.

This connection:
- Activates the life force in the body which triggers the ability for self-healing.
- Releases and transforms sick/negative energy.
- Creates a strong spiritual connection and higher awareness level.

Although this healing practice is easy to learn for anyone with enough interest and perseverance, the effectiveness of a treatment mainly depends on the level of energy (quantity/quality), the clarity of the connection of the healer with nature and Universal forces and the ability to see what the student really needs at that moment.

This strength and sensitivity can only be cultivated by doing the previously described meditations on a regular basis and fully integrating them into your daily life.

General Healing Session

For reasons of clarity this text only mentions one person or student; this session may however be performed with a group also. Before starting this session do some meditation practice and warm ups with your student(s).

There are two ways of doing this type of healing session:

One way is to focus on the specific location in your own body, using your hands and asking the other person to do the same. Together you go through the complete healing procedure.

Another way is to focus on your energy body and do the same step by step meditation. For details refer to the appropriate chapter.

1) Be aware of the Tan Tien and connect to the universe. Let the student sit back on the chair. Sit across from the student. Be aware of your sacrum area and feel the Chi; transfer this feeling up to the crown and to the universe. Spiral the Chi down to the energy body and it will go down to the student's physical body.
2) Draw the green light in with your palm and push it right through the sacrum to spread the sickness through to the other side of the universe. Pull the green light from the universe and push the sick Chi out to the universe. Do this 6 to 9 times until you feel the sacrum is clean. When you pull back, stop the green Chi right at the student's sacrum; there is no need to pull it back to you.

   Yellow light from the ground will help strengthen the sacrum bone. Visualize the sacrum and vitalize the complete bone-structure with yellow light.
3) Be aware of the energy body above the crown; extend yourself up from above your crown and channel down the white light from the center of the galaxy and the violet light

from the Polar star. Using your mind-power, invite the inside of the bone to open, allowing the white and violet light to flow into the marrow. Focus on the energy body; you can picture the energy body's sacrum and bone structure to guide the energy inside and see the whole body light up from deep inside.

Next, focus on the Door of Life and the navel. First flush them through with green light, to clean them out. Draw the yellow light from the Door of Life through to the navel and then push back through. To cool down the Door of Life (if necessary), draw the blue light and push it through from the navel to the Ming Men, connecting with the universe. Then bring the white or violet light down and activate the lower Tan Tien. Teach people about their Tan Tien. It is like an ocean and the body is like a hollow bamboo. The bamboo can bring the water up. This way energy will never dry up.

4) Concentrate on the solar plexus and the Chi Kung (T-11). Again, draw the green light in, spiral it, flush with the green light, then energize with white and violet light. As before, always allow the energy to stream through both points fully. When working on the solar plexus, which holds all the emotions, the most important thing to remember is to connect the backside of the solar plexus to the universe. There is literally no end to this connection. Just allow the Chi to come all the way down and pull a little. Simply clean out the path. Allow the information to condense, allow any images to form and be released. Then stabilize the energy. Picture the Chi field encompassing the person as a big protective bubble. Cool down with blue.

5) Proceed to the heart and the Shen Dao (T5/ T6). Draw the green light in and push it through; repeat several times; now scan the heart with your palm, judging its strength; next select the strength of the red color, (never too dark); send the red light through the heart, strengthening it.

6) Cool down any excess heat in the heart, flushing down and out, using blue. Draw in the white Chi; push it through to the Wing Point (T5/T6). Energize the center at the back of the heart using violet and golden Chi. Picture the heart surrounded by a golden aura.

7) Move up to the throat center, flushing through to C-7, using green light first. The throat center responds very well to the blue light; it opens and clears it.

8) Next activate the mid-eyebrow. Focus on the mid-eyebrow in your own body. Attract the golden yellow color and use it to flush and stabilize. Flush it all the way through to the back of the head. Energize with violet and golden light.

9) Proceed up to the third eye in the middle of the forehead. Connect to the 'Kun Lun' at the back of the crown. Flush through both points using the light violet light. Energize with electric white golden light.

10) Concentrate on the crown. Invite the violet golden light to enter and flush all the way down through the center channel, leaving the body at the perineum. Cool down the system by showering blue light over the whole body.

Du Mai Information

The co-author of this book Dirk Oellibrandt, together with his wife Katrien Laurens, leads an organization called Du Mai.

This organization is active in Belgium and has side branches in Holland, Sweden and France. The Du Mai philosophy promotes the practice of 4 Dimensional Life and Taoism and uses the Taoist principles in a complete approach of healing and the art of bodywork, called 4 Dimensional Bodywork.

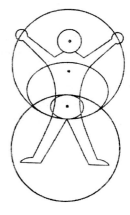

The Du Mai organization offers possibilities in four different fields for deepening and improving the quality of your life and for reaching a higher level of health, happiness and awareness.

In the Du Mai therapeutic clinic many western bodywork techniques are combined with food prescriptions, herbs and other forms of therapy. All this is based on the unique Taoist view of the universe and is structured upon a treatment approach called 4 Dimensional Bodywork.

The Du Mai program is organized into three categories:
1. Personal development.
2. Three to five years in therapeutic education.
3. Courses of up to three years of training for professional therapists.

An Overview of the Du Mai Course and Training Activities
Universal Tao Belgium

Evening, weekend and weekly courses that will teach you to heal yourself, understand your true nature and your task in life, and discover vitality, happiness and freedom in daily life.

Basics: Inner Smile
Six Healing Sounds
Iron Shirt Chi Kung I
Chi Self Massage
Microcosmic Orbit
Tao Yin
Taoist Secrets of Love
Advanced Bone Marrow Nei Kung
Fusion I - II - III Inner Alchemy
Tai Chi Chi Kung I - II - III
Pushing Hands
Pakua Palm

Chi Nei Tsang
 - Level I, II, III
Cosmic Healing
 - Level I, II

4 Dimensional Life Training

1 year/12 weekends training in the art of 4-Dimensional awareness and understanding man, in the world, the universe and the intelligence that connects and governs all these processes called life.

Goals in this training are :
- Spiritual : awakening
- Mental : clearness and presence
- Emotional : understanding, using and transforming emotions
- Fysical : building the fundament for a strong/vital/healthy body

Much time is invested in becoming aware through touch and bodywork of the different layers systems and frequencies in your body, so that the deep information and energy potential is awakened.

4-Dimensional Bodywork

A 3 year (500 hours) or 5 year (850 hours) training to became an all round healer/ bodyworker with a strong ground of 4-Dimensional self realization. The Du Mai school offers you a unique training according to quality and variety. Truly understanding life and its play in our manifestation as a human being is the fundament of the school. Within this unique view, a complete circle of all possible bodywork and healing techniques is offered. These techniques come from traditional and modern, eastern and western origin. Or from sjamanistic traditions or Taoist cosmology or simply from our own body intelligence. The main guidance into this network of information is the students message and information system, showing us a constant flow in priorities in the treatment approach.

For already professional therapists and bodyworkers (prerequisites are 400 hours of training as a bodyworker/healer/natural therapist). We offer a 3 year training in 4-Dimensional Bodywork that will push your already achieved therapeutic level to a wider and stronger platform. Individual therapeutic limitations are removed and the circle of therapeutic possibilities is enlarged.

Some of the topics are (a specific personal development program for each year) :
- 4-Dimensional life/bodywork
- Natural healing - diagnostics
- Universal Tao : Basics, Iron Shirt I, Healing Love, Tai Chi I, Fusion I
- Chi Nei Tsang I
- Cosmic Healing I
- Chakra + Aura Healing
- Reflexology
- Shiatsu - Thai massage
- Craniosacral Therapy
- Osteopatic Techniques
- Fascia and Visceral Therapy
- Structural Corrections
- Sjamanistic Healing
- Food prescriptions
- Frequency Healing
- Spiritual Healing
- 4-Dimensional Integration
- Following the priority

In the near future, books on 4 Dimensional Life and 4 Dimensional Bodywork will be published. Please contact us for book availability.

If you want more information please contact:

Du Mai Belgium:
Dirk Oelllibrandt / Katrien Laurens
Drapstraat 13A
9220 Hamme
Belgium
Tel: +32-(0)52-48 02 19
Fax: +32-(0)52-48 06 63
Email: dumai97@hotmail.com
Web site: www.dumai.org

Du Mai Holland:
Letty Moerel
Zonnebaars 11
2661 KK Bergschenhoek
Holland
Tel: +31-(0)10-521-1172

Du Mai Sweden:
Philippe Vandenabeele
Drottninggatan 28
80311 Gavle Sweden
Tel: +46-(0)290-71407
     +46-(0)26-123660
Email: dumai_se@yahoo.com
Web site: www.dumai.nu

Bibliography

Chia, Mantak: *Taoist Secrets of Love*, 1984, Aurora Press, NY
Iron Shirt Chi Kung, 1986, H.Tao books Huntington, NY
Fusion of the Five Elements I, 1989, H.Tao books Huntington, NY
Healing Love through the Tao, 1986,H.Tao books Huntington, NY
Chi Nei Tsang, 1990, H.Tao books Huntington, NY
Awakening Healing Light, 1993 H.Tao books Huntington, NY

Kushi, Michio: *One Peacefull World*, St Martin's Press, NY
The Teachings of Michio Kushi vol. 2
Other Dimensions, 1992, Avery Publishing group

Mann, A.T.: *The Round Art*, 1979, Dragon's World, Limpsfield, GB

Bleckschmidt, E. and Gasser, M.D.& R.F. PH.D.:
Biokinetics and Biodynamics of Human Differentation, Thomas Books

Upledger, John: *Craniosacral therapy*, 1983, Eastland Press, Washington

Veltman: *Mensen en Planeten*, 1993, Christofoor Zeist, NL

West, John, : *Tempel van de Mens* (translation of "The serpent in the sky: the high wisdom of ancient Egypt"), 1978, Bres, Den Haag, NL

Milne, Hugh: *The Heart of Listening*, 1995, North Atlantic Books, California

Liang, Yang & Wu: *Bagua Zhang -Emei Bagua Zhang*, 1994, YMAA, Publication Center, Jamaica Plain, MA, USA

Ni, Hua Ching: *Taoist Inner View of the Universe and the Immortal Realm*, 1979
The Book of Changes and the Unchanging Truth, 1977

Masunaga: *Zenshiatsu*, 1979, Ank Hermes, Deventer, NL, (translated from Zen Shiatsu, Japan publications, Tokyo)

Sadler: *Langman's Medical Embryology*, 1966, Williams and Wilkins Company, Baltimore, MD, USA

Carus, Paul: *Chinese Astrology*, 1992, Pelanduk Publications, Malaysia

Walter, Derek: *Chinese Astrology*, 1987, The Aquarian Press, London
The Chinese Astrology Workbook, The Aquarian Press, London

Moore & Nicolson: *The Universe*, 1985, Equinox, Oxford

Matsumato & Birch: *Hara Diagnosis: Reflection on the Sea, Stems and Branches*

Gerber, Richard : *Vibrational Medicine,* 1988, Bear & Company, Santa Fe, USA

Planetary & Stellar Images from: *www.astro.uni-bonn.de/~webgk/mc_pic.html*
www.geocities.com and http://nssdc.gsfc.nasa.gov/photo

Universal Tao Center
Overview of the System

Mantak Chia

The Universal Tao is a practical system of self-development that enables individuals to complete the harmonious evolution of their physical, mental and spiritual bodies. Through a series of ancient Chinese meditative and internal energy exercises, the practitioner learns to increase physical energy, release tension, improve health, practice self-defense and gain the ability to heal oneself and others. In the process of creating a solid foundation of health and well-being in the physical body, one also creates the basis for developing their spiritual potential. By learning to tap the natural energies of the Sun, Moon, Earth, Stars and environmental forces around us, the practitioner attains the ability to develop and nurture a solid spiritual body. The ultimate goal of Taoist practice is to transcend physical boundaries through the development of the soul and the spirit within the human.

The Universal Tao practices are derived from ancient techniques rooted in the processes of nature. They have been gathered and integrated into a coherent, accessible system for well-being. Universal Tao Center is not a religion and does not require the belief in any set of deities or gods. The techniques work directly with the life force, 'Chi,' flowing through the meridian system of the body. The aim of the Universal Tao Center is to restore the individual to a condition of harmony with the flow of the forces of nature. Master Chia's method of teaching is direct and practical. Years have been spent developing and perfecting techniques for passing these traditional practices to students around the world. The emphasis is always on mastering the actual practice. The system includes a complete set of practices divided into the Four Branch Healing Arts System of the Universal Tao Center.

Instructor & Practitioner Training - Certification Codes

Next to many of the courses in the System Course Chart and in the Course Description section, you will notice a code letter in parentheses. The code letter indicates that the course is required as part of an Universal Tao instructor and practitioner training. One or more courses may be required for instructor and practitioner certification for the level represented by the letter. A prospective instructor and practitioner must be experienced and competent in the practices taught in the course. An instructor and practitioner candidate must also demonstrate the ability to teach the related contents of the course to the public. For example: Cosmic Inner Smile, Wisdom Chi Kung, Cosmic Six Healing Sounds, Awaken Cosmic Healing Energy (Microcosmic Orbit), World Link Meditation and Chi Self-Massage each have the "(M)" code letter beside it. This means that these courses are part of the Microcosmic Orbit instructor certification. New instructor candidates must be proficient in each of these courses. Previously certified instructor must update their training to include the more recent modifications in the courses offered. The following list shows the codes for Universal Tao instructor and practitioner categories.

Universal Tao Center
Four Branch Healing Arts System
Instructor and Practitioner Certification Key

Living Tao Practices

Level I

AI	Associate Instructor
AT	Simple Tai Chi Chi Kung
C	Certified Instructor:
M	Microcosmic Orbit Set
I1	Iron Shirt Chi Kung I
HL	Healing Love
Y1	Tao Yin 1
CC	Cosmic Cleansing I
TT	Tan Tien Chi Kung
T1	Tai Chi Chi Kung I

Level II

F1	Fusion of Five Elements I
F2	Fusion of Five Elements II
F3	Fusion of Five Elements III
S	Senior Instructor
I2	Iron Shirt Chi Kung II
BM	Bone Marrow Nei Kung
Y2	Pakua Palm Tao Yin II
T2	Tai Chi Chi Kung II

Level III

T3	Tai Chi Chi Kung III (Wu)
T4	Tai Chi Chi Kung Sword
T5	Tai Chi Chi Kung Stick
T6	Tai Chi (36 Movements)
T7	Tai Chi (108 Movements)
G1	Hsing I

Chi Nei Tsang

Level I

C1	Practitioner

Level II

C2	Intermediate Practitioner
C3	Assistant Teacher
CT	Teacher

Level III

ST	Senior Teacher

Cosmic Healing

Level I

H1	Practitioner

Level II

H2	Advanced Practitioner
H3	Assistant Teacher
HT	Teacher

Level III

SH	Senior Teacher

Immortal Tao

Level I

K1	Lesser Kan & Li
K2	Greater Kan & Li
K3	Greatest Kan & Li

Level II

IS	Alchemy Senior Instructor
SF	Sealing of the Five Senses
HE	Congress of Heaven/Earth
HM	Reunion of Heaven/Man

Universal Tao Center
Four Branch Healing Arts Course Chart

Living Tao Practices (Emotional Body)	Chi Nei Tsang (Physical Body)	Cosmic Healing (Energy Body)
Level I	**Level I**	**Level I**
Basic Meditations:	*Internal Organ Massage:*	*Activating Empty Force:*
Cosmic Inner Smile (M)	Chi Nei Tsang I (C1)	Cosmic Chi Kung (H1)
Wisdom Chi Kung (M)	*Basic Chi Kung:*	Six Directions (H1)
Six Healing Sounds (M)	Elixir Chi Kung (C1)	Opening 3 Tan Tiens (H1)
Cosmic Orbit (M)		Cosmic Practitioner (H1)
World Link Meditation (M)	**Level II**	Advanced Practitioner (H2)
Six Directions (M)	*Mastering 12 Winds:*	*Basic Chi Kung:*
Opening 3 Tan Tiens (M)	Chi Nei Tsang II (C2)	Fire Ring Chi Kung (H1)
Chi Self-Massage (M)	*Advanced Chi Kung:*	Pakua Palm I (P1)
Basic Chi Kung:	Sword Finger Kung Fu(C2)	10 Branch (P1)
Simple Chi Kung (A1)		
Cosmic Cleansing (CC)	**Level III**	**Level II**
Iron Shirt Chi Kung I (I1)	*Opening Body Meridians:*	*Connecting the Universe:*
Healing Love (HL)	Chi Nei Tsang III (C3) (ST)	Color Healing (H3)
Tao Yin (Y1)		Assistant Teacher (H3)
Tan Tien Chi Kung (TT)		Cosmic Teacher (HT)
Tai Chi Chi Kung I (T1)		*Advanced Chi Kung:*
		Chi Field Chi Kung (HT)
Level II		Universal Linking (HT)
Advanced Meditations:		Pakua Palm II (P2)
Fusion 5 Elements I (F1)		12 Heavenly Stems (P2)
Fusion 5 Elements II (F2)		
Fusion 5 Elements III (F3)		**Level III**
Advanced Chi Kung:		*Taoist Cosmology:*
Iron Shirt Chi Kung II (I2)		Senior Teacher (SH)
Bone Marrow Nei Kung (BM)		
Pakua Palm Tao Yin (Y2)		
Tai Chi Chi Kung II (T2)		

Immortal Tao (Spirit Body)

Living Tao Practices	Level I	Level II
Level III	*Spiritual Foundation:*	*Realm of Soul and Spirit:*
Advanced Chi Kung Forms:	Lesser Kan & Li (K1)	Sealing 5 Senses (SF)
Tai Chi Chi Kung III (Wu)(T3)	Greater Kan & Li (K2)	Congress Heaven/Earth (HE)
Tai Chi (Sword) (T4)	Greatest Kan & Li (K3)	Reunion Heaven/Man (HM)
Tai Chi (Stick) (T5)		
Tai Chi (36 Movements)(T6)		
Tai Chi (108 Movements) (T7)		
Hsing I (G1)		

Universal Tao Center

Overview of the System and Course Descriptions

Courses are generally taught as part of a retreat, workshop, seminar, or ongoing class. Depending on time constraints, several courses, or fewer, may be offered within the given format.

Following each course description is a list of Universal Tao supporting reference materials that are available. One may order from the Universal Tao Fulfillment Center or from other sources. Beside the name of each item, there are identifying letters and numbers. The letters indicate the kind of item as follows: book (B__), video (V__), cassette (C__), chart (CH__), poster (P__), comic book (CB__), booklet (BL__) and teaching booklet (TB__).

Living Tao Practices - First Branch (Emotional Body)

Level I – Basic Foundation of Universal Tao

1. Basic Sitting Energy-Mastering Meditations (Nei Kung)

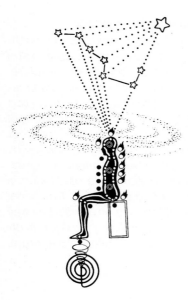

A. Awaken Cosmic Healing Light
(General Retreat – Summer & Winter)

Basic Manual TB-BM $5.95

1) Cosmic Inner Smile (M)

With the advent of the new millenium, the Cosmic Inner Smile serves as a more powerful beginning practice for new students and experienced practitioners alike. In addition to the fundamentals taught previously, one learns to connect the positive virtue energy of the vital organs with corresponding universal energy by using the simple smile that we learned as a baby. This has the effect of increasing our positive power for health, happiness and spiritual evolution.

The Cosmic Inner Smile is a powerful relaxation technique that utilizes the expanding energy of happiness, love and of nature as a language with which to communicate with the internal organs of the body, the 'Second Brain' in the abdomen and the universe. By learning to smile inwardly to the organs and glands, the whole body will feel loved and appreciated. Stress and tension will be counteracted, and the flow of Chi will be increased from within and from the universe. One feels the energy descend down the entire length of the body like a waterfall.

Transform Stress Into Vitality (B03) $11.95

Western medical doctors have only recently discovered the disastrous effects on health of stressful living and their ways of coping with it are still in their infancy. They know nothing of the ancient, successful tradition of the Tao and its long record of transforming stress into vitality and power.

Here, in this book, the Taoist way is set forth and illustrated. The meditation technique of the Inner Smile teaches you how to get in touch with your inner organs, feel love for them and smile to them, so that stress and negative emotions are transformed into creativity, learning, healing and peak performance energy.

Also included is the Taoist way of the Six Healing Sounds, which help to cool down the system, eliminate trapped energy, clean toxins out of the organs and make it possible for the organs to be in peak condition.

Along with these methods, you are taught how to freely circulate your Chi throughout your Microcosmic Orbit. These are the Taoist foundations of true success, power and health.

Cosmic Comics "The Inner Smile" (CB01) $6.95

A lighthearted and humorous look at our world and the teachings of the Taoist sages in a modern context. The inspiration and guidance of the Inner Smile, the energy medicine of the future. Our first theme comic book. The Inner Smile provides explanation and guided instruction for learning to feel the sensation of a smile on your face and then moving that sensation throughout your body – "Smiling" to all of your internal organs and your spine and brain. Smiling in this way is both calming and joyful. This video guides you through an easy twenty-minute progression known as the Inner Smile Meditation. This meditation is part of the ancient and often overlooked science of Traditional Chinese Medicine. The simple act of focusing on a smile this way calms the autonomic nervous system, revitalizing the internal organs by increasing the flow of blood and 'Chi' (life force energy).

Inner Smile (C09) $9.95

Inner Smile (V42) $29.95

This joyful meditation can be learned in a matter of a few days or a few weeks. Healing the internal organs is a necessary first step toward physical health, emotional stability and spiritual unfolding. This tape takes you right into the classroom during an annual summer retreat. You will follow the same step-by-step instruction that the students received at the retreat. This video, shot in a high resolution format, combines rich detail and clear organization. The Inner Smile provides guided instruction for learning to feel the sensation of a smile on your face and then moving that sensation throughout your body – "smiling" to all of your internal organs, your spine and brain. This meditation is part of the ancient and often overlooked science of Traditional Chinese Medicine. The simple act of focusing on a smile this way calms the autonomic nervous system, revitalizing the internal organs by increasing the flow of blood and "Chi" (life force energy).

Chi Cards – Level 1 (CC01) $9.95

The Chi Cards are designed to give short, concise reminders of what to do. Books are reduced to formulas on a few cards. The Universal Tao practices are arranged in Chi Card Levels 1-4. Instead of fumbling through the books when you practice, you can now simply have a Chi Card available to help you complete the formula and proceed smoothly in your practices. You can use the Chi Cards to help clarify, purify, transform, regenerate and transcend your energy, and further discover its relationship to the energy surrounding you. There are twenty cards in a packet (playing card size), which are easy to read and you can carry them anywhere you go. The front side of the card is the actual formula written down step by step and on the reverse side there are visual colored illustrations of the formulas, so you can follow them visually.

Cosmic Inner Smile
Transform Stress into Vitality
Front Line - Functional Channel *(Pg 43)*
1. Be aware of smiling **Cosmic Energy** in front of you: **Breathe it into your Eyes**. Smile **down** to **Nose, Cheeks,** & lift up corners of Mouth (**Tongue to Palate**).
2. Smile in **Neck, Throat, Thyroid, Parathyroid** & **Thymus**.
3. Smile in **Heart** feeling joy & love spread out to the **Lung, Liver, Spleen, Pancreas, Kidneys** & **Genitals**.

Middle Line - Digestive System *(Pg 49)*
1. Bring smiling Energy into Eyes; then Down to Mouth - **Swallow Saliva** smiling down **Stomach, Small Intestine** (Duodenum, Jejunum & Ileum), **Large Intestine** (Ascending - Transverse - Descending), **Rectum** & **Anus**.

Back Line – Governor Channel *(Pg 51)*
1. Smile - Look up into mideyebrow to **Pituitary Gland (3")** **Breathe in** Bright Golden Light shining through Brain.
2. Smile (Spiral) into **Thalamus, Pineal Gland (Crystal Room)**, left & **Right Brain** to **Crown** & **Base of Skull**.
3. Smile **down to each** Vertebrae: 7 Cervicals (Neck), 12 Thoracics (Chest), 5 Lumbar (Lower Back), & Sacrum.

All 3 Lines – Entire Body *(Pg 55)*
1. Smile down **Front, Middle** & **Back Lines**; then **do all simultaneously** feeling like a Cooling Waterfall or Glowing Sunshine of Cosmic Energy, **Smiles, Joy** & **Love**.

Collect Energy in Navel *(Pg 56)*
1. **Smile in Navel** (1") - Spiral with Mind or Hands outwardly **36x** (Diaphragm to Pubic Bone) reverse **24x** back to Navel (**Male** spiral Clockwise to Counter/Clockwise, **Female** reverse) storing the Energy safely in Navel.

CC 1 (1)

(Actual Size)

Chi Card Sets

Level 1 – *Inner Smile, Healing Sounds, Chi Self Massage, Six Direction, Cosmic Orbit, Healing Love, Wisdom Chi Kung, Iron Shirt I.*
Level 2 –*Bone Marrow Nei Kung, Fusion I, Tai Chi I, Heart Chi Kung, Sun & Moon Chi Kung.*
Level 3 – *Fusion II, Cosmic Healing Chi Kung & Chi Nei Tsang, World Link & Tree Chi Kung.*
Level 4 –*Tao Yin, Iron Shirt II, Fusion III, Tan Tien & Simple Chi Kung, Empty Force & Cosmic Cleansing.*

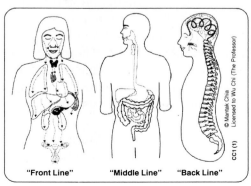

"Front Line"   "Middle Line"   "Back Line"

2) Wisdom Chi Kung (M)

Using the power of the Cosmic Inner Smile, one learns how to rest the brain when it is not needed and to use the Second Brain in the abdomen, which is the seat of awareness. Once the brain in the head comes to rest and is emptied of restless energy, the organs will become filled with Chi. With the power of the Cosmic Inner Smile the organs' Chi will become transformed and full with positive energy. The transformed Chi will then fill the brain with enhanced and purified energy with which to develop the brain and increase the wisdom. Over thousands of years of experimenting with the life force energy, the Taoist sages discovered the power of our inner smile and that energy could be stored in the Tan Tien (abdomen) and the organs, but not in the brain. By emptying the attention of the mind down into the Tan Tien and filling the Tan Tien with chi from the brain, we can activate our inner awareness. Once the brain becomes inactive, the awareness in the abdomen and the consciousness in the heart will be activated. When the mind is empty and the Tan Tien is full we continue the process by emptying the mind down to the specific organs as we smile to them. At the same time we maintain our awareness in the Tan Tien. We charge and fill the brain with the transformed energy of the respective organs. When the brain is filled with this improved Chi, we can open ourselves to the Universal energy.

Wisdom Chi Kung (CH51) $7.50
Use the chart to learn how to rest the brain when not in use, and how to use the second brain which is the seat of awareness.

3) Cosmic Healing Sounds (M)

A basic relaxation and self-healing technique, the Cosmic Healing Sounds meditation utilizes skills developed in the Cosmic Inner Smile. They are used for connecting with the Second Brain and extending the positive chi of the vital organs out to the universe. These skills are combined with simple arm movements and special sounds to produce a cooling, balancing effect on the internal organs and the emotional energy that is stored there. These special sounds vibrate specific organs. The arm movements, combined with posture, guide heat and pressure out of the body.

The results are improved digestion, reduced internal stress, reduced insomnia and headaches, more balance in our emotional energy and a greater vitality. The Chi flow increases through the different organs and the connective tissues surrounding these organs. The Cosmic Healing Sounds method is beneficial to anyone practicing various forms of meditation, martial arts or sports, in which there is a tendency to build up excessive heat in the system.

Transform Stress Into Vitality (B03) $11.95
For Book description, see Overview page 6

Sounds That Heal (V43) $29.95

Sounds that heal presents detailed instruction on the postures, sounds and emotional tunings that constitute the Six Healing Sounds. The Sounds are easy to learn and joyful to practice. They are part of the ancient and often overlooked science of Traditional Chinese Medicine. For centuries they have been used for detoxifying, strengthening, and regenerating the internal organs. The healing of the internal organs has a positive effect on physical health, emotional stability and spiritual unfolding. By using this videotape on a regular basis, in a matter of a few days or a few weeks you will begin to manifest the benefits of the Six Healing Sounds in your body and mind.

Sounds That Heal takes you right into the classroom during an annual summer retreat. You will follow the same step-by-step instruction that the students at the retreat received.

Six Healing Sounds (C10) $9.95

The Six Healing Sounds are a series of simple arm movements and vocalizations, which produce a cooling effect on the internal organs. The six healing sounds are useful in reducing stress, indigestion, insomnia, headaches and fatigue, and are used in conjunction with the Inner Smile and Microcosmic Orbit meditation.

Chi Cards - Level I (CC01) $9.95

4) Awaken Cosmic Healing Light (Microcosmic Orbit) (M)

Opening the Microcosmic Orbit inside you is one of the cornerstones of your Healing Tao practice. An open Microcosmic Orbit enables you to circulate the Chi (life force) through your body and to expand outward to connect with the forces of Nature, the six directions of the Universal energy and with the Earth power. Through unique relaxation and concentration techniques, this practice awakens, circulates, directs, and preserves the generative life-force, or Chi, through the first two major accupuncture channels (or meridians) of the body. The Functional Channel runs down the chest, and the Governor Channel ascends the middle of the back. You will also learn to activate the three internal fires and open the three Tan Tiens.

Basic Manual TB-BM $5.95   Awaken Healing Light (B11) $17.95

Awaken Healing Light of the Tao teaches how; to heal yourself by pulsing Chi through the key points of the body, relax and smile your way to enlightenment with the Cosmic Inner Smile, redirect sexual passion into a loving heart and accelerte your spiritual growth, quickly energize any meditation with Spinal Chi Kung warm-ups, and how to tap the three primordial forces of Earth, Heaven and Higher Self to achieve immortality. This manual shows how to circulate the life-force or Chi in a simple loop up the spine and down the front acupuncture channels of the body. Balancing these yang (male) and yin (female) currents of bio-electrical energy is the most direct path to physical, emotional, mental and spiritual well-being. In this sequel to his widely acclaimed classic, Awaken Healing Energy through the Tao, Taoist Master Mantak Chia reveals the universal system of Taoist mind, body, spirit practices. He shares new methods of activating the life force refined while teaching thousands of Western students over the past decade.

Awaken Healing Light (V61) $59.95
Home Basic Sitting Meditation (V40) $29.95

Through consistent use of this half-hour video, you will begin to experience more vital health, a more balanced emotional life and a deeper feeling of connection with everything around you. Guided sitting meditation is an energy-enhancing half-hour meditation in which you orbit the healing light (your life-force energy or "Chi") up your spine and down the front of your body through specific energy pathways. It is considered to be the foundation of all higher Taoist meditations and practices. This tape guides you in a continuous flow through all the details of the complete Seven Stage Microcosmic Orbit Meditation taught on the Awaken Healing Light, Instruction and Theoretical videos. In the course of the meditation you will activate your internal energy, draw on the energy of the Earth and the "Chi" of the air, harmonize your sexual energy with your heart energy, connect with the energy of the stars and planets, and circulate all this "Chi" through the major energy centers up your spine and down the front of your body. This video, shot in a high resolution format, combines rich detail and clear organization to give you a truly complete experience of the teachings.

Home Basic Standing Meditation (V41) $29.95

Guided Standing Meditation is a full one-hour standing meditation, in which you will orbit the healing light (your life force energy or "Chi") up your spine and down the front of your body through specific energy pathways. It is considered to be the foundation of all higher Taoist meditations and practices. Master Chia guides you through all Seven Stages of the Microcosmic Orbit Meditation, as taught on the Awaken Healing Light Instruction and Theoretical video. In the course of the meditation you will activate your internal energy, draw on the energy of the Earth and the "Chi" of the air. You will harmonize your sexual energy with your heart energy, connect with the energy of the stars and planets, and circulate all this "Chi" through the major energy centers up your spine and down the front of your body. He also incorporates circulation of the sexual energy as taught on the Healing Love video. In the course of the meditation you will use subtle breathing methods, and more powerful internal locking methods to lead the sexual energy up the spine to the brain.

Morning Practice Establishing the Root (V79) $29.95

Body/Mind/Spirit Chart (CH47) $7.50

The Organs and their relationships with the Five Elements, the Six Healing Sounds, the points on the Microcosmic Orbit, Lunar and Solar influences, Centers for higher level practices and the development of the Spirit.

Microcosmic Orbit – Functional Channel (Yin) (P31) $7.50

The Microcosmic Orbit Meditation is the key to circulating internal healing energy, and is the gateway to higher Taoist Mediatations.

Microcosmic Orbit – Governor Channel (Yang) (P32) $7.50

The Governor Channel of the Microcosmic Orbit Meditation allows the Yang (hot) energy to flow from the base of the spine to the brain.

Microcosmic Orbit (C11) $9.95

The Microcosmic Orbit meditation awakens and circulates healing energy, called Chi or Prana, through the primary acupuncture channels of the body. This practice is the ancient foundation for healing and martial arts and is essential for developing increased life force.

Sitting Meditation for Home (C14) $9.95

Through consistent use of this half-hour video, you will begin to experience more vital health, a more balanced emotional life and a deeper feeling of connection with everything around you. Guided sitting meditation is an energy-enhancing meditation in which you orbit the healing light (your life-force energy or "Chi") up your spine and down the front of your body through specific energy pathways. It is considered to be the foundation of all higher Taoist meditations and practices.

Standing Meditation for Home (C15) $9.95

Guided Standing Meditation is a standing meditation, in which you will orbit the healing light (your life force energy or "Chi") up your spine and down the front of your body through specific energy pathways. It is considered to be the foundation of all higher Taoist meditations and practices. Master Chia guides you through all Seven Stages of the Microcosmic Orbit Meditation. In the course of the meditation you will activate your internal energy draw on the energy of the Earth and the "Chi" of the air, harmonize your sexual energy with your heart energy, connect with the energy of the stars and planets, and circulate all this "Chi" through the major energy centers up your spine and down the front of your body. He also incorporates circulation of the sexual energy as taught on the Healing Love video. In the course of the meditation, you will use subtle breathing methods and more powerful internal locking methods to lead the sexual energy up the spine to the brain.

Chi Cards - Level I (CC01) $9.95

5) World Link Meditation (M)

Through the World Link practice you learn to empty the upper brain so your awareness and consciousness can be awakened. You link your own awareness and conscious centers, connect your personal star to other people's stars around the world and join an effort to link with the Universal/Cosmic/God Force. This will create an endless source of Chi that can be used for healing and spiritual development for yourself and others.

The Universe has abundant energy to enhance our life. All that we need to do is to be connected to the source. It helps to understand the principle of fusing the three minds. The first mind is in the brain. The second is called the conscious mind in the heart. The third mind is the awareness mind in the lower abdomen. The three minds combine to fuse together in the abdomen, creating one mind, called 'Yi' in Taoist practices. This World Link Healing Meditation takes around 15 to 30 minutes. When people from all around the world link together at the same time to perform this meditation, the meditation is greatly empowered. This meditation can be practiced easily, even by those who have never worked with the Universal Tao practices.

Times to Link: Thailand 12:00 Noon; New York 12.00 Midnight; Europe 6:00 am. in the Morning. (Find your Time Zone, and it can be one hour before or after these morning and evening times.)

For this meditation we surround ourselves with the Protective Ring, Sacred Circle of Fire and the Golden Dome so that we are protected by the divine love.

The **Sacred Circle of Fire** has the power to protect us from all evil, whether it is sickness, misfortune or negative thinking from those around us. It allows us to connect with the power of the universe. It helps us remove doubts in our own worthiness, so that we might reclaim the best that life has to offer. Additionally, the **Protective Ring** connects us with the elemental essences of Forces in the Universe which both strengthen and protect us.

World Link Meditation Booklet (BL01) $6.95
World Link Meditation booklet, second edition, is a 'how-to-do-it' guide for connecting oneself and others to the power of the Universe. This 32 page booklet crystallizes 'step-by-step' instructions that enable one to create a protective field around themselves and to access healing energy from the universe. It also shows how to link others to this healing energy, how to strengthen the immune system and how to use the universal energy to create a better life for oneself. The instructions are thoroughly supported with color illustrations throughout.

Chi Cards – Level 3 (CC01) $9.95

6) Chi Self-Massage (M)

Chi Self-Massage is a method of hands-on self-healing work using one's internal energy or Chi to strengthen and rejuvenate the sense organs (eyes, ears, nose, tongue), teeth, skin and inner organs. Using internal power (Chi) and gentle external stimulation, this simple yet highly effective self massage technique enables one to dissolve some of the energy blocks and stress points responsible for disease and the aging process. Taoist rejuvenation dates back 5000 years to the Yellow Emperor's classic text on internal medicine.

Chi Self-Massage (B04) $11.95
Virtually all Western style massage is massage primarily of the muscles. Whatever its virtues, Western massage is altogether different from Chi Massage. From ancient times to the present, Taoist Masters have been remarkably youthful, appearing and functioning at least twenty years younger than their actual ages. Tao Rejuvenation employs one's own internal energy, Chi energy, to strengthen and rejuvenate the sense organs – eyes, ears, nose, tongue, teeth and skin – and the inner organs. The techniques used by Taoists are some five thousand years old and, until very recently, were closely guarded secrets passed on from a Master to a small group of students.

Often, too, each Master knew only a small part. Now Master Chia has pieced together the entire system of Chi Massage in a logical sequence in such a way that once you have it shown to you, you need only five or ten minutes of daily practice. In short order you will note improvement in complexion, taste, vision, hearing, sinuses, gums, teeth, tongue, the internal organs and general stamina.

Chi Self-Massage (V52) $ 29.95

Use these simple, highly effective, self-massage techniques to dissolve the energy blocks and stress points that are responsible for disease and the aging process. This form of massage is very different from muscular massage. Chi Self Massage presents a method of hands-on self healing work using your own internal energy, or Chi, to strengthen and rejuvenate your sense organs (eyes, ears, nose, tongue), your teeth, your skin and your inner organs.

Taoist Rejuvenation dates back 5000 years to the Yellow Emperor's classic text on Taoist internal medicine. Master Chia shows you how to use your internal concentration, along with gentle external stimulation, to activate healing energy (your Chi) in whatever area of you body you are working on. Practicing only five to ten minutes a day will improve your complexion, vision, hearing, sinuses, gums, teeth, tongue, internal organs and general stamina.

Chi Cards – Level I (CC01) $9.95

Completion of the Microcosmic Orbit, the Cosmic Inner Smile, the Cosmic Healing Sounds and Chi Self-Massage techniques are prerequisites for any student who intends to study the more advanced practices of the Universal Tao Center.

B. Healing Love, Multi-Orgasmic Energy (HL) (General Retreat – Summer & Winter)

The pillars of Healing Love are cultivating, conserving, transforming and circulating sexual energy. Doing so enables us to use this energy (Ching Chi) for healing and nourishing our body and mind. It is also necessary for our spiritual development in the higher practices of the Taoist internal alchemy.

Although the principle of conservation applies to both men and women, the actual practice of conserving Ching Chi differs. The main way men lose Ching Chi is through ejaculation. Women, by contrast, lose little sexual energy through orgasm, but instead lose it primarily through menstruation and childbearing.

In studying the nature of sex, Taoist masters found a way to control and use sexual energy without celibacy through the practice of Testicle and Ovarian Breathing, Breast Massage, Power Lock and the Orgasmic Upward Draw. Men and women learn to have a total body orgasm without indiscriminate loss of Ching Chi (vital energy). The conservation and transformation of the sexual energy acts as a revitalizing factor in the physical, mental and spiritual development of both women and men. Cultivating, conserving, redirecting and circulation of the generative force from the sexual organs to higher centers of the body invigorates and rejuvenates all the vital functions and activates the higher forces. Mastering these practices produces a deep sense of respect for all forms of life.

Healing Love is one of the main branches of the Universal Tao Center.

Multi-Orgasmic Energy (seminar – European /US Tour)

Healing Love (TB – HL) $5.95

**Taoist Secrets of Love
(Cultivating Male Sexual Energy) (B02) $17.95**

Master Mantak Chia reveals to the general public for the first time, the ancient sexual secrets of the Taoist sages. These secrets enable men to conserve and transform sexual energy through its circulation in the Microcosmic Orbit, invigorating and rejuvenating the body's vital functions. Hidden for centuries, these esoteric techniques and principles make the process of linking sexual energy and transcendent states of consciousness accessible to the reader.
This revolutionary and definitive book teaches:

A. *Higher Taoist practices for alchemical transmutation of body, mind and spirit.*
B. *The secret of achieving and maintaining full sexual potency – The Taoist "Valley Orgasm" Pathway to higher bliss.*
C. *How to conserve and store sperm in the body.*
D. *The exchange and balancing of male and female energies, within the body and with one's partner.*
E. *How this practice can fuel higher achievement in career and sports.*

Healing Love Through the Tao (B06) $15.95

The sexual guidance and exercises presented in this book are being introduced plainly to the Western public for the first time. For thousands of years Taoist masters taught these secrets only to very small numbers of people in the royal courts and in esoteric circles, who were sworn to silence. Now, this young Taoist Master practitioner of this ancient sexology feels the need to share this knowledge with the world. There are two main practices that teach women to cultivate and enhance their sexual energy. One is Ovarian Breathing which can shorten menstruation, reduce cramps and compress more life force energy (Chi) into the ovaries for more sexual power. Another, the Orgasmic Upward Draw can be done solo or with one's sexual partner. When this practice is mastered one can experience a total body orgasm that is beyond ordinary vaginal orgasm, without losing life-force energy. There are two other preparatory exercises taught by  *Mantak Chia. They are a series of exercises with an egg of jade or stone, which is used to strengthen the urogenital and pelvic diaphragm, the glands, tendons and nervous systems. These exercises lend themselves to titters by the uninformed, but in fact have been successfully practiced for thousands of years to enhance the potency and pleasure of the woman fortunate enough to know about them.*

Multi-Orgasmic Man (B13) $15.00

In this book co-written by Master Mantak Chia and Doug Arava, and published by Harper Collins, you'll learn the amazing facts about the multi-orgasmic capabilities of men. By learning to separate orgasm and ejaculation – two distinct physical processes – men can transform a momentary release into countless peaks of whole body orgasms without losing an erection. In addition to becoming better sexual partners, multi-orgasmic men enjoy increased vitality and longevity because they minimize the fatigue and depletion that follow ejaculation.

Multi-Orgasmic Couple $24.00

Every man, every woman and every couple can become multi-orgasmic. Men and women have different sexual energies – and too often this leads to disharmony, preventing us from fully exploring our sexual potential. The Multi-Orgasmic Couple shows how to create the ultimate sexual harmony between partners so you can make your bedroom a place for totally fulfilling passion and intimacy. By harnessing the power of an ancient tradition of sexual wisdom you and your partner can learn to use physical and psychological techniques to experience the bliss of a whole body sexual experience with orgasm after orgasm. Hot sex is here for us all – long-term couples, new partners, young adults and mature lovers. And if you've ever had a sexual problem you can be sure this book will help you to see it in a new light – and deal with it for good. There are no complicated theories – The Multi-Orgasmic Couple is for real couples everywhere. With tips for fine tuning your technique that are guaranteed to drive your partner wild, this is quite simply the best ever straight-talking guide for couples you'll ever read. Published by Harper Collins.

Healing Love Through the Tao (C11A) $9.95

Use your sexual energy to strengthen your body, deepen your spiritual awareness, and experience a new level of sensual pleasure. Healing Love presents Mantak Chia's teachings on cultivating sexual energy for health, spiritual development and sexual and emotional fulfillment.

Taoist Secrets of Love (P36) $7.50

The Taoists teach woman to regulate their menstrual flow and transmute sexual orgasm into higher spiritual love. The techniques of Seminal and Ovarian Kung Fu allow the practitioner to harness sexual impulses so that sex does not control the person. By controlling sexual impulse, people are able to move from the mortal level into higher levels of consciousness.

Healing Love Through the Tao (V63) $59.95

Use your sexual energy to strengthen your body, deepen your spiritual awareness and experience a new level of sensual pleasure. Healing Love presents Mantak Chia's complete teachings on cultivating sexual energy for health, spiritual development and sexual and emotional fulfillment. On these tapes Master Chia guides you through the steps for conserving and transforming your generative force by circulating it from the sexual organs to the higher energy centers via the Microcosmic Orbit. Master Chia teaches you how to circulate the sexual energy without a partner in order to redirect the force back into your body for healing and spiritual development. He also teaches how to deepen your level of orgasm and how to exchange this energy with a partner, for physical, emotional and spiritual balancing.

Chi Cards – Level I (CC01) $9.95

2. Basic Standing & Moving-Energy Mastering Meditations(Chi Kung)

A. *Iron Shirt Chi Kung I (I1)* (General Retreat – Summer & Winter)

The Iron Shirt practice is divided into three parts: Iron Shirt I, II, and III. Iron Shirt Chi Kung is the martial aspect of the Universal Tao System. It develops internal power and structure and a well-conditioned body through simple techniques that build and store Chi. The body becomes open and relaxed. The joints are strengthened, the muscles, tendons and ligaments become soft and strong, and the bones and bone marrow become strong and healthy. Iron Shirt Chi Kung helps us to become rooted to the earth, thereby keeping our body centered and balanced. In the long run, Iron Shirt offers a way of perfecting our inner selves, allowing us to reach higher spiritual levels. The grounding practice provides a firm rooting for the ascension of the spirit.

IRON SHIRT CHI KUNG I
Once a Martial Art, Now the Practice that Strengthens the Internal Organs, Roots Oneself Solidly, and Unifies Physical, Mental and Spiritual Health

MANTAK CHIA

The core of Iron Shirt I consists of the chi packing and breathing process and the Iron Shirt postures. By using certain standing postures, muscle locks and breathing techniques, one learns how to draw and circulate energy from the earth, nature and the universe and how to pack the chi into the vital organs and connective tissues, the spine and the bones. This will strengthen and rejuvenate them, as well as the tendons, muscles, and bone marrow. As the internal structure is strengthened through layers of Chi energy, the problems of poor posture and circulation of energy are corrected. The practitioner learns the importance of being physically and psychologically rooted in the Earth, a vital factor in the more advanced stages of Taoist practice.

Iron Shirt I (TB – IS) $5.95

Iron Shirt Chi Kung I (B05) $15.95

In the days before gunpowder, Iron Shirt Chi Kung was one of the principle martial arts, which built powerful bodies able to withstand hand to hand combat. Even then, however; martial use was only one aspect of Iron Shirt and today, its other aspects remain vitally significant for anyone seeking better health, a sane mind and spiritual growth. "Iron Shirt" refers to the fact that its unique system of breathing exercises which permanently pack concentrated air into the fascia (connective tissues), surrounding the vital organs, make them close to impervious to injuries from accidents or blows. We also learn how to root ourselves in the Earth's power and thus how to direct the Earth's gravitational and healing power through our bone structure. Iron Shirt's strengthening of the organs is of special interest to athletes and performers, for it teaches them how to increase the performance of the organs during sports, speech, singing, dancing and playing music. For the Taoist masters, these practices lay the groundwork for higher spiritual work. Every step of the way is made clear in the numerous line illustrations by Juan Li.

Iron Shirt Chi Kung I (V57) $29.95

The strength and vitality of your internal organs are the real keys to the overall health of your body. In Strengthen Your Internal Organs Master Chia guides you through certain standing postures, muscle locks, and breathing techniques, known as Iron Shirt Chi Kung. These practices direct internal power to the organs, the twelve tendon channels, and the connective tissues. By directing more energy into your internal organs you can perfect your body, increase performance, fight disease, and lay the groundwork for higher spiritual work.

The standing postures teach how to connect the internal structure (bones, muscles, tendons and fasciae) with the earth, so that rooting power is developed. By following along with the detailed instruction that Master Chia presents on this tape, you will learn how to draw and circulate energy from the earth.

Iron Shirt Chi Kung I (C13) $9.95

Using standing postures, muscle locks and breathing techniques, this vigorous Chi Kung (energy mastering exercise) teaches the ability to draw energy from and feel connected – or rooted – to the ground. Over time, Iron Shirt strengthens the tendons, muscles, bones and organs. It aids in achieving increased stamina and developing the body's ability to fight disease and protect the organs from unexpected injury. Recommended prerequisite: Microcosmic Orbit.

Chi Cards – Level I (CC01) $9.95

B. Tao Yin (Y1)

(Tao Yin, Tan Tien Chi Kung and Tai Chi: Combined, Summer Retreat Week)
In the old days when people still lived close to nature, the heat that was released by the body was absorbed by the woods. These days, the artificial environments that we live in don't provide us with this kind of release. Heat is more and more trapped in the body, causing it to overheat and to damage the internal organs. This may cause various diseases including heart attacks.

Tao Yin lying and sitting positions contain a set of postures, breathing exercises, and meditation that are designed to move the excess heat out of the body. They stretch, detoxify and revitalize the muscles and the tendons. While in the relaxation period after the active phase of movement and stretching, we guide the Chi with the breath to that particular part of the body affected by the exercise. This yin phase of the practice expels the heat and opens the muscles, tendons, ligaments and joints that are emphasized in the postures.

In general, the combination of active and passive phases of the practice conditions the spine, tendons, ligaments, muscles and diaphragm in ways that cannot be achieved in standing and moving positions. A balanced session of practice opens chi flow throughout all the meridians, removes toxins and tension throughout the body and engenders a deep sense of relaxed peace and calm – yet wonderfully energized at the same time.

In particular, Tao Yin focuses especially on the Psoas muscle because of its central role in our body. The Psoas muscle connects and moves the hips, spine and legs; all movements of Tai Chi Chi Kung come from the Psoas muscle. The kidneys are connected to the Psoas muscle, and the nerves move it from behind. While doing Tao Yin, one also trains the Second Brain in the abdomen as the control and coordination center of awareness for the body. Practicing Tao Yin is very helpful for the practice of Iron Shirt and of Tai Chi Chi Kung.

Tao Yin (B07) $17.95

The Tao Yin exercises included in this book are all performed in either lying or sitting positions. They provide unique benefits that cannot be so readily achieved in standing or moving practices, such as Iron Shirt Chi Kung or Tai Chi. Improved patterns of physical alignment and movement will recondition the spine and refresh the body by opening chi flow in the meridians. Tendons and psoas muscles will be imbued with the power of elasticity, and the spine becomes more flexible. Employing the dynamic principle of 'finding the straight in the curve' enables the practitioner to grow and strengthen the tendons and to cultivate their elasticity.

Tao Yin exercises are moving meditations. Using the inner smile, one trains the feeling and awareness brain, the Second Brain in the abdomen, to coordinate and direct the actions in the body. They integrate the subtle power of the breath and mind in the process. The practitioner learns to train and develop 'Yi,' the mind-eye-heart power. The practice cultivates gentleness while developing strength. One learns to breathe consciously with the light in order to release tensions and toxins and to energize tired or weak areas during rest between exercises. A balanced Tao Yin session ends with 'Yin Meditation.' With the body deeply relaxed, the mind calm, the tan tien full of Chi and Chi flowing in the meridians – one might experience the fullness of delightful yang 'cell massage' or the refined yin state of inner 'embryonic breathing.' This foundation practice supports all other practices.

Chi Cards – Level 4 (CC04) $9.95

Tao Yin (V69) $59.95

Tao Yin exercises help your internal life force (Chi), to circulate more freely, for the purpose of refreshing, attuning, adjusting and regenerating your personal energy. All the Tao Yin movements are based on ancient spiritual development. Through the gradual process of Taoist Chi cultivation, the physical energy of the body is transformed into spiritual energy. Tao Yin contains a wide variety of movements from many systems. An important aspect of Tao Yin is that it has alternating phases of activity and relaxation. During the relaxation phase you will learn to feel & gently guide the Chi flow to specific areas of your body. You will learn to absorb the nutrition from the air & the surrounding energy so you can open each cell to the fresh vitality of the universal force. This practice will help you relieve any energy stagnancy. Master Chia demonstrates the exercises.

Advanced Empty Force Tao Yin (V72) $29.95

This set of Empty Force Tao Yin has been regarded as very secretive. The practice is intended to cool the body down after long meditation and to ignite the internal fire. The knees, joints, spine and neck can become very stiff especially when the meditator leaves the body for extended periods. If practiced every day, this set will activate all the glands and the five major systems of the body; energy meridians, glands/organs, tendons/fascia, blood/lymph and bones/nerves. Each is comprised of one yin and one yang part.

Breathing is a very important part of this practice. There is both a yin and a yang pattern. One is used for tonifying the body and the other for cooling. Both rely on the Empty Force inside. For each position, be sure to hold the Empty Force breath for a moment and then release. Later on you will learn how to direct and vibrate the energy in a special channel. It is very important to practice this together with Jin Suei (Water of Life). This will help to cool you down. These two techniques alone can give you the perfect physical body and stop the aging process.

C. Internal Power & Internal Gym.

The Internal Gym along with Tao Yin and Tan Tien Chi Kung helps to improve the practices of Iron Shirt and Tai Chi Chi Kung. It helps to open the body to the flow of energy and to strengthen the muscles and the internal power. In performing the exercises we make use of our internal structure, Tan Tien power and the breath to work smoothly and gently, with amazing results of increased health and vitality.

D. Tan Tien Chi Kung (TT)

Tan Tien Chi Kung consists of specific breathing and animal exercises. It is one of the Taoist practices used to develop the power of the Tan Tien and the Perineum. We have a constant air pressure in our body that we call Chi pressure. In the Tan Tien Chi Kung we learn to develop and enhance this Chi pressure. We can actually increase our vitality, strengthen our organs and promote self- healing by increasing the Chi pressure in the organs and body cavity. The circulatory system, the lymphatic system, the nervous system and the endocrine system will be activated and Chi and blood will flow more easily through the body. It is also the Chi pressure (Internal Power) in the Tan Tien that roots our body and mind. It is like an electric wire in the earth. Tan Tien Chi Kung is therefore very important for our Iron Shirt and Tai Chi Chi Kung and even for the sitting meditation practices.

TB-TT $5.95

3. Cosmic Cleansing

Every day our bodies are affected by environmental pollution, improper diet or eating habits, medication, substance abuse and stress. Our body is the house in which we live. The kind and the quality of the food we put into our body is of vital importance to every phase of our existence. Good nutrition not only regenerates and rebuilds the cells and tissues which constitute our physical body, but is also involved in the processes by which the waste matter, the undigested food, is eliminated from our body to prevent corruption in the form of fermentation and putrefaction. When the mineral elements which compose the foods we eat are saturated with oil or grease, the digestive organs cannot process them efficiently and they are passed out of the small intestine into the colon as debris. When "demagnetized" food passes through the body system with little or no benefit, these foods leave a coating of slime on the inner walls of the colon like plaster on a wall. In the course of time this coating may gradually increase its thickness until there is only a small hole through the center, and the matter slowly passes through containing much undigested food from which the body derives no benefit. The consequent result is a starvation of which we are not conscious but that causes old age and senility. This detoxification program is designed to cleanse all the eliminative organs in a systematic way, helping the body to effectively rid itself of these toxic substances and recover vibrant health. We take our detoxification program step by step until at last the all-important lymphatic system is cleansed and your body is rid of toxins on a cellular level. Cosmic Cleansing (Summer & Winter Retreat)

Chi Cards – Level 4 (CC04) $9.95

Level II – Internal Practice

1. Advanced Sitting Meditations – Beginning Internal Alchemy
Fusion of the Five Elements

The Fusion of the Five Elements is the second level of UTC internal Alchemy meditation. The concept of Internal Alchemy is grounded in the Taoist belief that the inner Universe is identical to the outer Universe. They share the same "cosmology." The knowledge of the Internal Alchemy is a necessary step in becoming connected to the outer universe, from which an unlimited power can be derived for one's individual benefit. The Taoist Masters reasoned that to become connected to the outer universe, one needs first to gain control of his or her own inner universe. The Fusion of the Five Elements practice is a big step in this direction. One begins with the understanding of the dynamics of the universe, the planet Earth, and the human body with respect to their relationship to the Five Agents of Nature (or Energy Phases) and the Eight Forces of Nature. In our inner universe, our organs correspond with these Five Phases of Energy in three distinct ways: controlling, creating and balancing. The Fusion practice combines the energies of the Five Phases of Energy into one harmonious whole. Fusion I, II, III, (Combined course, Summer & Winter retreat)

A. Fusion of the Five Elements I (F1)

Fusion I uses pakuas to call forth and connect with the five energies and eight forces of nature for protection, to enhance one's energy and to increase the mind power. The pakuas are energetic figures controlled by the mind to guide energy. In this practice of internal alchemy, the student also learns to transform the negative emotions of worry, sadness, cruelty, anger, and fear into pure energy. This process is accomplished by identifying the source of the negative emotions within the five organs of the body. After the excessive energy of the emotions is filtered out of the organs, the state of psycho-physical balance is restored to the body. Freed of negative emotions, the pure energy of the five organs is crystallized into a radiant pearl or crystal ball. The pearl is then circulated in the body and attracts energy from external sources – Universal Energy, Cosmic Particle Energy and Earth Energy. The pearl plays a central role in the development and nourishment of the soul or energy body. The energy body is then nourished with the pure (virtue) energy of the five organs.

Fusion of the Five Elements I: Basic Practice (TB-F1) $5.95

Fusion of the Five Elements I (B09) $13.95

Fusion of the Five Elements I is the first level of meditation in a Taoist practice also known as Fusion of the Five Forces in the Universe. It is the beginning of Inner Alchemy, a scientific process by which you gain control over the energies of your inner Universe so that a connection can be made to the tremendous energy of the Universe beyond the body. This energy becomes useful for self-healing, day-to-day living, and reaching spiritual goals.

Fusion I meditation is the first step in learning to control the generation and flow of emotional, mental, and physical energies within your body. The practice teaches you how to locate and dissolve the negative energies hidden inside your body. Using the Taoist Five Element Theory, a connection is made between the five outer senses—eyes, tongue, mouth, nose, ears—and the five major emotions — anger, hate, worry, sadness, and fear. Once the negative emotion is identified with the organ in which it is stored in, it can be controlled.

Fusion I meditation shows you step by step how the negative emotions are removed from the organs. Negative emotions are neither suppressed nor expressed. Instead, their negative energy is brought to specific points in the body where it is easily neutralized, purified, and then transformed back into your original positive, creative energy.

The great secret of crystallizing and storing your original positive energy in a mysterious pearl, is revealed for the first time in the Fusion alchemical formula. This pearl is the essence of our life force energy, or Chi. It is central to nourishing the physical body, and later to nourishing the soul, or energy body. In more advanced Fusion practices, your soul/energy body becomes very controllable and its power can be balanced, strengthened, and expanded to connect with the essence of the Earth and Star energies.

The Fusion of the Five Elements I practice is the essential first step toward complete emotional and spiritual development. In this useful and informative work, Master Mantak Chia leads you step by step to becoming an emotionally balanced, controlled, and strong individual, while offering you the key to an immortal existence.

Fusion of the Five Elements I (V64) $59.95

Transform Negative Emotions continues the process of physical and psychological self-healing that was begun in the Microcosmic Orbit and Inner Smile meditations. On this two tape set Master Chia will present the theory and explanation of the Taoist meditation known as the Fusion of Five Elements, Level II. Then he will guide you through the Five Formulas that rebalance negative emotions to become pure, unblocked life force energy.

Much of our life force energy is chronically trapped inside our internal organs and causes us to experience anger, worry, sadness, fear, and cruelty. In Taoist practice, using images from nature, these emotional energies are expressed as extreme weather conditions – hot, cold, wet, dry and damp. Fusing these imbalanced energies together in one place creates a state of "ideal weather" within your body—giving you access to a very focused, pure and dynamic source of energy within yourself.

Pakua (P42) $7.50

Ancient Taoist symbol of integration of the Eight forces and the Five Phases of Energy in the Tai Chi. A powerful image used for self-cultivation and protection.

Fusion of the Five Elements I: (P37)

Each organ stores a separate emotional energy. When fused into a single balanced Chi at the navel, the opening of the six special channels becomes possible.

Fusion of the Five Elements I (C16) $9.95

This meditation cleans out negative emotions by balancing and rechanneling emotional energy. You will learn how the five elements with their corresponding seasons, senses, organs, emotions and colors can be experienced, fused, harmonized and then circulated through the Microcosmic Orbit. The effect is to continue the process of physical and psychological self-healing which characterized the early stages of the Taoist meditation system. Recommended prerequisite: Microcosmic Orbit. **Chi Cards – Level 2 (CC02) $9.95**

B. Fusion of the Five Elements II (F2)

The second level of Fusion practice teaches additional methods of circulating the pure energy of the five organs once they are freed of negative emotions. When the five organs are cleansed, the positive emotions of kindness, gentleness, respect, fairness, justice and love are combined into compassion energy that emerges as a natural expression of internal balance. The practitioner is able to monitor his/her state of balance by observing the quality of emotions arising spontaneously within. The energy of the positive emotions is used to open the three channels running from the perineum, at the base of the sexual organs, to the top of the head. These channels collectively are known as the Thrusting Channels or Routes. In addition, a series of nine levels called the Belt Channels is opened, encircling the nine major energy centers of the body.

Fusion of the Five Elements II (TB-F2) $5.95

Fusion of the Five Elements II (C17) $9.95

This meditation formula focuses on generating spiritual values, opening the eight special channels, and balancing and controlling the increased energy that accompanies the work on this level. The first of these channels is the Belt Route which spirals around the whole body, strengthening the auric field and provides a form of psychic self-defense. The second is the Thrusting Route which runs through the center of the body, linking the "Chakra" centers and connecting the body between Earth and Heaven. Recommended prerequisite: Fusion of Five Elements I.

Fusion of the Five Elements II (V65) $59.95

Feelings of love, kindness, gentleness and courage can be consciously cultivated in your body. Cultivate Healing Emotions presents the complete teaching of the Taoist meditation, which is known as the Fusion of Five Elements, Level Two. On this two tape set Master Mantak Chia will present the theory of the Fusion II meditation as well as an explanation of the practice. Then he will guide you through the Five Formulas that multiply healing emotional energy in your organs and circulate it through new energy pathways.

By following the guided meditations on these tapes, you will learn to move the "pearl of radiant energy" (created in Fusion I) through your internal organs, one by one, multiplying the natural virtues that reside there. With this vital energy you can open the Thrusting Route, which runs through the center of the body linking the "Chakras", and open the Belt Route, which spirals around your whole body, strengthening your auric field and providing a form of psychic protection.

Fusion II (P38, 39, 40, 43, 44) $7.50

(P38) Fusion of the Five Elements II—*Enhancing and Strengthening the Virtues. Fusion of the Five Elements II strengthens positive emotions, balances the organs,and encourages in men and women the natural virtues of gentleness, kindness, respect, honor and righteousness.*

(P39) Fusion of the Five Elements II—*Thrusting Channels. Running through the center of the body, the Thrusting Routes allow the absorption of cosmic energies for greater radiance and power.*

(P40) Fusion of the Five Elements II—Nine Belt Channel. *The Taoist Belt Channel spins a web of Chi around the major energy vortexes in the body, protecting the psyche by connecting the power of Heaven and Earth.*

(P43) Fusion of the Five Elements III—Yin Bridge and Regulator Channels. *Fusion of the Five Elements III uses special meridians to cleanse the aura and regulate high-voltage energy absorbed during the meditation.*

(P44) Fusion of the Five Elements III—Yang Bridge and Regulator Channels. *Fusion of the Five Elements III teaches the yogic secrets of safely regulating the release of the kundalini energy using special meridians.*

Chi Cards – Level 3 (CC03) $9.95

C. Fusion of the Five Elements III (F3)

The third level of Fusion practice completes the cleansing of the energy channels in the body by opening the Bridge and Regulator channels. You also learn in this level to build some extra psychic protection, You learn techniques to drive out negative energy entities that attach to the spine and other areas. There are specialized practices to protect the spine and to clear the brain. The opening of the Microcosmic Orbit, the Thrusting Channels, the Belt Channel, the Great Regulator, and Great Bridge Channels makes the body extremely permeable to the circulation of vital energy. The unhindered circulation of energy is the foundation of perfect physical and emotional health. The Fusion practice is one of the greatest achievements of the ancient Taoist masters, as it gives the individual a way of freeing the body of negative emotions and, at the same time, allows the pure virtues to shine forth.

Fusion of the Five Elements III (TB – F3)

Fusion of the Five Elements III (V66) $59.95

Free flowing circulation of energy is the foundation of physical and emotional health. Open Psychic Energy Channels presents the complete teaching of the Taoist meditation known as Fusion of Five Elements, Level Three. On this two tape set Master Mantak Chia will present theory of the Fusion III meditation as well as an explanation of the practice. Then he will guide you through the three Formulas that open energy routes throughout your body, making your whole body extremely permeable to the circulation of vital "Chi".

In this meditation you will use the "pearl of compassionate energy" and use it (formed in Fusion II) to open the Great Bridge and Regulator channels in your body. These four channels, combined with the Microcosmic Orbit, the Thrusting Route and the Belt Route comprise the eight special or "psychic" meridians that channel the basic constitutional energy of your body and create a personal psychic protection.

Fusion of the Five Elements III (C18) $9.95

This tape completes the Fusion formulas as you continue to "wire" the body and clean the aura through the system of eight special or "psychic" channels. This process began with the Microcosmic Orbit and now includes the positive and negative arm and leg meridians, various spiral routes and numerous combinations of energy pathways and grids. Recommended prerequisite: Fusion of Five Elements II.

Chi Cards - Level 4 (CC04) $9.95

2. Advanced Standing and Moving Meditations

Level I – Developing Internal Power

A. Tai Chi Chi Kung I (T1)

(Tao Yin, Tan Tien Chi Kung and Tai Chi: Combined, Summer Retreat Week)
Tai Chi Chi Kung consists of thirteen movements which are performed in all the four directions, clockwise and counterclockwise. Tai Chi Chi Kung is comprised of four parts:

1. Mind:
   a) How to use one's own mass together with the force of gravity;
   b) How to use the bone structure to move the whole body with very little muscular effort;
   c) How to learn and master the thirteen movements so that the mind can concentrate on directing the Chi energy.
2. Mind and Chi: How to use the mind to direct the Chi flow.
3. Mind, Chi, and Earth force: How to integrate the three forces into one unit moving unimpeded through the bone structure.
4. Learn applications of Tai Chi for self-defense.

In the practice of Tai Chi Chi Kung, the increased energy flow developed through the Microcosmic Orbit, Fusion work, Iron Shirt, Tao Yin and Tan Tien Chi Kung practices are integrated into one unified movement, so that the body learns more efficient ways of utilizing energy in motion. Improper body movements restrict energy flow causing energy blockages, poor posture and, in some cases, serious illness. Quite often, back problems are the result of improper posture, accumulated tension, weakened bone structure and psychological stress. One result of increased body awareness through movement is an increased awareness of one's environment and the potentials it contains. Since Tai Chi is a gentle way of exercising and keeping the body fit, it can be practiced well into advanced age because the movements do not strain one's physical capacity as some aerobic exercises do.

Before beginning to study the Tai Chi Chi Kung I form, the student must complete: (1) Opening of the Microcosmic Orbit, (2) Iron Shirt Chi Kung I, and (3) Seminal and Ovarian Kung Fu. Tai Chi Chi Kung I, Tan Tien Chi Kung and Tao Yin are combined in one week of summer retreat.

Inner Structure of Tai Chi: Tai Chi Chi Kung I (B12) $15.95

This book is designed for Tai Chi practitioners of all levels. This book strips away the unnecessary mystery surrounding Tai Chi. Taoist Master Mantak Chia and Juan Li demonstrate with the help of hundreds of drawings and detailed illustrations, the relationship of the inner structure of Tai Chi to the absorption, transformation, and circulation of the Three Forces, or energies – the Universal Force, the Cosmic Force and the Earth Force – that enliven us. The inner structure of Tai Chi is an indispensable resource for anyone who now practices or wants to learn a form of Tai Chi.

Tai Chi Chi Kung I (V50) $59.95

On this tape Master Chia will guide you through a Tai Chi form that is short, simple and easy to learn. Within this simple form Master Chia reveals the real treasure of Tai Chi: the energetic movement that comprises the inner structure. Through the regular practice of Tai Chi you can learn to move your body effortlessly, utilizing energy, or Chi, rather than muscle tension. By feeling the circulation of Chi through the acupuncture channels, muscles and tendons, your body learns more efficient ways of utilizing energy in motion.

The Inner Structure of Tai Chi presents the Nine Levels of Tai Chi Chi Kung, including: Yin & Yang Form, Rootedness Form, Spinal Cord Chi Transfer Form, Changing the Tendons Form, Tan Tien Chi Form, Organ Healing Form, Skin Breathing & Bone Marrow Form, Inner Structure and Applications, and the Combined Form.

Tai Chi Chi Kung I (TB-TC)   **Tan Tien Chi Kung (TB-TT)**

Tai Chi Chi Kung I (C12) $9.95   **Chi Cards – Level 2 (CC02) $9.95**

B. Iron Shirt II (I2)

In the second level of Iron Shirt, one learns how to combine the mind, heart, bone structure and Chi into one moving unit. The static forms learned in the first level of Iron Shirt evolve at this level into moving postures. The goal of Iron Shirt II is to develop rooting and internal power and the ability to absorb and discharge energy through the tendons. A series of exercises allow the student to change, grow and strengthen the tendons and joints, to stimulate the vital organs and to integrate the fascia, tendons, bones and muscles into one structure. The student also learns methods for releasing accumulated toxins in the muscles and joints of the body. Once energy flows freely through the muscles and joints, accumulated toxins can be discharged out of the body very efficiently without resorting to extreme fasts or special dietary aids. Iron Shirt I is a prerequisite for this course.

Iron Shirt II (V59) $59.95

You can actually grow your tendons, making them supple and elastic like a child's. Your joints can open and become free passageways for the "Chi" life force energy to circulate through your body. The key to these changes is the use of slow, gentle movements that activate the tendons, followed by quiet meditation that directs the internal energy. Enliven Your Joints and Tendons presents exercises to train you to combine the mind, heart, bone structure and Chi flow into one moving unit.

In Enliven Your Joints and Tendons, Master Chia leads you through a set of moving postures that evolve out of the static forms learned in the first level of Iron Shirt Chi Kung. You will learn these postures as individual exercises and as partner exercises. You will also learn how to absorb and discharge energy through your tendons. Also, Master Chia teaches the use of a Mung bean filled cloth hitter that will release accumulated toxins in your joints and muscles.

C. Bone Marrow Nei Kung (Iron Shirt III) (BM)

In the third level of Iron Shirt, one learns how to strengthen the bones by increasing bone density and structure & to regrow the marrow through bone breathing and internal sexual organ massage. One also learns how to direct internal power to the higher centers. This level of Iron Shirt works directly on the organs, bones and tendons in order to strengthen the entire system beyond its ordinary capacity. An extremely efficient method of vibrating the internal organs allows the practitioner to shake toxic deposits out of the inner structure of each organ by enhancing Chi circulation. This was once a highly secretive method of advanced Iron Shirt, also known as the Golden Bell System.

Prerequisites: Iron Shirt Chi Kung I and Healing Love.

Bone Marrow Nei Kung (B08) $15.95

Bone Marrow Nei Kung is a system of health developed by the ancient Taoist masters for the cultivation of internal power. They discovered that, through the process of absorbing energy into the bones, bone marrow can be revitalized to replenish the blood and nourish the life force within. Many healers have sought these methods which are known to make the body impervious to illness and disease. In ancient times, the "Steel Body", attained through this practice was a coveted asset in the fields of Chinese medicine and martial arts.

Today, the copious health benefits of this art are sought after by health enthusiasts from all walks of life. The Taoist methods of "regrowing" the bone marrow are crucial in the rejuvenation of the body, which in turn rejuvenates the mind and spirit. These secrets have never before been revealed but now their disclosure is necessary to instill the sensibilities of the masters into an energy deficient society. In this book, Master Mantak Chia divulges the step by step practices of his predecessors in a useful and informative work, written for the health and spiritual well-being of today's world.

Chi Cards – Level 2 (CC02) $9.95

Bone Marrow Nei Kung (V58) $59.95

You can revitalize you bone marrow, replenish your blood, and strengthen your bones through the simple process of absorbing energy into your bones. In Revitalize Your Bone Marrow Master Chia presents the practice of Bone Marrow Nei Kung, a system for cultivating internal power. In this third level of Iron Shirt Chi Kung you will learn to cleanse and purify the Chi life force energy in your bones and organs so that they resist aging and disease. On this tape you will learn methods for leading the energy produced in your sexual organs into your bones and up to higher energy centers. You will also learn an extremely efficient method of vibrating your internal organs to shake toxic deposits out of the inner structure of each organ. These methods are crucial to rejuvenating your body, which in turn rejuvenates your mind & spirit. Revitalize Your Bone Marrow takes you right into the classroom during an annual summer retreat. You will follow the same step by step instruction that students at the retreat received. (2 tapes)

D. Tai Chi Chi Kung II (T2)

Tai Chi Chi Kung II is the higher level of moving meditation using the Discharge technique to absorb and transmit the Universal and Earth Forces. The practice consists of the 13 movements performed clockwise & counterclockwise, as in Tai Chi Chi Kung I, with Push Hands applications. This discipline improves postural alignment and body and mind coordination with self-defense applications.

Tai Chi Chi Kung II (V51) $59.95

Through the regular practice of Tai Chi you can learn to move your body effortlessly, utilizing Chi, rather than muscle tension. With the Inner Structure of Tai Chi II you will learn a fast discharge form of Tai Chi. The Tai Chi form Master Chia will guide you through on these tapes is very short and simple, and is easy to learn. Within this simple form Master Chia reveals the real treasure of Tai Chi: the energetic movement that comprises the inner structure. In these tapes you will learn how to move fast in the five directions. You will learn how to move the entire body structure as one piece. And you will learn how to discharge the energy from the Earth through the body structure. Also, on these tapes Master Chia shows Single and Double Push Hands. He shows the energetic quality of the different directions of force, and he demonstates the self defense applications.

E. Pakua Palm Tao Yin (Y2)

F. Senior Instructor (S)
Certification Requirements:
1) 8 years of practice in the Living Tao Practices
2) Certified in Iron Shirt Chi Kung I, Healing Love, Fusion of the Five Elements I, II, III and Tai Chi Chi Kung I
3) Approved by other Senior Instructors

Level II – Advanced Internal and Discharge Power

A. Tai Chi Chi Kung III – Wu Style (T3)

Tai Chi Wu Style is the advanced level moving meditation using twisting and leaning techniques to open the kua and sacrum for transferring the Cosmic Forces. The practice consists of eight movements performed in the Eight Directions, connecting with the Eight Forces. This discipline balances the hip and sacral alignment, opens the Tan Tien and Kidney fires, and coordinates body and mind movement with self-defense applications.

B. Tai Chi Chi Kung IV (Sword) (T4)

C. Tai Chi Chi Kung V (Stick) (T5)

D. Tai Chi Chi Kung VI (36 Movements) (T6)

E. Tai Chi Chi Kung VII (108 Movements) (T7)

F. Hsing I (G1)

Chi Nei Tsang - Second Branch (Physical Body)

Level I

A. Chi Nei Tsang I (C1)

The practice is divided into three parts: Chi Nei Tsang I, II, and III. Chi Nei Tsang, or Organ Chi Transformation Massage, is an entire system of Chinese deep healing that works with the energy flow of the five major systems in the body: the cardiovascular system, the lymphatic system, the nervous system, the tendon/muscle system, and the acupuncture meridian system.

In the Chi Nei Tsang practice, one is able to increase energy flow to specific organs through massaging a series of points in the navel area. In Taoist practice, it is believed that all the Chi energy of the organs, glands, brain, and nervous system are joined in the navel; therefore, energy blockages in the navel area often manifest as symptoms in other parts of the body. The abdominal cavity contains the large intestine, small intestine, liver, gall bladder, stomach, spleen, pancreas, bladder and sexual organs, as well as many lymph nodes. The aorta and vena cava divide into two branches at the navel area, descending into the legs. Chi Nei Tsang works on the energy blockages in the navel and then follows the energy into the other parts of the body. Chi Nei Tsang also prepares the body to receive the higher frequencies of the spiritual energy.

In Chi Nei Tsang I one studies specific techniques of abdominal and organ massage that can release and clear blockages, toxins, excessive heat and negative emotions. Prerequisite: Microcosmic Orbit.

Chi Nei Tsang (B10) $17.95

Chi Nei Tsang presents a whole new understanding and approach to healing with detailed explanations of self-healing techniques and methods of teaching others to heal themselves. This book presents many hands-on techniques for detoxifying and rejuvenating the vital organs. Chi Nei Tsang is full of new ideas and ancient healing techniques gathered from thousands of years of experience. The art evolved in an era when there were few physicians and people had to know how to heal themselves. For many today, the situation remains the same. Chi Nei Tsang teaches people how to take full charge of their health and well being. The first known techniques that could be applied to the navel's center. The navel's center is where negative emotions, stress, tension, and sickness accumulate and congest. When this occurs, all vital functions stagnate. Using Chi Nei Tsang techniques in and around the area of the navel provides the fastest method of healing and the most permanent results. Many techniques of other systems only work at the body's extremities, far from the navel's center and the organs. The Chi Nei Tsang techniques taught in this book can be applied to the abdominal center where the Universal, Cosmic and Earthly Forces are combined and stored.

Chi Nei Tsang (V67) $59.95

Chi Nei Tsang: Internal Organs Massage presents a whole new approach to healing that teaches you how to heal yourself and how to facilitate the healing of others through their own efforts. Chi Nei Tsang teaches you how to take full charge of your health and well-being. From this tape you will learn techniques for massaging all of the internal organs as well as the skin, the circulatory system, the lymphatic system and the reproductive system. The technique of Chi Nei Tsang is to massage directly into the navel center and the surrounding abdominal area. In the navel center, stress, tension, and negative emotions accumulate and congest. When this occurs, all vital functions stagnate. This stagnation slowly weakens the internal organs and decreases your energy and vitality. Chi Nei Tsang massage quickly releases the negative emotions, tensions and sickness, bringing comfort and relief to the abdomen and vital energy to the internal organs.

Chi Nei Tsang's Healing Power (V68) $29.95

On this tape Master Mantak Chia shows you how to work with the energy of trees, both to ground toxic energy and to accumulate healing energy. He also shows you how to use self massage to heal yourself and how to cultivate internal energy to protect yourself while doing Chi Nei Tsang massage. Chi Nei Tsang's Healing Power Practice presents important techniques for developing your internal energy in order to be more effective in doing Chi Nei Tsang massage.

The technique of Chi Nei Tsang is to massage directly into the navel center and the surrounding abdominal area. In the navel center, stress, tension, and negative emotions accumulate and congest. When this occurs, all vital functions stagnate. Chi Nei Tsang massage quickly releases the negative emotions, tensions and sickness, bringing comfort and relief to the abdomen and vital energy to the internal organs.

Chi Cards – Level 3 (CC03) $9.95

B. Golden Elixir Chi Kung (Five Finger Kung Fu)

This consists of 11 postures; nine of these involve gathering the forces through the saliva. The remaining two are tendon stretching and strengthening exercises.

Chi Nei Tsang I (Summer Retreat)

Level II - Chi Nei Tsang II (C2)

Chi Nei Tsang II (B14) $16.95

Chi Nei Tsang II works primarily with the trapped winds of the body that become sick or evil winds which can lead to (for example) a heart attack, if not released. The students will learn the Ten Different Winds, and how to chase and discharge them out of the body and to inject good Chi back into the vital organs and glands.

Chi Nei Tsang II & III $16.95

Level III - Chi Nei Tsang III (C3) (CT) (ST)

Chi Nei Tsang III uses the One Finger Technique working primarily with the Left side of the navel (Left Hand) and moving up the Spine (Right Hand) releasing any blockages or tension of the nerves and tendons, moving up into the heart, neck & head. The students will learn how to loosen the nervous system through the sacrum, legs and arms; and how to open up the nerve endings filling them with revitalized Chi.

Senior Teacher (ST)
Certification Requirements:
1) 2 years of teaching as a Chi Nei Tsang Teacher (CT)
2) 200 Case Studies: 40 Students per 5 Sessions each or 240 Sessions with no more than 80 Students
3) Evaluated in Theory & Practice and approved by Chi Nei Tsang Committee with 2 Chi Nei Tsang Senior Teachers

Chi Nei Tsang II & III (Combined Summer Retreat)

Cosmic Healing - Third Branch - Energy Body

Level I

1. Cosmic Healing

Taoists believe in the underlying unity that permeates the Universe. Cosmic Healing is a Chi Kung meditation that strengthens and opens us up to the forces and Energy within Nature and the Universe. We are dynamically connected to the infinite. "As above, so below," is an echo of wisdom heard from sages and mystics from all ages. When we can channel the energy that surrounds us, the pathway reveals the many splendors of the Cosmos. We are a reflection of the light and energy in the Universe, drawing in the life force of the sun in the air we breathe, the food we eat and through all of our senses. We exist because of the unique combination of forces that surround us. By tapping into our internal resources and channeling the energy around us, we can perceive much more than the senses normally report to the mind.

This course teaches a hands-on technique using acupuncture points on the hand, such as the palm, to activate and open acupuncture meridians throughout the body. Through Cosmic Chi Kung, the practitioner learns to channel external forces such as cosmic energy and energy around us through the palms for healing. The energy being channeled can be used to heal oneself as well as others. Cosmic Chi Kung integrates both static and dynamic exercise forms in order to cultivate, channel and mix the cosmic force with the saliva to nourish Chi, and to direct it to the hands and fingers for healing and creativity. Practitioners of body centered therapies and massage systems will greatly benefit from this method. Prerequisite: Microcosmic Orbit.

A. Cosmic Chi Kung (Buddha Palm) (H1)

Cosmic Healing Chi Kung I is the ability to absorb and transmit Chi with your hands using Bone Marrow Washing, Earth & Heaven Channeling, Tiger Mouth and Open Index Finger techniques. The students learn to activate the Bridge, Regulator & Functional Channels using the Beaming & Cosmic absorbing techniques of the Six Directions.

Cosmic Healing I: Cosmic Chi Kung (B16) $19.95

This healing technique uses Cosmic Chi Kung postures and movements to absord Chi from Nature's Cosmic and Universal Forces. The student will develop the Cosmic Chi Kung (Buddha Palm) practices to heal themselves and others. This is a practical guide using Empty Force Chi Kung, meditation and color to effect the student's continuing self-healing. The student will learn to connect with the Six Directions and the Galaxies, to draw these energies down for their self-healing. The students will also learn how to reach out into the Universe and bring down these life giving forces directly to others.

Cosmic Healing (Summer Retreat)
Healing Energy Seminar (Europe/North America)

Chi Cards – Level 4 (CC04) $9.95

Cosmic Healing Chi Kung – Channeling Cosmic Energy (V60) $29.95

Cosmic Healing Chi Kung presents an elegant set of slow, Tai Chi-like movements of the arms and hands that cultivates and channels the Cosmic Force or "Chi" in the air all around us. As you learn these movements, you will learn to feel the Cosmic Chi and to direct it to your hands and fingers for healing and creativity. On this tape Master Chia guides you through the four-part Chi Kung form. He also discusses the theory of channeling energy and shows you how to direct energy into someone's internal organs for healing.

With this Chi Kung you use major acupuncture points in your hands to activate, open and balance acupuncture meridians throughout your body. Practice of this set will balance and harmonize your internal energy. It will also produce a great activation of Chi in your hands, enabling you to have the energy to help others to heal themselves. This practice is highly recommended for massage therapists and other practitioners of body-oriented therapies.

Cosmic Healing Chi Kung – Six Directions Channeling (V76) $29.95

We live in and are surrounded by the energy of the earth, the bio-cosmos, and the universe. We need many different kinds of energy to sustain our life, not only the physical. Taoists refer to breathing as taking in the essence of the earth and the cosmic order. Nature and the universe are above, below, in front and behind, and to the left and right of us; the six directions. Our glands and organs need each of these energies to support our life.

In this video we would like to share a simple method to expand your mental power to connect to the Six Directions of nature, the cosmos, and the universe. By doing the opening the three Tan Tien to the Six Directions together with the Cosmic Healing Chi Kung form with the colors, you can learn to create the Chi field.

These energies come to us as light and we can separate the light into individual colors, known as Healing Color. When we can train the body to absorb these energies or light then we can transform it to be our own energy. Taoists regard this as containing a higher octane than just food. These energies are abundant all around us. All we need to do is learn how to take in and transform them to use for ourselves and to help heal other.

Cosmic Healing Chi Kung – Empty Force Practice (V77) $29.95

Cosmic Healing is training in expanding our mind and Chi to the universe. By learning to relax, smile and let go, we can expand ourselves into the Universe, the empty space, extending out a Chi pattern, so it can grow, multiply and be absorbed back for our use.

Cosmic Healing Chi Kung consists of four sets of simple postures and movements for absorbing the life force energy of nature and the Universe. By practicing this art you can learn to take color healing Chi from empty space into yourself or to direct it from the source straight into others for healing. Each of the four sections of Cosmic Healing Chi Kung develops a different type of energy mastery. Each of the four sections begins and ends the same way, yet has different movements in the middle part: 1. Connecting to Heaven and Earth. 2. Opening the Bridge and Regulator Channels and extending your Chi outwards. 3. Opening and energizing the Governor and Functional Channels. 4. Activating One Finger Art and the Chi belt.

Cosmic Healing Chi Kung – Healing Practice (V78) $29.95

In this tape you will learn a series of specific healing patterns and techniques applicable to different illnesses, applying what you have been learning in the Six Directions and Empty Force practices. The applications refer to and develop the different healing powers of each of the Chi colors. By expanding our awareness to a distant energy source such as a Galaxy, we can draw different distinct kinds of Color Chi for healing.

You will learn the practices of: a. Building an energy-field, b. Organizing the Chi field, c. Using Color Chi for healing, d. Working with the Universal Chi, e. The description of each healing color Chi and f. How to use the Galaxy, Universe, nature and color Chi to help others.

Cosmic Healing Chi Kung (CH50) $5.50

B. Pakua Palm I (P1)

Level II

A. Cosmic Healing II (HT) (H2) (H3)

Cosmic Healing Chi Kung II is the ability to form & build an energy field with the six directions gathering Nature's Forces, Original Force, Earth Force, Universal Forces and the students' own energy fields to heal themselves. The students learn to create and focus this healing vortex from all Five Levels using Nature's Healing Colors to balance and heal any body areas (Organs, Senses, or Systems – the immune system), and how to bury sick energy into the earth.

Cosmic Healing II: Taoist Cosmology and Universal Healing Connections (B17) $19.95

Building on the knowledge and experience of Cosmic Healing I, this book takes you to our solar system, out to our galaxy and deeper into the Outer Universe so as to connect more profoundly with the Inner Universe. Chinese astronomy and astrology is demystifed and integrated with the western system. The students will learn planetary and stellar meditations to increase your awareness and sensitivity that will support and encourage your healing potential.

B. Pakua Palm II (P2)

Level III

Senior Teacher (SH)
Certification Requirements:
1) 2 years of teaching as a Cosmic Healing Teacher (HT)
2) Retake Cosmic Healing I, II, III Retreat Weeks
3) Practices with students completing (100) Cosmic Healing Questionnaires & mail with address to Tao Garden for certificate
4) Evaluated in Theory & Practice and approved by Cosmic Healing Committee with 2 Cosmic Healing Senior Teachers

Immortal Tao - Fourth Branch (Spiritual Body)

Level I - Foundations of Spiritual Practice

A. Lesser Enlightenment Kan & Li (K1)

Lesser Enlightenment of Kan and Li (Yin and Yang Mixed): This formula is called Siaow Kan Li in Chinese, and involves a literal steaming of the sexual energy (Ching or creative) into life-force energy (Chi) in order to feed the soul or energy body. One might say that the transfer of the sexual energy power throughout the whole body and brain begins with the practice of Kan and Li. The crucial secret of this formula is to reverse the usual sites of Yin and Yang power, thereby provoking liberation of the sexual energy.

This formula includes the cultivation of the root (the Hui-Yin) and the heart center, and the transformation of sexual energy into pure Chi at the navel. This inversion places the heat of the bodily fire beneath the coolness of the bodily water. Unless this inversion takes place, the fire simply moves up and burns the body out. The water (the sexual fluid) has the tendency to flow downward and out. When it dries out, it is the end. This formula reverses normal wasting of energy by the highly advanced method of placing the water in a closed vessel (cauldron) in the body, and then cooking the sperm and the egg (sexual energy) with the fire beneath. If the water (sexual energy) is not sealed, it will flow directly into the fire and extinguish it or it will be consumed. This formula preserves the integrity of both elements, thus allowing the steaming to go on for great periods of time. The essential formula is never to let the fire rise without having water to heat above it, and never allow the water to spill into the fire. Thus, a warm, moist steam is produced containing tremendous energy and health benefits to rejuvenate all the glands, the nervous system and the lymphatic system and to increase pulsation. The formula consists of:

1. Mixing the water (Yin) & fire (Yang), (Male & Female) to give birth to the soul;
2. Transforming the sexual power (creative force) into vital energy (Chi), gathering and purifying the Microcosmic outer alchemical agent
3. Opening the twelve major channels
4. Circulating the power in the solar orbit (cosmic orbit)
5. Turning back the flow of generative force to fortify the body and the brain and restore it to its original condition before puberty
6. Regrowing the thymus gland and Lymphatic system
7. Sublimation of the body and soul: self-intercourse: giving birth to the immortal soul (energy body).

Lesser Kan & Li (Winter Retreat)   **Lesser Kan & Li (TB-K1)**

Lesser Kan & Li (Retreat Set) (C29) $99.50

Inner Alchemy of the Tao (CH48) $9.50

Ancient diagram, beautifully rendered in full color depicts the secrets of Taoist Inner Alchemy as a universe within the body. Hidden meaning described in detail in an accompanying 8 page booklet.

The Eight Immortals (CH49) $9.50

The Eight Directions, the Eight Forces and an accompanying detailed history of each of the legendary Eight Immortals. Full color, laminated, suitable for framing.

B. Greater Enlightenment Kan & Li (K2)

This formula comprises the Taoist Dah Kan Li (Ta Kan Li) practice. It uses the same energy relationship of Yin and Yang inversion but increases to an extraordinary degree the amount of energy that may be drawn up into the body. At this stage, the mixing, transforming, and harmonizing of energy takes place in the solar plexus. The increasing amplitude of power is due to the fact that the formula not only draws Yin and Yang energy from within the body, but also draws the power directly from Heaven and Earth or ground (Yang and Yin, respectively), and adds the elemental powers to those of one's own body. In fact, power can be drawn from any energy source, such as the Moon, Wood, Earth, Flowers, Animals, Light, etc.

The formula consists of:
1. Moving the stove and changing the cauldron;
2. Greater water and fire mixture (self-intercourse);
3. Greater transformation of sexual power into the higher level;
4. Gathering the outer and inner alchemical agents to restore the generative force and invigorate the brain;
5. Cultivating the body and soul;
6. Beginning the refining of the sexual power (generative force, vital force, Ching Chi);
7. Absorbing Mother Earth (Yin) power and Father Heaven (Yang) power. Mixing with sperm and ovary power (body), and soul
8. Raising the soul
9. Retaining the positive generative force (creative) force, and keeping it from draining away
10. Gradually doing away with food & depending on self sufficiency & universal energy
11. Giving birth to the spirit, transferring good virtues and Chi energy channels into the spiritual body
12. Practicing to overcome death
13. Opening the crown
14. Space travelling

Greater Kan & Li (Winter retreat) (TB-K2)   **Greater Kan & Li (TB-K3)**

Greater Kan & Li (Retreat Set) (C30) $99.50

C. Greatest Enlightenment Kan & Li (K3)

This formula is Yin and Yang power mixed at a higher energy center. It helps to reverse the aging process by re-establishing the thymus gland and increasing natural immunity. This means that healing energy is radiated from a more powerful point in the body, providing greater benefits to the physical and ethereal bodies.

The formula consists of:

1. Moving the stove and changing the cauldron to the higher center
2. Absorbing the Solar and Lunar power
3. Greatest mixing, transforming, steaming and purifying of sexual power (generative force), soul, Mother Earth, Father Heaven, Solar and Lunar power
4. Mixing the visual power with the vital power
5. Mixing (sublimating) the body, soul and spirit

Greatest Kan & Li (Winter retreat)   **Greatest Kan & Li (TB-K3)**
Greatest Kan & Li (Retreat Set) (C31) $99.50

D. Senior Inner Alchemy Instructor (IS)

Certification Requirements:

1) Certified in all 3 Levels of Kan & Li Practices.

Level II - The Realm of Soul and Spirit

A. Sealing of the Five Senses (SF)

This very high formula effects a literal transmutation of the warm current or Chi into mental energy or energy of the soul. To do this, we must seal the five senses, for each one is an open gate of energy loss. In other words, power flows out from each of the sense organs unless there is an esoteric sealing of these doors of energy movement. They must release energy only when specifically called upon to convey information. Abuse of the senses leads to far more energy loss and degradation than people ordinarily realize. Examples of misuse of the senses are as follows: if you look too much, the seminal fluid is harmed; listen too much and the mind is harmed; speak too much and the salivary glands are harmed; cry too much and the blood is harmed; have sexual intercourse too often and the marrow is harmed. Each of the elements has a corresponding sense, its elemental force may be gathered or spent. The eye corresponds to fire; the tongue to water; the left ear to metal; the right ear to wood; the nose to earth.

The fifth formula consists of:

1. Sealing the five thieves: ears, eyes, nose, tongue, and body
2. Controlling the heart, and seven emotions (pleasure, anger, love, hate, and desire)
3. Uniting and transmuting the inner alchemical agent into life-preserving true vitality
4. Purifying the spirit
5. Raising the spirit; stopping the spirit from wandering outside in quest of sense data
6. Eliminating decayed food and depending on the undecayed food, the Universal energy, is the True Breatharian

Sealing of the Five Senses (Winter Retreat)   **Sealing of the Five Senses (TB-SF)**

B. Congress of Heaven and Earth (HE)

This formula is difficult to describe in words. It involves the incarnation of a male and a female entity within the body of the adept. These two entities have sexual intercourse within the body. It involves the mixing of the Yin and Yang powers on and about the crown of the head, being totally open to receive energy from above and the regrowth of the pineal gland to its fullest use. When the pineal gland has developed to its fullest potential, it will serve as a compass to tell us in which direction our aspirations can be found. Taoist Esotericism is a method of mastering the spirit, as described in Taoist Yoga. Without the body, the Tao cannot be attained, but with the body, truth can never be realized. The practitioner of Taoism should preserve his physical body with the same care as he would a precious diamond, because it can be used as a medium to achieve immortality. If, however, you do not abandon it when you reach your destination, you will not realize the truth.

This formula consists of:

1. Mingling (uniting) the body, soul, spirit and the universe (cosmic orbit)
2. Fully developing the positive to eradicate the negative completely
3. Returning the spirit to nothingness

Congress of Heaven & Earth (Winter Retreat)

C. Reunion of Heaven and Man (HM)

We compare the body to a ship, and the soul to the engine and propeller of a ship. This ship carries a very precious and very large diamond which it is assigned to transport to a very distant shore. If your ship is damaged (a sick and ill body), no matter how good the engine is, you are not going to get very far and may even sink. Thus, we advise against spiritual training unless all of the channels in the body have been properly opened, and have been made ready to receive the 10,000 or 100,000 volts of super power which will pour down into them. The Taoist approach, which has been passed down to us for over five thousand years, consists of many thousands of methods. The formulae and practices we describe in these books are based on such secret knowledge and the author's own experience during over twenty years of study and of successively teaching thousands of students.

The main goal of Taoists:

1. This level—overcoming reincarnation, and the fear of death through Enlightenment
2. Higher level—the immortal spirit and life after death
3. Highest level—the immortal spirit in an immortal body. This body functions like a mobile home to the spirit and soul as it moves through the subtle planes, allowing greater power of manifestation.

Universal Tao Centers

For further information about any of our courses or centers, or to order books, posters, etc., please write or call:

North, Central, South American Distribution Outlet
140 Bonhomme Avenue,
Hackensack, NJ 07601 U.S.A
Tel. (1)(201) 343 5350 **Fax.** (1)(201) 343 8511
E-mail: kasorvik@juno.com

European, Asian, African, Australian Fulfillment Center
274 Moo 7, Luang Nua, Doi Saket,
Chiang Mai 50220, Thailand
Tel. (66) (53) 495596 to 9 **Fax.** (66) (53) 495852
Email: universaltao@universal-tao.com

Universal Tao Center Online Order
Web Site: www.universal-tao.com

There are also Universal Tao Centers in:

North America	Kansas	South America	Europe
• BERMUDA	Maine	• BRAZIL	• AUSTRIA
• CANADA	Maryland	• CHILE	• BELGIUM
Ontario	Massachusetts	**Asia**	• CYPRUS
British Columbia	Michigan	• CHINA	• DENMARK
Quebec	Minnesota	• INDIA	• ENGLAND
New Brunswick	New Hampshire	• JAPAN	• FINLAND
Prince Edward Island	New Jersey	• KOREA	• FRANCE
• UNITED STATES	New Mexico	• MALAYSIA	• GERMANY
Alaska	New York	• PHILIPPINES	• GREECE
Alabama	North Carolina	• RUSSIA	• ISRAEL
Arizona	Oklahoma	• SINGAPORE	• ITALY
California	Oregon	• THAILAND	• NETHERLANDS
Los Angeles	Pennsylvania	• UKRAINE	• PORTUGAL
San Francisco	South Dakota	**Australia**	• SCOTLAND
Colorado	Texas	• AUSTRALIA	• SPAIN
Connecticut	Utah	New South Wales	• SWITZERLAND
Delaware	Virginia	Queensland	• SWEDEN
District of Columbia	Virgin Islands	South Australia	• TURKEY
Florida	Washington	Victoria	• WALES
Hawaii	Wisconsin	Western Australia	**Africa**
Illinois	• MEXICO	• NEW ZEALAND	• SOUTH AFRICA

Our new center in Thailand holds retreats during the winter and summer seasons, and is located in Chiang Mai. For more information, please call, fax, or write to the above Thailand address.

Universal Tao Instructor Associations

Asian/Australian Instructors Association (AAIA)
Tao Garden Training Center
274 Moo 7, Luang Nua, Doi Saket,
Chiang Mai 50220, Thailand
Tel. (66) (53) 495596 to 9 **Fax.** (66) (53) 495852
Email: universaltao@universal-tao.com

North America Healing Tao Instructors Association (HTIA)
FDR Station P.O. Box 6314 New York,
New York 10150-6314 U.S.A.
Tel: (1)(718) 933-3109 (888-444-7426 toll free)
Fax: (1)(718) 965-9447
Email: winn.tao@worldnet.att.net

European Instructors Association (EIA)
c/o Zentrum Waldegg
3823 Wengen, SWITZERLAND
Tel: (41)(33) 855 44 22 Fax: (41)(33) 855 50 68
Email: info@waldegg.ch

Universal Tao Publishing - Foreign Publishers

Bulgarian

Dimitar Ilev
Odysseus Publishing
17 Alabin Str.,
1000 Sofia, Bulgaria
(359) (2) 807-513 (T/F)

Czech

F.R. Hrabal
Cad Press
Luda Zubka 23 Dubravka Cad
SK-84101 Bratislava 42 Slovakia
(421)(7) 769-928
Email: cadpress@inecnet.sk

Danish

Grete Damgaard & Steen Piper
Forlaget Hovedland
Stenvej 21
8270 Hojbjerg, Denmark
(45)(86) 276-500 (Fax) 276-537
Email: hovedland@isa.dknet.dk

Dutch

Emy ten Seldam
Ankh-Hermes Publisher
Smyrnastraat 5,
7413 BA Deventer, Netherlands
(31)(570) 678-911 (Fax) 624-632
Em:ankh-hermes.uitg@planet.nl

Chris Van Gelderen
Gottmer-Becht-Aramith
Postbus 160,
2060 AD Bloemendaal, NE
(31)(23) 525-7150 (F) 527-4404

Annette Derksen
Stichting Healing Tao Holland
P.O. Box 15450
1001ML Amsterdam, NE
(31)(20) 620-4970 (F) 624-2011
Email: healingtao@xs4all.nl

English

Heide Lange
Sanford Greenburger Assoc.
55 Fifth Ave. 15 Floor
New York, NY 10003 USA
(1)(212) 206-5608 (F) 463-8718

Karen Bouris & Peter Evans
Harper San Francisco
160 Battery St.
San Francisco CA 94111 USA
(1)(415) 415-4490

Barbara Somerfield
Aurora Press
P.O. Box 573
Santa Fe, MN 87504 USA
(1)(505) 989-9804 (F) 982-8321
Email: aurorep@aol.com

Y.S. Tan
Asia Publication
35 Kallang Pudding #03-01
Tong Lee Bldg., Block A
Singapore 349314
(65) 747-5301 (Fax) 748-7020

Jendy Gozali
Delapratasa Publisher
Jl. maatraman Raya No 56
Jarkarta 13150, Indonesia
(62)(21) 851-2510 (F) 851-2511

French

Guy Tredaniel
Edition de la Maisnie
65, rue Claude-Bernard
75005 Paris France
(33)(1) 4336-4105 (F) 4331-0745
Email: tredaniel@courrie.com

J.Y. Anstet Dangles
Edition Dangles
18, rue Lavoisier
45801 St.Jean Braye, France
(33)(2) 3886-4180 (F) 3888-7234

Jacques Maire
Edition Jouvence
Chemin du Guillon 20, #143
1233 Geneve, Switzerland
(41)(2) 757-6220
Em: jouvence@mail.dotcom.fr

German

Eckhard Graf
Scherz Verlag
Theaterplatz 4-6
CH-3000 Berne 7, Switzerland
(41)(31)327-7125 (F) 327-7169
Email: e.graf@sc-service.net

Peter Schaper
Droemer Verlag
Rauchstr. 9-11
81679 Munich, Germany
(49)(86) 92710 (Fax) 927-1168

Wolfgang Dahlberg
Weichsel Gertenstr, 22
8000 Munich 71, Germany

Greek

Alederaran
Laskaridou 160, Kallithea
17675 Athens, GREECE
(30)(1) 951-1051

Stinis or Voudouris
Trito Mati
Armodiou 14
Athens 10552, GREECE
(30)(1)321-5627 (Fax) 323-7007

Maria G. Parissianos
Medical/Scientific Publishing
20, Navarinou St.
Athens 106 80 Greece
(30)(1) 361-5047 (Fax) 361-6424

Hebrew

Shoshanna Shatz
Or'am Publishing House, LTD
28 Yitzhak St., P.O. Box 22096
TelAviv 61220, ISRAEL
(972)(3) 537-2277 (Fax) 537-2281
Email: orishatz@shani.net

Ariel Sa'ar, **Inbar Publishing**
Hagalil via Moran ISRAEL 20107
(972)(6) 698-7302 (Fax) 698-7537
Email: inbarinn@mail.inter.net.il

Hungarian

Erzsebet Toth & Gyula Edelenyi
Lunarimpex Publishing Corp.
Rozsa U. 10 VI/31
1045 Budapest, Hungary
(36)(1) 189-4492 (T/F)
Em: lunar@globenet.hu

Indonesian

Jendy Gozali
Delapratasa Publishing
Jl. Matraman Raya, 56
Jakarta 13150, INDONESIA
(62)(21) 851-2510 (Fax) 851-2511
Email: ceo@centrin.net.id

Italian

Ganonica
Edizioni Mediterranee Roma
Via Flaminia, 109
00196 Rome, ITALY
(39)(6) 320-1656 (F) 322-3540
Email: edimedit@flashnet.it

Sperling Kupfer Editoria
Via Borgonuvo, 24
20121 Milano ITALY
(39)(2) 290341 (Fax) 659-0290

Luigi DiPalma
M.I.R Edizioni
Via Montelupo, 147
50025 Montespertoli
Firenze, ITALY
(39)(571) 671-106
Email: mirediz@logo.it

Japanese

Hiroyuki Makihara
Eneterprise Publishers
2-1-3 Honkomagome,
Bunkyo-ku Tokyo, JAPAN
(81)(3) 3942-8096 (F) 3942-7804

Noriko Hasegawa
English Agency LTD.
Sakuragi Bldg. 4F
6-7-3 Minami-Aoyama
Minato-Ku, Tokyo 107 JAPAN
(81)(3)3406-5385(F)3406-5387/97

Korean

Lee Young-Joo
Spiritual Culture Publishing Co.
Dongwon Bldg, Room 202
119-1 Waryong-Dong 110-360
Jongro-Gu Seoul, KOREA
(82)(2) 765-3270 (Fax) 765-3271

Hanam Publishing
198-16 Kwanhundong,
Chongroku,Seoul 110-300

Lithuanian

Amalijus Narbutus
A.S.Narbuto Leidykla
Klevu 9, 5400 Siauliai, Lithuania
(370)(1) 420-868 (Fax)429-335
Email: amalijus@siauliai.aiva.lt

Malaysian

Eesah Sulaiman
Albaz Publishing
1223, Taman Jasa Tiga,Taman
Jasa 68100 Batu Caves
Selangor Darul Ellsan, Malyasia
(60)(3) 6897-570 (Fax) 6878-525

Polish

Jacek Santorski
Jacek Santorski Publishing
Nobla 25/3,
03-930 Warsaw, Poland
(48)(2) 220-7100
Em:tomasz.pankowski@swipnet.se

Dariusz Mynarczyk Publishing
Luban 59-800
Ul. Tkacka 28/1, Poland
(48)(71) 448-505(T/F)

Stanislaw Jedrzejewski
Pol Books Ltd.
Ul. Wislana 4
85-773 Bydgoszcz, Poland

Portugese

Editoria Objective Ltda.
Rua Cosme Velho 103
22241-090 Rio de Janeiro, Brasil
(55)(21) 556-7824 (Fax) 556-3322
Email: marisebarros@ibm.net

Russian

Yuriy Smirnov & Andriy Kostenko
Sophya Publishing House
P.O. Box 41
Kiev 01030 Ukraine
(380)(44) 244-0759 (T/F)
Email: kostenko@carrier.kiev.ua

Serguei Orchkine
Matveevskay 20-139
Moscow 119517 Russia
(7)(095) 441--0945 (Fax) 120-2331
Email: serguei@imce.ru

Serbo-Croatian

Ljiljana Stojanovic-Popin
Stojanovic-Popin Publishing
Biblioteka Horus, Sarajevska 70
1000 Belgrade, Serbia,
(38)(1) 145-4581

Slovenian

Jimmy Dusan Doblanovic
Doblanovic/Dusan
Streliska 6
61000 Ljubljana, Slovenia
(386)(61)125-4688

Spanish

Pilar Llanes
Editorial Sirio, S.A.
C/Panaderos 9
29005 Malaga, Spain
(34)(95) 222-4072 (Fax) 223-7435
Email: edisirio@vnet.es

Gutierrez Meliado
Editorial Mirach, S.A.
15 Ventura Rodriquez
Villaviciosa de Odon
28670 Madrid, Spain
(34)(1) 616-2684

Turkish

Cem Sen, **Dharma Press**
Dharma/Kuzey Yildizi Kkulturve
Spor Merkrzl SiraselvilerCaddesi
Havyar Sokak 30
Cihangir-Istanbul, Turkey
(90)(212) 243-1016 (F) 243-0633
Email: cemsen@intcafe.com

Tao Garden Health Resort

Eighty-Acre Resort with Year-Round Housing for 200 Guests, Daily Exercise and Meditation, Closed Circuit Security System, Facilities Available for Group Rates. Chiang Mai International Airport nearby in northern Thailand.

For Information: Fax(66)(53)495-852
Em:universaltao@universal-tao.com

Tao Garden Guest Quarters:

Standard Rooms: Modern rooms with two single beds in a two-storey building with 24 rooms surrounding a landscaped inner courtyard. All rooms have private toilets, showers and balcony.

Deluxe Rooms: One of three large guestrooms in a town house with private bath and balcony. Most guestrooms have two single beds. Some have Double Beds, which you can request at registration. All rooms are equipped with overhead fans. Some standard and some deluxe rooms are equipped with air conditioning at an extra charge.

All accommodations can be private or shared with another person.

Tao Garden Organically Grown and Freshly Prepared Meals Daily - Breakfast - Lunch - Dinner - Fruit Breaks:

Fruits: Papaya, Banana, Pineapple, Lime, Cantaloupe, Honeydew Melon, Pomello, Watermelon, Mango, Jack Fruit, Guava, Dragon Eyes,

Juices: Orange, Guava, Pineapple, Soymilk, Green Vegetable, Aloe Vera

Whole Grains: Hot Cereals & Breads, Oats, Rice, Buckwheat, Millet, Barley

Nut Butters: Peanut, Cashew, Sesame, Sunflower, Almond, Pine Nut

Jams: Tamarind, Pineapple, Kumquat, Hibiscus, Tangerine, Pomello

Salad Bar: Sunflower, Buckwheat, Pea, Mung Bean (Sprouts), Leaf & Romaine Lettuce, Cabbage, Carrots, Chestnuts, Scallions, Peppermint Basil leaf, Tarot Root, Red Bean, Tomato, Cucumber, Onion, Green Papaya, Mushrooms, Truffles and Homemade Dressings

Soups: Chicken, Corn, Cucumber, Miso, Mixed Vegetable, Noodle, Rice, Pumpkin, Red Bean, Seaweed, Sweet/Sour, Tofu, Radish, Mushroom

Vegetables: Steamed or Stir Fried with Gluten or Tofu

Fish, Shrimp & Chicken (Eggs): Pooled & free range, raised organically

Thai Deserts: Banana Cake, Banana & Papaya Ice Pureed, Mung Bean, Lotus Seed, Herb or Banana Hot Pureed Sweet Soups

Herb Teas: Safflower, Lemon Grass, Pandamus, Ginger, Lingzhi with Stevia Leaf, Chrysanthemum, Green, Jasmine, Mint (Wild Flower Honey)

Drinking Water: 5 Phase Reverse Osmosis Filtered Purification System

Anytime: Teas, Dried Bananas & Papaya, 3 Types Fresh Ripe Bananas

How to Order from USA, North, Central & South America

Prices and taxes:
Subject to change without notice. New York State residents add 8.25% sales tax.

Payment:
Send traveler's check, money order, certified check, or bank cashier's check to:

Universal Tao Center
140 Bonhomme Avenue,
Hackensack, NJ 07601 U.S.A.
Tel: (1)(201) 343 5350 **Fax:** (1)(201) 343 8511
Email: universaltao@universal-tao.com

Universal Tao Online Order
WEB SITE: www.universal-tao.com

All foreign checks must be drawn on a U.S. bank. Mastercard, Visa, and American Express cards accepted.

Shipping
Domestic Shipping: Via UPS requires a complete street address.
Please include special mailing requests. Allow 3-4 weeks for delivery.

Order Total	U.S.A. Zones 1-6	U.S.A. Zones 7 & 8
9.95 or less	5.50	5.50
10.00-29.95	8.75	9.45
30.00-50.00	10.70	11.70
50.01-70.00	12.45	12.95
70.01-100.00	13.70	15.95
100.01-120.00	14.95	17.70
120.01-140.00	16.70	19.45
140.01-160.00	17.95	21.50
160.01-180.00	18.95	23.70
180.01-200.00	19.70	25.40
over 200.00 add $5.95/every $50.00		

Order Total	Book Rates Canada	S.America
14.99 or less	17.95	23.10
15.00-29.99	25.75	30.75
30.00-49.99	35.90	48.75
50.00-100.00	53.85	74.40
Over 100.00	64.10	82.15
Plus	5.95 per 10	7.75 per 10
Non-Book Rates		
34.95 or less	24.50	22.00
35.00-74.99	24.50	26.50
75.00-149.99	32.00	34.75
Over 150.00	37.50	43.00
Plus	1.00 per 20	1.50 per 20

Zones 7 & 8: Zip codes with the first 3 digits:
577, 586-593, 677-679, 690, 693
733, 739, 763-772, 774, 778-799
800-899, 900-994
All other Zip codes are Zones 1-6

For Central America shipping rates please contact the above address

Please call or write for additional information in your area.

How to Order from the Rest of the World

Payment: Send traveler's check, money order, certified check, or bank cashier's check to:

> **Universal Tao Center**
> 274 Moo 7, Luang Nua, Doi Saket, Chiang Mai, 50220, THAILAND
> **Tel:** (66)(53) 495-596 **Fax:** (66)(53) 495-852 **E-mail:** universaltao@universal-tao.com

Universal Tao Online Order

Web Site: www.universal-tao.com

Mastercard, Visa, and American Express cards accepted.

Foreign Shipping:

International Orders are shipped Worldwide from Thailand by EMS: Air courier shipping & handling charged by region, see chart below. Shipment will be made within 6 business days.

BOOK RATES	Western Europe	Eastern Europe & Middle East	Southeast Asia	Japan	Australia/NZ
Order Total	By Air	By Air	By Air	By Air	By Air
$14.99 or less	$23.50	$15.38	$8.35	$9.00	$13.00
$15.00 - $29.99	$28.25	$19.25	$10.50	$12.95	$18.00
$30.00 - $49.99	$38.50	$30.75	$15.50	$18.00	$25.75
$50.00 - $100.00	$51.50	$45.00	$20.50	$26.00	$43.75
Over $100.00	$64.50	$51.50	$26.00	$30.75	$48.75
Plus	$5.60 per $10	$4.80 per $10	$2.10 per $10	$3.00 per $10	$4.65 per $10

NON-BOOK RATES	Western Europe	Eastern Europe & Middle East	Southeast Asia	Japan	Australia/NZ
Order Total	By Air	By Air	By Air	By Air	By Air
$34.95 or less	$24.50	$16.25	$11.75	$12.00	$13.50
$35.00 - $74.99	$27.00	$19.00	$11.75	$12.00	$16.00
$75.00 - $149.99	$32.00	$24.00	$13.75	$15.50	$21.00
Over $150.00	$37.25	$29.00	$16.00	$18.75	$26.50
Plus	$1.00 per $20	$1.00 per $20	$0.45 per $20	$0.60 per $20	$0.90 per $20

Western Europe:
Austria, Belgium, Switzerland, Germany, Denmark, Estonia, Spain, Finland, France, Gibraltar, Ireland, Italy, Lithuania, Luxembourg, Latvia, Netherlands, Norway, Portugal, Sweden, United Kingdom

Eastern Europe & Middle East:
United Arab Emirates, Afghanistan ,Albania, Armenia, Azerbaijan, Bosnia, Herzegovina, Bulgaria, Belarus, Cyprus, Czech Republic, Egypt, Ethiopia, Georgia, Greece, Croatia, Hungary, Israel, Jordan, Kyrgyzstan, Kuwait, Kazakhstan, Lebanon, Macedonia, Mongolia, Nepal, Poland, Romania, Russia, Slovenia, Slovak Republic, Syria, Tajikistan, Turkmenistan, Tunisia, Turkey, Ukraine, Uzbekistan, Yugoslavia

Southeast Asia:
American Samoa, Bangladesh, China, Hong Kong, Indonesia, Cambodia, Korea (North), Korea (South), India, Laos, Sri Lanka, Myanmar, Mongolia, Malaysia, Philippines, Pakistan, Singapore, Thailand, Viet Nam
Posters will be shipped separately with separate shipping charge.